W9-CKD-543

02/24

STAND PRICE
$ 5.00

Travels with Our Fellow Creatures

Most Perigee Books are available at special quantity discounts for bulk purchases for sales promotions, premiums, fund-raising or educational use. Special books, or book excerpts, can also be created to fit specific needs.

For details, write: Special Markets, The Berkley Publishing Group, 375 Hudson Street, New York, New York 10014.

Travels with
Our Fellow Creatures

Edited by
Phyllis Hobe

A Perigee Book

A Perigee Book
Published by The Berkley Publishing Group
A division of Penguin Putnam Inc.
375 Hudson Street
New York, New York 10014

Copyright © 1999 by Merit Books
Book design by Tiffany Kukec
Cover design by Charles Björklund

A list of acknowledgments can be found on pages 301–304.

All rights reserved. This book, or parts thereof,
may not be reproduced in any form without permission.

Perigee hardcover edition: October 1999

Published simultaneously in Canada.

The Penguin Putnam Inc. World Wide Web site address is
http://www.penguinputnam.com

Library of Congress Cataloging-in-Publication Data

Travels with our fellow creatures / edited by Phyllis Hobe.
    p.   cm.
  Includes bibliographical references.
  ISBN 0-399-52551-3
  1. Animals Literary collections.   2. Human-animal relationships
Literary collections.   1. Hobe, Phyllis.
PN6071.A7T68   1999
808.8'0362—dc21   99-28101
                                                          CIP

Printed in the United States of America

10 9 8 7 6 5 4 3 2 1

CONTENTS

Preface by Phyllis Hobe   ix

Part 1
CLOSE COMPANIONS

MAY SARTON, from *The Fur Person*   3

JOHN WRIGHT, *Grammer and Two-Tom*   14

CLEVELAND AMORY, from *The Cat Who
    Came for Christmas*   18

J. R. ACKERLEY, from *My Dog Tulip*   29

GARY ALLEN SLEDGE, *My Father's Way*   44

JAMES THURBER, *A Snapshot of Rex*   50

RUDYARD KIPLING, *Garm—A Hostage*   55

ANTON CHEKHOV, *Grief*   73

ROBERT GRAVES, *In the Wilderness*   80

Part 2
PARTNERS

WILLIE MORRIS, from *My Dog Skip*   85

MACKINLAY KANTOR, *The Horse Looked
   at Him*   96

HECTOR CHEVIGNY, from *My Eyes Have a
   Cold Nose*   101

PAUL GALLICO, from *Honorable Cat*   117

JOHN STEINBECK, from *Travels with Charley*   124

Part 3
NEIGHBORS

FLOYD SKLOOT, *Daybreak*   137

HOPE RYDEN, from *Lily Pond*   139

DIAN FOSSEY, from *Gorillas in the Mist*   157

FARLEY MOWAT, from *Never Cry Wolf*   167

STERLING NORTH, from *Rascal*   173

Part 4
ANIMALS AFAR

JACK LONDON, from *White Fang*   183

ERNEST HEMINGWAY, from *The Short Happy Life
   of Francis Macomber*   200

ELIZABETH MARSHALL THOMAS, from *The Tribe
   of Tiger*   210

ROGER CARAS, from *Animals in Their Places*   218

Part 5
FELLOW CREATURES

WALT WHITMAN, from *Song of Myself*   237

FRED BODSWORTH, from *Last of the Curlews*   238

PAUL GALLICO, from *The Snow Goose*   248

CHRISTINA ROSSETTI, from *To What Purpose
This Waste?*   253

ALDEN STEVENS, from *The Way of a Lion*   254

DIAN FOSSEY, from *Gorillas in the Mist*   260

FARLEY MOWAT, from *A Whale for the Killing*   273

DIANE ACKERMAN, from *Whales*   280

BARRY LOPEZ, *Caring for the Woods*   292

ALBERT SCHWEITZER, from *The Ethics of Reverence
for Life*   300

Acknowledgments   301

PREFACE
by Phyllis Hobe

There are as many ways to know animals as there are people, because each of us knows them in a different way. Some of us count animals as friends or family members, some work with them, some study them, some interpret them in works of art. Some depend on animals to help us through life's difficulties, and some struggle to help them survive. The nature of animal-human relationships is as fascinating as the natures of the individuals involved.

Fortunately, many of the people who know animals well also have written about them—beautifully. Stories, articles, poems, and books about animals of all kinds have become a substantial and memorable part of good fiction and nonfiction. Authors have introduced us to many animals we probably wouldn't have met on our own, in ways we can't forget.

My own acquaintance with animals has been deepened by many superb writers who have known animals in ways that I did not. Years ago, reading Sheila Burnford's *The Incredible Journey,* I was made aware that the breed characteristics of dogs and cats have more to do with their ability to survive in the wilderness than with taking Best in Show. Fred Gipson's *Old Yeller* introduced me to dogs as coworkers and protectors. Farley Mowat's *Never Cry Wolf* changed my impression of wolves from one of movie-type random attackers to one of hardworking providers in an ancient culture facing extinction.

No matter how many times I reread *The Snow Goose* by Paul Gallico, I sense an almost mystic bond between human and animal as the big white bird hovers over the drifting boat bearing the body of the lonely man who befriended it. I am also indebted to Gallico for *Honorable Cat,* a book that could have been written only by someone whose respect for cats was at least as great as his passion for them.

A respect for animals as they are, rather than as we would have them be, is an important criterion for the selections in this anthology. Another is that the reader learns something about the writer as well as the animal through their relationship. The third, and most important, criterion is that each selection must be a good read. My aim is for readers who like animals to enjoy them more because they know them better— and good writing makes this possible.

In five sections, *Travels with Our Fellow Creatures* will portray our relationships with animals that are familiar to most of us, as well as those we usually know from a distance. Some selections, such as "A Snapshot of Rex," by James Thurber, are complete works. Some, such as the passages from *The Tribe of Tiger,* by Elizabeth Marshall Thomas, are excerpts. They all illustrate the rich diversity of animal literature.

"Close Companions" describes some of the animals who share our homes and our lives. It includes chapters from *The Fur Persons* by May Sarton, the reminiscence "Grammar and Two-Tom," by John Wright, an excerpt from *My Dog Tulip,* by J. R. Ackerley, "My Father's Way," by Gary Allen Sledge, "A Snapshot of Rex," by James Thurber, "Garm—a Hostage," by Rudyard Kipling, and "Grief," by Anton Chekhov.

"Partners" is about animals who share our struggles and lighten our burdens. Its selections include an excerpt from

John Steinbeck's *Travels with Charley,* MacKinlay Kantor's short story "The Horse Looked at Him," chapters from Hector Chevigny's *My Eyes Have a Cold Nose,* and poems and an excerpt from *Honorable Cat,* by Paul Gallico.

"Neighbors" acquaints us with some of the wildlife we might meet near our homes or in woods, plains, and mountains. For example, Floyd Skloot's poem "Daybreak" captures the sudden intake of breath that comes with the unexpected sight of deer. Chapters from Hope Ryden's *Lily Pond* involve us with a colony of beavers in a daily struggle for survival.

"Animals Afar" is about animals in distant, vast places, such as rain forests, the desert, glaciers, and the sea. Excerpts from "The Short Happy Life of Francis Macomber," by Ernest Hemingway, *The Tribe of Tiger,* by Elizabeth Marshall Thomas, and *Animals in Their Places,* by Roger Caras, give us insights into the cultures of the lion and the bear.

"Fellow Creatures" explores the common destiny of human beings and animals. We meet animals who need our help to survive as a species, implying the question, "If they can't, can we?" Among the selections are excerpts from Walt Whitman's "Song of Myself"; Christina Rossetti's "To What Purpose This Waste?"; Alden Stevens's short story "The Way of a Lion"; Diane Ackerman's *New Yorker* article, "Whales"; "Caring for the Woods," by Barry Lopez; and an excerpt from *The Ethics of Reverence for Life,* by Albert Schweitzer.

The selections in this anthology range from classic to contemporary animal literature. They were found in magazines, newspapers, and books, some of them shiny and new and some so old that the pages were brown and cracked. In a few instances, a book I knew existed but couldn't find was tracked down by librarians who gave new meaning to the word determination. Although many of the works are or once were widely read, those that aren't deserve to be. Collecting them has been a pleasure and a discovery.

One

CLOSE COMPANIONS

May Sarton

THE FUR PERSON

When he was about two years old, and had been a Cat About Town for some time, glorious in conquests, but rather too thin for comfort, the Fur Person decided that it was time he settled down. This question of finding a permanent home and staff was not one to be approached lightly of a May morning like his casual relationships with various grocers in the neighborhood, kind but vulgar people who did not know how to address a Gentleman Cat. Not at all. This was to be a systematic search for a housekeeper suitable in every way. Every cat knows that the ideal housekeeper is an old maid, if possible living in a small house with a garden. The house should have both an attic and a cellar, the attic for fun and games, the cellar for hunting. Children, I regret to say, are to be avoided whenever possible. They are apt to distract the housekeeper from her duties, and their manners leave much to be desired.

The Fur Person owed his life to a small freckled boy, but he was very good at forgetting things he wished to forget, and this was one of them. It was quite true that the boy named

Alexander had howled so loudly when a man from the Animal Rescue League came with a black bag that his mother had relented and said, looking down at the litter, "Well, you may keep just one, Alexander. But you'll have to choose quickly."

"The one with the rather long tail," Alexander said without a moment's hesitation, and dived into the box to rescue the small wobbly velvet pillow who was to turn into the Fur Person, but who was still so small that his ears were not yet unbuttoned and he could barely see out of vague blue eyes. The discomfort of having no mother but only an awkward boy was considerable, but his own proper mother, who would have licked him into shape and provided warm milk whenever he so much as murmured, had disappeared shortly after giving birth to five kittens with very high desperate voices. Instead, Alexander came (when he remembered it) with a medicine dropper and some inferior cow's milk, carried the kitten around inside his leather jacket and was apt to squeeze him rather too tight; that may be why the Fur Person grew into a somewhat long and straggly cat. He slept on Alexander's bed and on very cold nights sometimes wound himself round Alexander's neck, and thus came to be known as Alexander's Furpiece. He bore with Alexander and Alexander's whims until he was nearly six months old. Then one fine summer day, having licked his shirt front into white splendor and examined with pride the white tip of his tail, and seen that every stripe was glossy along his tiger back, he swaggered out like any young dandy, and what began as an extended rove and ramble ended in a way of life, for he never came back.

As a Cat About Town he developed a stiff hippy walk; he had a very small nick taken out of one ear; and sometimes he was too busy to bother about washing for days at a time. His shirt front became gray, the white tip of his tail almost disappeared, and his whiskers sprang out from his cheeks with the strength and vitality of porcupine quills. He learned a great variety of street songs, how to terrify without lifting a paw, how to wail a coward into retreat, how to scream a bully into attacking just a fraction of a second too soon, how to court a gentle middle-aged tabby as well as many a saucy young thing; he was kept extremely busy right on into the fall, and, I am afraid, he forgot all about Alexander. His expeditions and conquests took him far afield and when he did, at an off moment, remember the soft bed of his kittenhood he was not quite sure where to find it again. I am myself, he thought, lashing his tail back and forth, a formidable, an irresistible Cat About Town, and that is enough to be. It was a full-time job. The question of food, for instance, continually interrupted other and more interesting pursuits. A Cat About Town must be wily as well as ferocious, must know every inch of a territory for the wobbliest garbage-can lids, must learn the time when local grocers are apt to fling a few tasty haddock heads and tails to anyone who may be about just then; he must learn how to persuade old ladies into handing out bowls of milk, or even an occasional saucer of cream, without ever allowing himself to be captured, must in fact hunt out kindness with ruthless self-interest, but never give in to any such dreams of comfort as might involve a loss of Independence. It is an arduous life and the Cat About Town is a lean mocking character for whom human beings are to be used for what they are worth, which is not much.

The Fur Person, at this time of his life, was no exception; he conformed to type, except when he was curled up into a tight ball under a hedge and sometimes made a small whirring noise which resembled a purr, and sometimes even opened his paws and closed them again as if he were remembering something delicious, but when he woke up he had always forgotten what it was. Only once in a while he felt rather wistful and gave his face and shirt front a lick to cheer himself up, and swaggered down the street a fraction more aggressively than usual, and then stopped, looked back, seemed for a moment not to know where he was, or even perhaps who he was.

By the time he was two years old, he was still a Cat About Town, but he was a Cat About Town who had strange dreams, dreams of an open fire and himself with his paws tucked in sitting in front of it, of a gentle hand quite unlike a small boy's hand, of a saucer of warm milk—very strange dreams indeed. They required concentrated yoga exercises to forget, and sometimes he was haunted by one for as much as a whole day.

And one morning when he woke up purring from his dream, he washed his face very carefully and decided that it was time he settled down. His whiskers shone in the sun. He stretched, yawned, and then amused himself for a few moments by scaring the pigeons waddling under an elm a few yards away. But in the middle of this childish game, he suddenly sat quite upright, narrowed his eyes, then opened them very wide and looked at nothing for a long time. It was here at this very spot that he realized that he was an orphan. His face grew quite pointed with self-pity and it was all he could do to maintain his dignity and not utter the long wail of loneliness which he felt rising within him.

This experience was followed by a hard day, a day of aimless wandering and of painful encounters with fat sleek cats sitting on porches, whom he now regarded in an entirely new light; they had found housekeepers; they had snug warm beds. By the time dark was falling, the Fur Person was very tired, walking down a strange street alone, and he knew in his bones that the time for decision was at hand.

Then he heard a gentle human voice calling, "Here kitty, kitty, kitty," from somewhere quite far away. Even a week ago this sound would not have concerned him at all. But now in an instant he was alert and trotted amiably along to reconnoiter. He could see a stout woman with gray hair standing in the lighted doorway of a house, all surrounded by a garden. There was no little boy in sight, and the Fur Person felt strongly drawn to the place. He ran around a barberry bush and sat down where he could observe matters, and he was about to make up his mind, when a very peculiar-looking cat suddenly raced up the steps and disappeared inside as the door closed. The cat was beige colored with dark brown paws and ears and—was the Fur Person in a slightly hallucinated state?—seemed to have blue eyes like a human being.

It was a moment of bitterness even to a nature as philosophical, as used to Hard Knocks as the Fur Person. Another cat was already in possession! Another cat was lord of the garden, the little pear tree, the beautifully soft earth in the flower beds (just right for certain purposes), and above all of the kindly old woman with the gentle voice. He had found this perfect haven too late.

The Fur Person raced up the pear tree just to give himself confidence, and then raced down again, without even stopping to sharpen his claws. On an impulse he ran to the back door, for there were lights in what must be the kitchen. Then gently and politely he scratched a little at the screen door. There was no response. He began to miss Alexander. He even thought without distaste of the boring food from a can with a stupid-looking cat face on it, which was all Alexander ever fed him. He was, in fact, ravenously hungry and exhausted. He scratched a little again and gave a very polite mew, a restrained mew, considering the violence of his feelings, considering that only a day before he had been a wild and wily Cat About Town. He imagined the peculiar cat lifting a paw toward some delicious lamb or beef liver being cut up at this very moment by the kind old lady into convenient small pieces and lightly sautéed in bacon fat. It was really too much, and now suddenly under the full force of emotion he found himself singing an entirely new song, a song he made up himself. It went something like this:

> Dear Lady, please
> Open the door.
> Do not keep me any longer
> Faint from thirst and hunger
> But have pity

> On an orphan kitty,
> Hear, my mews!

It was not too bad a song, he felt, for a first try and when it was finished, because he was a Gentleman Cat, he turned his back and sat down, as if perfectly indifferent, though his heart was beating very fast, and one ear cold not be persuaded to stay pointed forward, but turned backward, rather inelegantly, to listen. Sure enough, the door opened.

"Well," said a not very pleased voice, "where did you come from? Hungry, are you?"

The Fur Person, according to the First Commandment of the Gentleman Cat ("When addressed, do not move a muscle. Look as if you hadn't heard."), just gazed soulfully in the opposite direction.

"You'd better go home now," the voice said, not unkindly. Unfortunately at this moment a cloud of scent, the scent of fresh cod boiling on the stove, came and settled around the Fur Person like a nimbus. He was, after all, still a young cat, and at this instant karma was stronger than any rule or regulation. He really did not know how it happened, but the next thing he did know was that he was in the kitchen, spirited there as Odysseus into the arms of Circe by the ineffable cod (sacred, as you all know, and hence having perhaps some attributes of a mystical kind). He was also, unfortunately, spirited into the furious presence of the peculiar cat, who sprang at him and succeeded in scratching him on the small cinnamon square of his nose in the tenderest place. This was no time for poetry; the Fur Person gave a scream of outrage and shot out into the night. "Hear my mews" indeed, he said to himself, growling. And he went on his way shouting in a very piercing voice, so the whole neighborhood was alarmed:

> May your milk turn sour;
> May your fish taste queer,
> And your meat look strange,

From this very hour;
May your blue eyes blear;
May you get the mange.

It was such a good curse that he repeated it, making a few changes in the inflection, just to try it out. He was so pleased with it that he forgot to be hungry and lonely any more and curled up in some delicious wood shavings in a basket outside the grocery store, and slept the sleep of satisfied anger.

———

Early in the morning he was still curled up into a ball, one paw clasping his nose, so he was perfectly airtight and warm, when he was roused from a delicious dream about some affectionate and playful mice by an infernal noise, a noise so tremendous that it sounded as if several houses were collapsing, and all the china and saucepans in them being hurled violently about by a giant. The Fur Person sprang up without even opening his eyes and vanished behind the grocery store. When he was able to open his eyes—they seemed to be glued together—he crept back to see if there was anything left of the world, but just then there was another huge crash and bang. Luckily this time his eyes were open and he saw that this earthquake was merely the ashman emptying the barrels. So, like any Gentleman Cat who has just been badly scared (Second Commandment: "When frightened, look bored."), he sat very erect and still and did some yoga exercises to calm himself down. This meant sitting with his paws tucked in and forcing himself to think of nothing at all; it is quite hard to do.

What with the events of the night before and the fact that his bed had now disappeared into the ashman's truck and was on its way to the town dump, what with the cold gray morning light and the thought of that horrible blue-eyed cat having a sumptuous breakfast no doubt at this very moment, the Fur Person felt very depressed. He lifted one paw in hesitation, looked at it thoughtfully and then became absorbed in washing it, so that all decisions were put off for the time being. For the first thing a Gentleman Cat does in the morning is to be sure that his suit is thoroughly pressed and damped, and his shirt front immaculate. While busy with this absorbing job, he considered himself with an impersonal and thoughtful eye. Perhaps he was rather too thin and his tail a trifle long, but after all, he reminded himself, it does have a small white tip. That is quite a distinction. And no one could deny that a white shirt front and white paws went very well with a glossy tiger coat and set off the wide black bands looped across his breast, rather like a Lord Mayor of London's chains. He told himself that he was not the handsomest cat in town, but reasonably distinguished as cats of his family went, and he gave his whiskers a good deal more than a lick and a promise. In fact his right front paw had been moistened and rubbed his face at least fifty times that morning, and his tongue was quite tired.

He had just stopped to rest, giving a long stretch first of his front legs then of his back, so that he looked longer than ever, when the grocer drew up in a big black car, got out, swinging his keys in a rather cheerful way, and began to open the various locks on the door of his shop. The Fur Person instantly thought of milk, even a small piece of cheese perhaps, or some hamburger, and explained his plight to the grocer by rubbing against the doorjamb and then slipping in, his tail straight up in the air like a flag, and every bit of his person saying, "Thank you very much, nice morning, isn't it?"

"I haven't seen you before, have I?" said the grocer. "Hungry?"

It was delicious to feel the low thunder of purrs rumbling inside him. During his years of being a Cat About Town he had only purred in his sleep, but now he began to roar with pleasure like a little stove. He could feel every hair of his fur coat trembling with the force of these purrs; he swayed slightly as he sat down, lifting his head in pure hope to the grocer's face. Of course the grocer, a simple fat man of no graces, could hardly appreciate the refinement of ecstasy which he was witnessing. But he did seem to get the crude point even if he did not appreciate its nuances. In a very few moments, he had poured out some milk in a saucer and laid beside it on a piece of newspaper some hamburger, of uncertain age. The Fur Person approached the milk, breathed above it for a few seconds, and then actually settled down, wrapping his tail around him, his two front paws close together. When the saucer was empty he moved over to the hamburger with eager anticipation. Alas, it was not worthy of a Gentleman Cat, and though he was still very hungry, he rose up with immense dignity and scratched at the newspaper as if to cover up this unfortunate meal, that it never be seen again.

"Not as hungry as you look, eh?" said the grocer cruelly. The Fur Person gave him a long indignant look, his green eyes as wide open as they could be, then slowly shut them on the vulgarity of the grocer. Still, it was not to be supposed that he would find the perfectly suitable establishment on the very first day of his search, and, all things considered, the grocer's shop might be as good a base camp as he could find. So the Fur Person assumed his usual habits; as it was now time to read the newspaper, he jumped up into the big window and settled down comfortably, his paws tucked in, to see what was going on in the world. Clever cats know that this time in the morning is dogtime and generally sit indoors looking out. It is very thrilling to learn the news in this way. The Fur Person opened his eyes wide when a St. Bernard sauntered past, and then a poodle went by like lightning. But when Hannah came into sight, he was quite beside himself with excitement and pressed his nose to the pane, for Hannah lived on Alexander's street. Every morning she ran the whole length of the street announcing the morning news in a series of loud excited barks and thus she was known as "the barky dog." She was a beagle and very much too fat, the Fur Person thought; being so thin himself, the fat of others disgusted him.

It lacked elegance. He was amazed to see Hannah so far from home. Whatever could she be doing? She stood by the window and seemed to recognize him, for she became very barky indeed. The Fur Person, offended by so much noise, withdrew and turned his back on her. The only sign that he was paying attention was a slight raising of the fur along his spine (he could not prevent this though Hannah was beneath such notice, noisy gossip that she was). His long thin tail had suddenly become enormous.

He had been so busy not listening to Hannah and pretending not to mind her voice that he had not noticed the arrival of a customer.

"Good morning, Mrs. Seaver, you're an early bird," said the grocer in the falsely jovial tone that grocers often employ. It was a tone the Fur Person recognized at once, the tone people used who said "Nice Kitty" but really did not like cats.

"I ran out of coffee," said Mrs. Seaver, helping herself to a bag on the shelf. "Want to grind this for me, percolator—" but she had hardly finished this sentence when she saw the Fur Person, glorious, every hair shining in the sun, his tail beautifully enlarged by his anger at Hannah, his green eyes observing her with obvious interest. "Ooooooh," she crooned, "you have a lovely kitty. Where did you come from, Kitty?" she asked in a foolish tone of voice, as if he were feeble-minded or only a few weeks old. But she leaned over and scratched him under his chin and no Gentleman Cat can resist such an attention. He got up, arched his back and thanked her kindly.

"He was out there, waiting at the door, like he belonged here," said the grocer. "Not even hungry," he lied without so much as batting an eyelash.

The customer was stroking the Fur Person down his arched back now, in a way very consoling to an orphan. "Mmmm" she murmured in his ear as if she were contemplating a lobster dinner, "I do love cats." The Fur Person should have been warned by something cannibalistic in this tone, but it must be remembered that he was young and inexperienced in the ways of human love, and besides he was very hungry. The ecstasy began to thrum inside him again and before he knew it, he was purring away, and even lifting one paw into the air and spreading out the claws, out and in, out and in, from sheer pleasure.

"Will you look at that? Isn't he the cutest thing?" the lady crooned. "You wouldn't let me have him, would you?" she asked the grocer.

"He ain't mine to give. Take him along if you like him."

The Fur Person had no time to consider this proposition or to get a word in edgewise. Before he knew what had happened, he was lifted up into the air and hanging down awkwardly over the lady's arm. He struggled, but she put a hand over his nose and said, "Oh no, you don't." Very well, he thought, wait and see. Maybe she had a little house with an attic and a cellar and garden with neat beds of flowers and good earth, and maybe she had lobster every day for lunch. He kept very quiet, but his eyes were enormous with expectation, and his long tail hanging down under her arm twitched back and forth with excitement.

He leaned way out to see where they were going. His ears pricked as they approached a dear little house and a garden, but they passed it by. He was rather disconcerted, and made a halfhearted attempt to jump down when the Lady turned in before a huge brick apartment house. By now it was too late. He looked up into the Lady's soft foolish face with alarm, for she had suddenly became a jailer. But he really did need some breakfast, and after breakfast he would try to make a discreet withdrawal. So he told himself, as she finally set him down in a tiny dark hall.

John Wright

GRAMMER AND TWO-TOM

My grandmother smelled like ripe lilacs and wore size 2 shoes and had long Gravel Gertie hair and a violin voice that sounded like Billie Burke who played Glenda the Good Witch in *The Wizard of Oz*.

Mostly, Grandmother loved to win at Parcheesi and look for ancestors in graveyards and cook sugar-soaked fudge on Sunday nights and write the history of the First Presbyterian Church and hunt for Two-Tom.

People in town called her Mrs. Wright or Carimae but underneath all that, she was just "Grammer."

How Two-Tom got his name is lost in family mist. Daddy claimed the first time he saw him wallowing in the rock garden, he thought, "Now there's a real two-ton tomcat." But Della, the maid, credited herself with "Two toms for the price of one."

The price was high. Anybody who ever saw Grammer flying up the path from the scuppernong arbor with a Sears hoe in one hand and Two-Tom slung over the other, knew that God had created one orange-and-yellow and ornery cat just to get Grammer's blood going and extend her days.

The cat made mistakes, but he didn't make big ones. Two-Tom had memorized the cat taboo list. No shedding on Mother's inherited, imitation Queen Anne chair. No digging in the rubber tree pot on the patio. No love rubbing against the visiting gams of Mrs. Monroe, whose sensitive nose extended beyond felines to 12-year-old boys.

Otherwise, he was a carte blanche cat. Like every Sunday when the three of us marched over Confederate Hill to Church Street Cemetery where most of the Wrights were gone but not forgotten by Grammer. And when Grammer arrived at any graveyard, she called roll. Notebook in hand, she'd check off the uncle under alabaster angels, the great-grand-somebody in a creepy mausoleum, and cousin Suzanne who left orders to be buried standing up facing Jerusalem.

But it was the kudzu-covered kin who were in danger of falling off Grammer's family tree. Throughout my childhood and puberty, we hunted in vain for Commodore Edmund Wright who, Grammer allowed, might have been buried mistakenly in the Indian Ocean. Still we searched.

These routine trips to the cemetery continued until February came hard in 1963. The gardenia died to its roots, the basin of the birdbath iced into three pieces, and Grammer got a sore throat that went to pneumonia. Soon I barely recognized the mischievous little lady who used to hop up at 5 a.m. "to see God light the fire."

The whole drama weighed heavily on Two-Tom. He spent normal mousing hours in her room and took his condensed milk on her window sill where, in Sphinxy pose, he eyed her lost in the eiderdown.

Neither of them gave an inch until spring was brewing. Then one morning after breakfast, he was gone. A full week went by and Grammer, who spoke very little now, stared at the window with anguish and anger. It appeared the saga of Grammer and Two-Tom had run its course. Appearances, however, are deceiving.

On a Sunday when my parents were at church, but I was pure enough to stay home with Grammer, she suddenly raised up on one elbow and said, "Merciful heavens, that cat is getting my goat." I was on the floor reading, and those words sent a chill down my adolescent spine. Then, to my abiding grief, she tossed back the blanket and swung her feet to the floor.

"Just because I'm flat on my back," she fumed, "Two-Tom thinks he can take on the world. Not over my dead body!"

"Wait 'till church is out," I stalled.

"Church is already out for that cat!"

I still dream today of straggling behind her and staring back down Church Street for Daddy's green Studebaker. Already I was envisioning Grammer's interment and Reverend Sawyer's accusation in his funeral oration about me letting her out.

So the graveyard seemed more prophetic than usual as we touched base with the mausoleum, the uncle under angels, and other historic haunts. As she waded through the undergrowth, Grammer looked strong as brandy.

"You hear that?" she whispered, "It's Two-Tom!" Sure, she was right. Back there behind a headstone garlanded with plump April blackberries.

That old melancholy feline song.

I straddled the sandstone marker, destroyed my pants on the brambles, and latched on to the scruff of his neck. Grammar was so overcome she forgot to shake him like a dirty rag.

Then I noticed she was calm, her gaze directed near our feet to a chalky headstone that had lost its sharp corners to the seasons but still retained the carved outline of an old schooner.

"Great Caesar's ghost!" Grammer recognized it at once.

I'm not naive like Della, who swears Two-Tom led Grammar to that particular grave, but I'm positive he set out to coax her from the bed. And that Sunday fury was the tonic that sent Grammer into six more healthy Aprils . . . three times as many as the old cat would be allotted.

It was Daddy and I who risked our own lives (at Grammer's suggestion) to bury a cat where you don't. And if you can find the ironwork arch and the blackberries and the chalk-white schooner, look closely at the inscription. Partly chiseled. Partly scratched:

Commodore Edmund Wright
& Two-Tom

Cleveland Amory

THE CAT WHO CAME FOR CHRISTMAS

I had just turned from the pleasant task of watching the snow outside to the unpleasant one of surveying the bills when the doorbell rang. If there had been anyone else to answer it, I would have told them to say to whoever it was that we already gave at home. But there was no one, so I went myself.

The caller was a snow-covered woman whom I recognized as Ruth Dwork. I had known Miss Dwork for many years. A former schoolteacher, she is one of those people who, in every city, make the animal world go round. She is a rescuer and feeder of everything from dogs to pigeons and is a lifetime soldier in what I have called the Army of the Kind. She is, however, no private soldier in that army—she makes it too go round. In fact, I always called her Sergeant Dwork.

"Merry Christmas, Sergeant," I said. "What can I do you for?"

She was all business. "Where's Marian?" she asked. "I need

her." Marian Probst, my longtime and longer-suffering assistant, is an experienced rescuer, and I knew Miss Dwork had, by the very look of her, a rescue in progress. "Marian's gone," I told her. "She left about five-thirty, saying something about some people having Christmas Eve off. I told her she was a clock-watcher, but it didn't do any good."

Sergeant Dwork was unamused. "Well, what about Lia?" she demanded. Lia Albo is national coordinator of the Fund for Animals and an extremely expert rescuer. She, however, had left before Marian on—what else?—another rescue.

Miss Dwork was obviously unhappy about being down to me. "Well," she said, looking me over critically but trying to make the best of a bad bargain, "I need someone with long arms. Get your coat."

As I walked up the street with Sergeant Dwork, through the snow and biting cold, she explained that she had been trying to rescue a particular stray cat for almost a month, but that she had had no success. She had, she said, tried everything. She had attempted to lure the cat into a Hav-a-Heart trap but, hungry as he was and successful as this method had been in countless other cases, it had not worked with this cat. He had simply refused to enter any enclosure that he could not see his way out of. Lately, she confessed, she had abandoned such subtleties for a more direct approach. And, although she had managed to get the cat to come close to the rail fence at the end of the alley, and even to take bite-sized chunks of cheese from her outstretched fingers, she had never been able to get him to come quite close enough so that she could catch him. When she tried, he would jump away, and then she had to start all over the each-time-ever-more-difficult task of trying again to win his trust.

However, the very night before, Sergeant Dwork informed me, she had come the closest she had ever come to capturing the cat. That time, she said, as he devoured the cheese, he had not jumped away but had stood just where he was—nearer than he had ever been but still maddeningly just out of reach.

Good as this news was, the bad news was that Miss Dwork now felt that she was operating against a deadline. The cat had been staying in the basement of the apartment building, but the superintendent of the building had now received orders to get rid of it before Christmas or face the consequences. And now the other workers in the building, following their super's orders, had joined in the war against the cat. Miss Dwork herself had seen someone, on her very last visit, throw something at him and hit him.

WHEN we arrived at our destination, there were two alley-ways. "He's in one or the other," Sergeant Dwork whispered. "You take that one, I'll take this." She disappeared to my left and I stood there, hunched in my coat with the snow falling, peering into the shaft of darkness and having, frankly, very little confidence in the whole plan.

The alley was a knife cut between two tall buildings filled with dim, dilapidated garbage cans, mounds of snowed-upon refuse, and a forbidding grate. And then, as I strained my eyes to see where, amongst all this dismal debris, the cat might be hiding, one of the mounds of refuse suddenly moved. It stretched and shivered and turned to regard me. I had found the cat.

As I said, that first sight was hardly memorable. He looked less like a real cat than like the ghost of a cat. Indeed, etched as he was against the whiteness of the snow all around him, he was so thin that he would have looked completely ghost-like, had it not been for how pathetically dirty he was. He was so dirty, in fact, that it was impossible even to guess as to what color he might originally have been.

When cats, even stray cats, allow themselves to get like that, it is usually a sign that they have given up. This cat, however, had not. He had not even though, besides being dirty, he was wet and he was cold and he was hungry.

And, on top of everything else, you could tell by the kind of off-kilter way he was standing that his little body was severely hurt. There was something very wrong either with one of his back legs or perhaps with one of his hips. As for his mouth, that seemed strangely crooked, and he seemed to have a large cut across it.

But, as I said, he had not given up. Indeed, difficult as it must have been for him from that off-kilter position, he proceeded, while continuing to stare at me unwaveringly, to lift a front paw—and, snow or no snow, to lick it. Then the other front paw. And, when they had been attended to, the cat began the far more difficult feat of hoisting up, despite whatever it was that was amiss with his hips, first one back paw and then the other. Finally, after finishing, he did what seemed to me completely incredible—he performed an all-four-paw, ears-laid-back, straight-up leap. It looked to me as if he was, of all things in such a situation, practicing his pounce.

An odd image came to my mind—something, more years ago than I care to remember, that my first college tennis coach had drilled into our team about playing three-set matches. "In the third set," he used to say, "extra effort for ordinary results." We loathed the saying and we hated even more the fact that he made us, in that third set, just before receiving serve, jump vigorously up and down. He was convinced that this unwonted display would inform our opponents that we were fairly bursting with energy—whether that was indeed the fact or not. We did the jumping, of course, because we had to, but all of us were also convinced that we were the only players who ever had to do such a silly thing. Now when I see, without exception, every top tennis player in the world bouncing like cork into the third set, I feel like a pioneer and very much better about the whole thing.

And when I saw the cat doing his jumping, I felt better too—but this time, of course, about him. Maybe he was not as badly hurt as at first I had thought.

In a moment I noticed that Sergeant Dwork, moving quietly, had rejoined me. "Look at his mouth," she whispered. "I told you they have declared war on him!"

Ours was to be a war too—but one not against, but for, the cat. As Sergeant Dwork quietly imparted her battle plan, I had the uneasy feeling that she obviously regarded me as a raw recruit, and also that she was trying to keep my duties simple enough so that even a mere male could perform them. In any case, still whispering, she told me she would approach the fence with the cheese cubes, with which the cat was by now thoroughly familiar, in her outstretched hand, and that, during this period, I apparently should be crouching down behind her but nonetheless moving forward with her. Then, when she had gotten the cat to come as close as he would, she would step swiftly aside and I, having already thrust my arms above her through the vertical bars of the fence, was to drop to my knees and grab. The Sergeant was convinced that the cat was so hungry that, at that crucial moment, he would lose enough of his wariness to go for the bait—and the bite—which would seal his capture.

Slowly, with our eyes focussed on our objective, we moved out and went over the top. And just as we did so, indeed as I was crouching into position behind Sergeant Dwork, I got for the first time a good look at the cat's eyes peering at us. They were the first beautiful thing I ever noticed about him. They were a soft and lovely and radiant green.

As Sergeant Dwork went forward, she kept talking reassuringly to the cat, meanwhile pointedly removing the familiar cheese from her pocket and making sure he would be concentrating on it rather than the large something looming behind her. She did her job so well that we actually reached our battle station at almost the exact moment when the cat, still proceeding toward us, albeit increasingly warily, was close enough to take his first bite from the Sergeant's outstretched hand.

That first bite, however, offered us no chance of success. In one single incredibly quick but fluid motion, the cat grabbed the cheese, wolfed it down, and sprang back. Our second attempt resulted in exactly the same thing. Again the leap, the grab, the wolf, and the backward scoot. He was simply too adept at the game of eat and run.

By this time I was thoroughly convinced that nothing would come of the Sergeant's plan. But I was equally convinced that we had somehow to get that cat. I wanted to get over that fence and go for him.

The Sergeant, of course, would have none of such foolhardiness, and, irritated as this made me, I knew she was right. I could never have caught the cat that way. The Sergeant was, however, thinking of something else. Wordlessly she gave me the sign of how she was going to modify her tactics. This time she would offer the cat not one but two cubes of cheese—one in each of her two outstretched hands. But this time, she indicated, although she would push her right hand as far as it would go through the fence, she would keep her left hand well back. She obviously hoped that the cat would this time attempt both bites before the retreat. Once more we went over the top—literally in my case, because I already had my hands through the fence over the Sergeant. And this time, just as she had hoped, the cat not only took the first bite but also went for that second one. And, at just that moment, as he was midbite, Sergeant Dwork slid to one side and I dropped to my knees.

As my knees hit the ground, my face hit the grate. But I did not even feel it. For, in between my hands, my fingers underneath and my thumbs firmly on top, was cat. I had him.

Surprised and furious, he first hissed, then screamed, and finally, spinning right off the ground to midair, raked both my hands with his claws. Again I felt nothing, because by then I was totally engrossed in a dual performance—not letting go of him and yet somehow managing to maneuver his skinny, desperately squirming body, still in my tight grasp, albeit for that split second in just one hand, through the narrow apertures of the rail fence. And now his thinness was all-important because, skin and bones as he was, I was able to pull him between the bars.

Still on my knees, I raised him up and tried to tuck him inside my coat. But in this maneuver I was either overconfident or under-alert, because somewhere between the raising and the tucking, still spitting fire, he got in one final rake of my face and neck. It was a good one.

As I struggled to my feet, Sergeant Dwork was clapping her hands in pleasure, but obviously felt the time had now come to rescue me. "Oh," she said. "Oh dear. Your face. Oh my." Standing there in the snow, she tried to mop me with her handkerchief. As she did so, I could feel the cat's little heart racing with fear as he struggled to get loose underneath my coat. But it was to no avail. I had him firmly corralled, and, once again, with both hands.

The Sergeant had now finished her mopping and become all Sergeant again. "I'll take him now," she said, advancing toward me. Involuntarily, I took a step backwards. "No, no, that's all right," I assured her. "I'll take him to my apartment." The Sergeant would have none of this. "Oh no," she exclaimed. "Why, my apartment is very close." "So is mine," I replied, moving the cat even farther into the depths of my coat. "Really, it's no trouble at all. And anyway, it'll just be for tonight. Tomorrow, we'll decide—er, what to do with him."

Sergeant Dwork looked at me doubtfully as I started to move away. "Well then," she said, "I'll call you first thing in the morning." She waved a mittened hand. "Merry Christmas," she said. I wished her the same, but I couldn't wave back.

JOE, the doorman at my apartment building, was unhappy about my looks. "Mr. Amory!" he exclaimed. "What happened to your face? Are you all right?" I told him that not only was I all right, he ought to have seen the other guy. As he took me to the elevator, he was obviously curious about both the apparent fact that I had no hands and also the suspicious bulge inside my coat. Like all good New York City doormen, Joe is the soul of discretion—at least from tenant to tenant—but he has a bump of curiosity which would rival Mt. Everest. He is also, however, a good animal man, and he had a good idea that whatever I had, it was something alive. Leaning his head toward my coat, he attempted to reach in. "Let me pet it," he said. "No," I told him firmly. "Mustn't touch." "What is it?" he asked. "Don't tell anyone," I said, "but it's a saber-toothed tiger. Undeclawed, too." "Wow," he said. And then, just before the elevator took off, he told me that Marian was already upstairs.

I had figured that Marian would be there. My brother and his wife were coming over for a drink before we all went out to a party, and Marian, knowing I would probably be late, had arrived to admit them and hold, so to speak, the fort.

I kicked at the apartment door. When Marian opened it, I blurted out the story of Sergeant Dwork and the rescue. She too wanted to know what had happened to my face and if I was all right. I tried the same joke I had tried on Joe. But Marian is a hard woman on old jokes. "The only 'other guy' I'm interested in," she said, "is in your coat." I bent down to release my prize, giving him a last hug to let him know that everything was now fine.

Neither Marian nor I saw anything. All we saw, before his paws ever hit the ground, was a dirty tan blur, which, crooked hips notwithstanding, literally flew around the apartment— seemingly a couple of feet off the ground and all the time looking frantically for an exit.

In the living room I had a modest Christmas tree. Granted, it was not a very big tree—he was not, at that time, a very big cat. Granted, too, that this tree had a respectable pile of gaily wrapped packages around the base and even an animal figure attached to the top. Granted even that it was festooned with lights which, at rhythmic intervals, flashed on and off. To any cat, however, a tree is a tree and this tree, crazed as he was, was no exception. With one bound he cleared the boxes, flashed up through the branches, the lights, and the light cord and managed, somewhere near the top, to disappear again. "Now that's a good cat," I heard myself stupidly saying. "You don't have to be frightened. Nothing bad is going to happen to you here."

Walking toward the tree, I reached for where I thought he would be next, but it was no use. With one bound, he vanished down the far side and, flashing by my flailing arms, tried to climb up the inside of the fireplace. Fortunately the flue was closed, thus effectively foiling his attempt at doing a Santa Claus in reverse.

When he reappeared, noticeably dirtier than before, I was waiting for him. "Good boy," I crooned, trying to sound my most reasonable. But it was no use. He was gone again, this time on a rapid rampage through the bedroom—one which was in fact so rapid that not only was it better heard than seen but also, during the worst of it, both Marian and I were terrified that he might try to go through the window. When he finally materialized again in the hall, even he looked somewhat discouraged. Maybe, I thought desperately, I could reason with him now. Slowly I backed into the living room to get a piece of cheese from the hors d'oeuvre tray. This, I was sure, would inform him that he was among friends and that no harm would befall him. Stepping back into the hall, I found Marian looking baffled. "He's gone," she said. "Gone," I said. "Gone where?" She shook her head and I suddenly realized that, for the first time in some time, there was no noise, there was no scurrying, there was no sound of any kind. There was, in fact, no cat.

We waited for a possible reappearance. When none was forthcoming, obviously we had no alternative but to start a systematic search. It is a comparatively small apartment and there are, or so Marian and I at first believed, relatively few hiding places. We were wrong. For one thing, there was a wall-long bookshelf in the living room, and this we could not overlook, for the cat was so thin and so fast that it was eminently feasible that he found a way to clamber up and wedge himself behind a stack of books on almost any shelf. Book by book, we began opening holes.

But he was not there. Indeed, he was not anywhere. We turned out three closets. We moved the bed. We wrestled the sofa away from the wall. We looked under the tables. We canvassed the kitchen. And here, although it is such a small kitchen that it can barely accommodate two normal-sized adults at the same time, we opened every cupboard, shoved back the stove, peered into the microwave, and even poked about in the tiny space under the sink.

At that moment, the doorbell rang. Marian and I looked at each other—it had to be my brother and his wife, Mary. My brother is one of only three men who went into World War II as a private and came out as a colonel in command of a combat division. He was, as a matter of fact, in the Amphibious Engineers, and made some fourteen opposed landings against the Japanese. He had also since served as deputy director of the CIA. A man obviously used to crises, he took one look at the disarray of the apartment. In such a situation, my brother doesn't talk, he barks. "Burglars," he barked. "It looks like a thorough job."

I explained to him briefly what was going on—and that the cat had now disappeared altogether. Not surprisingly, while Mary sat down, my brother immediately assumed command. He demanded to know where we had not looked. Only where he couldn't possibly go, I explained, trying to hold my ground. "I don't want theories," he barked. "Where *haven't* you looked?" Lamely, I named the very top shelves of the closet, the inside of the oven, and the dishwasher. "Right," he snapped, and advanced on first the closets, then the oven, and last the dishwasher. And, sure enough, at the bottom of the latter, actually curled around the machinery and wedged into the most impossible place to get to in the entire apartment, was the cat. "Ha!" said my brother, attempting to bend down and reach him.

I grabbed him from behind. I was not going to have my brother trust his luck with one more opposed landing. Bravely, I took his place. I was, after all, more expendable.

Actually, the fact was that none of us could get him out. And he was so far down in the machinery, even he couldn't get himself out. "Do you use it?" my brother demanded. I shook my head. "Dismantle it," he barked once more. Obediently, I searched for screwdriver, pliers, and hammer and, although I am not much of a mantler, I consider myself second to no one, not even my brother, as a dismantler. My progress, however, dissatisfied my brother. He brushed me aside and went over the top himself. I made no protest—with the dishwasher the Amphibious Engineer was, after all, at least close to being in his element.

When my brother had finished the job, all of us, Mary included, peered down at the cat. And, for the fist time since my first sight of him in the alley, he peered back. He was so exhausted that he made no attempt to move, although he was now free to do so. "I would like to make a motion," Marian said quietly. "I move that we leave him right where he is, put out some food and water and a litter pan for him—and leave him be. What he needs now is peace and quiet."

The motion carried. We left out three bowls—of water, of milk, and of food—turned out all the lights, including the Christmas lights, and left him.

That night, when I got home, I tiptoed into the apartment. The three bowls were just where we had left them—and every one of them was empty. There was, however, no cat. But this time I initiated no search. I simply refilled the dishes and went to bed. With the help of a Sergeant, a colonel, and Marian, I now had, for better or for worse, for a few days at least, a Christmas cat.

J. R. Ackerley

MY DOG TULIP

Some years ago, when I was walking with my dog in Fulham Palace Gardens, we overtook an old woman who was wheeling a baby carriage. She was chatting cheerfully to the occupant of it, and it was therefore, perhaps, not unreasonable of me to be surprised to find, when I caught up with her, that this too was a dog. He was lying upon his back, propped up by pillows, with a rug tucked round his middle; just above the top of the rug the edge of a thick bandage was visible. Very comfortable and peaceful the little dog looked as the old woman trundled him along among the flowers, chatting to him in that bright, encouraging way in which people address invalids.

I made some sympathetic remark to her as I passed, and she was all agog to tell me about her troubles, how the poor little dog had been so seriously ill with an internal tumor, but how he was well on the road to recovery now, thanks, oh thanks—she could not thank her enough—to the wonderful lady vet who had operated on him and been so clever and so kind, for had it not been for her, the little dog, who was such a good little dog, would undoubtedly have died.

"Wouldn't you, love?" said she to the invalid, who lay back motionless against the pillows, with his paws folded on his stomach and a very solemn expression on his small, pointed face.

This conversation made a deep impression upon me. I was then quite new to the dog world, for my present dog was the first I had ever possessed, and there was much that I did not know and wished to learn. It astounded me to hear that dogs underwent major operations and had their stomachs opened and shut as we do, and I tried to picture this little mongrel lying upon the operating table, under the glare of the head-lamps, with the grave faces of surgeons, nurses, and anesthetists bent over him. What on earth would happen to my dog, I wondered uneasily, if she should ever develop anything so serious as an internal tumor? Who would care to operate on her? Before parting from the old woman, I did not fail to take the name and address of the lady vet who had been "so clever and so kind."

MY own dog is an Alsatian bitch. Her name is Tulip. Alsatians have a bad reputation; they are said to bite the hand that feeds them. Indeed Tulip bit my hand once, but accidentally; she mistook it for a rotten apple we were both trying to grab simultaneously. One of her canines sank into my thumb-joint to the bone: when I held it under the tap afterwards I could see the sinews exposed. We all make mistakes and she was dreadfully sorry. She rolled over on the grass with all her legs in the air; and later on, when she saw the bandage on my hand, she put herself in the corner, the darkest corner of the bedroom, and stayed there for the rest of the afternoon. One can't do more than that.

But if you look like a wild beast you are expected to behave like one; and human beings, who tend to disregard the savagery of their own conduct, shake their heads over the Alsatian dog. "What can you expect of a wolf?" they say.*

Tulip made no conspicuous effort to improve this situation. If people were inclined to look at her askance she gave them every reason to do so. They distrusted her; she suspected them. In fact she repudiated the human race altogether—that is to say the remainder of it. *I* could do with her whatever I wished—except stop her barking at other people. In this matter, she seemed to say, she knew better than I. Yet she behaved always with exemplary dignity and good breeding wherever she went, so long as she was let alone: it was when anyone approached her, or even gave the impression of being about to approach her, that she spoke her mind. She spoke sharply and loud, and she had a good deal to say, though what precisely her mind was I did not know. In truth, although I was very anxious to know, I was less anxious to find out. Her sweetness and gentleness to myself were such that it was almost impossible for me to believe that these were not the prevailing characteristics of her nature; but the language she used to others certainly sounded pretty strong, and bad language, as is well known, does not always stop at that.

No doubt the reason why I took the constant care I did take to protect her from being put to the test of showing how far she would go, was that I had to admit I had an inkling; but the two bus conductors and the postman whom she had already bitten could hardly be accepted as a true sociological sample of her feelings for mankind. They had all been doing things, like coming soundlessly upon us in sneakers, or striking the bus a sudden sharp rat-tat alongside us with their ticket

---

* "Don't let that dog near me!" shouted a tramp to me one day on Brook Green. "They ain't to be trusted!"

"You don't look particularly trustworthy yourself," I replied, and might be thought to have hit a nail on the head, for he at once fumbled a jack-knife out of his miscellaneous garments and, opening it with some difficulty, flourished it after me.

racks to make it move on, of which it is in the nature of dogs to disapprove; in any case she had not hurt them, but merely taken them by the sleeve or by the arm; and though one of the conductors had rolled back his cuff to display the wound, he himself seemed disappointed that there was nothing to be seen but a small white dent in his flesh.

When children are called difficult the cause is often traced to their homes, and it was upon Tulip's first home that I blamed her unsociable conduct. She had originally belonged to some working-class people who, though fond of her in their way, seldom took her out. She was too excitable, and too valuable, to be allowed off the leash; on it she pulled. For nearly a year she scarcely left their house, but spent her time, mostly alone, for they were at work all day, in a tiny back-yard. She could hardly be expected, therefore, to learn the ways of a world she so rarely visited; the only "training" she ever received was an occasional thrashing for the destruction which her owners discovered when they returned home. Alsa-tians in particular do not take kindly to beatings; they are too intelligent and too nervous. It was from this life, when she was eighteen months old, that I rescued her, and to it that I attributed the disturbances of her psyche. Thereafter it was clear that if she could have her way she would never let me out of her sight again.

It is necessary to add that she is beautiful. People are always wanting to touch her, a thing she cannot bear. Her ears are tall and pointed, like the ears of Anubis. How she manages to hold them constantly erect, as though starched, I do not know, for with their fine covering of mouse-gray fur they are soft and flimsy; when she stands with her back to the sun it shines through the delicate tissue, so that they glow shell-pink as though incandescent. Her face also is long and pointed, basically stone-gray but the snout and lower jaw are jet black. Jet, too, are the rims of her amber eyes, as though heavily mascara'd, and the tiny mobile eyebrow tufts that are set like accents above them. And in the midst of her forehead is a kind of Indian caste-mark, a black diamond suspended there, like the jewel on the brow of Pegasus in Mantegna's "Parnassus," by a fine dark thread, no more than a pencilled line, which is drawn from it right over her poll midway between the tall ears. A shadow extends across her forehead from either side of this caste-mark, so that, in certain lights, the diamond looks like the body of a bird with its wings spread, a bird in flight.

These dark markings symmetrically divide up her face into zones of pale pastel colors, like a mosaic, or a stained-glass window; her skull, bisected by the thread, is two primrose pools, the center of her face light gray, the bridge of her nose above the long, black lips fawn, her cheeks white, and upon each a *patte de mouche* has been tastefully set. A delicate white ruff, frilling out from the lobes of her ears, frames this strange, clownish face, with its heavily leaded features, and covers the whole of her throat and chest with a snowy shirt front.

For the rest, her official description is sable-gray: she is a gray dog wearing a sable tunic. Her gray is the gray of birch bark; her sable tunic is of the texture of satin and clasps her long body like a saddle-cloth. No tailor could have shaped it more elegantly; it is cut round the joints of her shoulders and thighs and in a straight line along the points of her ribs, lying open at the chest and stomach. Over her rump it fits like a cap, and then extends on in a thin strip over the top of her long tail down to the tip. Viewed from above, therefore, she is a black dog; but when she rolls over on her back she is a gray one. Two dark ribbons of fur, descending from her tunic over her shoulders, fasten it at her sternum, which seems to clip the ribbons together as with an ivory brooch.

She had been to three vets already for various reasons. It was a measure of my naïvety in dog affairs that my first consultation with a vet was to inquire whether she was in heat. The question was never settled, that is to say by him, for when he was finally able to make himself heard, in his bleak surgery, above her deafening challenge and my own vain exhortations to her to calm herself, all he said, in a cold voice, was "Have you any control over your dog?"

In the face of the evidence it seemed idle to return anything but "No"; to which, still keeping his distance, he drily replied, "Then take her out of my surgery at once."

Some weeks later she sustained a small cut in one of her pads, which took so long to heal that I began to fear that it would never heal at all; another vet had been recommended to me, and I decided to try my luck with him. He was an ex-Army man, a Major, and the most that I asked of Tulip on this occasion was that she should allow me to flex her paw so that, without touching her, he could glance at the cut. But she would not permit even that. Having failed, as I had failed, to humor her or shout her down, the Major suddenly lost his temper, and exclaiming, "These Alsatians! They're all the same!" he swooped upon her and beat her about the body with his bare hands.

These dashing military tactics were not without effect; they drove her, trembling with astonishment and fear, beneath his operating table, from the shelter of which she looked out at him with an expression which I might secretly excuse but could not approve; but they did not enable him to examine her, if that was part of his plan, and they could hardly be construed as an invitation to call again. They implied also, I took it, a rebuke to myself, as well as the more obvious one they meted out to her; they were teaching me a much needed lesson in how to discipline an unruly dog: "Spare the rod and spoil the child!" was what the Major was, in effect, saying.

As I walked away from this establishment with Tulip, who was now in her gayest and most winning mood, I supposed myself to be in possession of an undoctorable dog; but this gloomy reflection was succeeded by two others of a more comforting nature. The first was that, after all, she hadn't bitten the Major. And he might truly be said to have asked for that. Flinging caution to the winds, he had set about her;

but she had not retaliated: whatever savagery had been exhibited in the surgery had not been exhibited by her. My other reflection was, in one way, even more comforting. "These Alsatians! They're all the same!" he had said. Tulip, then, was not exceptional in her tiresomeness. She was not, so to speak, a delinquent dog. If all Alsatians were the same, her peculiarities were of the breed and not an individual affair. But if all Alsatians were the same, did any of them ever receive medical attention?

It transpired that they did; and above all the conflicting emotions that rent me when we visited our third vet—this time for a most important service, to have her inoculated against distemper—was gratitude that he did not summon the police or the fire department. I had made the appointment by telephone, and had thought it politic to apologize for Tulip in advance and to explain that, although I did not believe there was really any harm in her, she was not the most amenable of patients. To this the vet had merely grunted: when I set out with her I was already unnerved by the thought of the struggle that lay ahead. Nor were my drooping spirits raised by the first sight that greeted us, a Spaniel who was being treated as we arrived. This creature was visible to us, like some callous admonishment, before ever we reached the surgery door, for its window looked out upon a yard through which we had to pass, and the Spaniel was all too plainly seen within.

He was standing quietly on a table with a thermometer sticking out of his bottom, like a cigarette. And this humiliating spectacle was rendered all the more crushing by the fact that there was no one else there. Absolutely motionless, and with an air of deep absorption, the dog was standing upon the table in an empty room with a thermometer in his bottom, almost as though he had put it there himself.

"Oh, Tulip!" I groaned. "If only you were like that!"

But she was not. When the vet returned from his dispensary and, the thermometer and the spaniel having been successively removed, was free to turn his attention to us, she was not in the least like that. Suspecting the place's character, no doubt, from the pervasive odor of medicaments and the howls and moans of the various sick animals penned in the kennel at the back, she had exhibited the strongest aversion from entering it, and was now imploring and cajoling me to take her away: as soon as the vet opened his mouth to speak, she replied. A gray little man with an unsmiling face, he stood with his syringe in his hand patiently waiting while I petted and coaxed poor Tulip, speaking soothingly to her in baby language, as she shrank, dribbled, and barked between my knees.

"Can you turn her back to me and hold her head still?" he inquired, in a momentary lull.

"I think so," I said nervously.

But to turn her back on this odious little man was the last thing that Tulip intended; she squirmed convulsively out of my grasp over and over again, eventually wrenching her head out of her collar. Under the vet's expressionless gaze I had to retrieve her and rebuckle it, with hands which, he probably noticed, shook as much as she did.

"May I give her the injection myself?" I asked. "You could show me where to do it and she wouldn't mind it from me."

The vet made no reply. Instead, he laid his syringe upon the table, rang the bell, selected a strip of bandage from a hook on the wall and made a loop in it—all without a word. The door opened, and an assistant came in.

"Good!" exclaimed the vet to me, with sudden briskness. "Now just keep her head like that for a moment!" and advancing the loop towards Tulip, who was still determinedly pointing her face at him, and now glared at the approaching contraption as though mesmerised, he abruptly noosed her nose, with what was plainly the dexterity of long practice, drew her jaws tightly and roughly together, turned the ends of the tape round her throat and knotted them behind her ears.

"Oh, I say!" I cried. "Don't hurt her! There's really no need."

I was, indeed, in no position, or even mind, to question whatever methods this busy and helpful man might think fit to employ to exercise over my animal the control I lacked, and my miserable ejaculation was only wrung from me by the sight of Tulip's horror-stricken face and the squawk of pain and despair she uttered before her powers of speech were cut rudely short.

My thoughts, in fact, were in the utmost confusion. I suffered to see my dear, affectionate dog ill-used, but I could hardly expect my tender feelings to be shared by a vet who was meeting her for the first time and clearly did not bring out in her, like myself, the sweetest and the best. What should I do, I pondered, if I were in his shoes, confronted with a strange, large, vulpine and unfriendly dog, possessed of an excellent set of teeth, into whom I was asked to stick a needle? Would I cheerfully grasp her with hands upon the wholeness of which my means of livelihood depended? Yet, on the other side, could it be good for a creature, already so nervous and mistrustful, to be subjected to such violent stratagems?

However, for all the attention the vet paid me, I might never have spoken. "Now, Bob!" was all he said, and, brushing me aside, he and his assistant took hold of the defenceless Tulip, who was foaming at the mouth with terror, and pulling her legs from beneath her, brought her heavily to the ground.

"Pass the syringe," said the vet.

AFTER this, my ambition in life was to keep Tulip in such a state of health that she need never visit a vet again. It was an ambition which she herself appeared to share. She would not, if she could help it, even enter the streets in which her last two experiences had taken place. If I happened to forget and turned down one of them when we were out, I would suddenly miss her from my side, an unheard-of-thing, and looking wildly round, espy her far behind me, motionless at the corner, staring after me with her exclamation-mark face. There is no getting away from Tulip's face; with its tall ears constantly focused upon one it demands an attention which it seems unremittingly to give. She fixes one, as one is sometimes claimed and fixed by those insistent bores who, when they have something to impart, hold one's gaze with a searching, inescapable stare, as though they know from experience that the attention of their listeners is apt to wander and are determined to exact that responsive gleam of intelligence which their remorseless personalities require. "Are you listening?" they say, irritably or plaintively, from time to time.

Tulip's face perpetually said the same thing, for with all its perpendicular lines, the tall ears, the long nose, the black streak down the forehead and the little vertical eyebrow tufts, it was not merely interrogatory but exclamatory also: it said both "What?" and "What!" Useless to call her now, she would not budge; I must return to her and reach my objective by another route; but later I discovered that she would consent to follow me down these unsavory roads so long as I reassured her, by passing the surgeries, that it was not my intention to enter them. Then she would come, but always with infinite distaste, crossing the road to make the widest possible detour and hurrying past the baleful buildings, casting at them every now and then a repugnant, sidelong glance.

But my disinclination to visit vets was in frequent conflict with my need to consult them; perplexities of all sorts troubled my ignorant and anxious mind, and not the least of my worries at the time of my encounter with the old woman in Fulham Palace Gardens was that, in spite of the nourishing food I provided, Tulip looked too thin; beneath her sable tunic all her ribs were visible. The distressing word "Worms" was dropped into my ear by a kind acquaintance, and soon afterwards I decided to take her along to see Miss Canvey, which was the name of the lady vet who had been "so clever and so kind." Her surgery was in Parsons Green, and to the kennel-maid who answered the phone I explained, in the apologetic manner which was now habitual with me, that my bitch was very difficult and I would prefer, if convenient, to bring her along out of surgery hours.

Miss Canvey was a short, thickset, young woman with bobbed hair, spectacles, and a homely peasant's face. She wore a white overall, not intimidatingly clean, and as she advanced across the large, bare room towards me, I took an impression of calmness and competence. I had spoken sternly to Tulip as we waited, exhorting her to good behavior for a change, but I had no expectation of any improvement and there was none; she accorded Miss Canvey her usual defiant reception—defiance which became the more emphatic the more it was ignored. Miss Canvey approached imperturbably and stood quietly in front of us, looking down at her, while I stumbled through some account of her past and present troubles, punctuated with irritable commands to the dog to pipe down.

"She's like this with everyone," I said ruefully, "but as sweet as pie to me. I can't make it out."

Miss Canvey did not speak, but continued to gaze down at the excited animal. Then she asked:

"What's her name?" I told her. "Well, Tulip, you *are* a noisy girl, aren't you? What's it all about?" and she extended her hand, back foremost. Tulip paused for a moment to sniff it, then, as the hand was moved closer, retreated, barking more violently than ever. How maddening, how intolerable it was that this creature, usually so attentive and obedient to my wishes, should always let me down in public in this stupid way! Suddenly yelling "Stop it, you brute!" I biffed her on the nose. The blow was harder than I intended. Tulip gave a little cry of pain and rubbed her nose with her paw. Then she rose up on her hind legs and gently licked my face.

"I see," said Miss Canvey promptly. "You're the trouble."

"I?" I exclaimed, astonished.

"Just slip the lead through her collar, will you. I'll examine her in another room."

"Are you sure it will be all right?" I asked anxiously, doing as I was bid.

"Perfectly all right." And twisting the lead round her strong wrist, she marched firmly out of the room, towing behind her the horrified and struggling Tulip who cast back at me agonized glances as she slid and sprawled across the linoleum. The door closed.

Alone in the surgery I listened apprehensively for sounds— screams from Miss Canvey, cries of pain or rage from Tulip, rushing feet, banging doors—sounds of any sort: none could be reassuring. But the place was as silent as the grave. Then, after what seemed an eternity but was only ten minutes, I heard a scuffling in the passage and a few barks, but of a very different timbre; the door opened and Tulip reappeared, this time with Miss Canvey in tow.

"No sign of worms," remarked the latter, dropping the lead. "She's in excellent condition."

"How did she behave?" I asked, while Tulip cast herself into my arms and lavished upon me a greeting more suitable in its extravagance to lovers who had been parted for years.

"Good as gold," said Miss Canvey.

"Did you tie up her nose?"

"Heavens, no! I never do that."

"But you had help?" I said, gazing mistily at her.

Miss Canvey smiled:

"Of course not. She was no trouble. I knew she wouldn't be."

"How did you know?" I asked humbly.

"Well, you learn by experience, I suppose. But it isn't difficult to tell a dog's character from its face. Tulip's a good girl, I saw that at once. You're the trouble."

I sat down.

"Do tell me," I said.

"Well, she's in love with you, that's obvious. And so life's full of worries for her. She has to protect you to begin with; that's why she's upset when people approach you: I expect she's a bit jealous, too. But in order to protect you she's naturally got to be free; that's why she doesn't like other people touching her; she's afraid, you see, that they may take hold of her and deprive her of her freedom to guard you. That's all the fuss is about, I should say. It's you she's thinking of. But when you're not there, there's nothing for her to do, of course, and no anxiety. Anyone can handle her then, I'm sure. That's all," she concluded with a smile. "Dogs aren't difficult to understand. One has to put oneself in their position."

Miss Canvey could have put herself in any position she wished, for I was already her slave and gazed at her with the veneration with which we behold a saint. I asked her some questions about Tulip's diet, paid the fee—half-a-crown, so far as I recall, was all that this miracle cost—and took my leave. As I was going, she suddenly said:

"Why do you shout at her?"

"I don't know," I stammered, rather taken aback. "She exasperates me sometimes. She doesn't seem to hear what I say."

"She can hear a pin drop!" said Miss Canvey briefly. "Look at her ears!" Then on a milder note: "Try not to. It's bad for her. She's very highly strung. Speak to her quietly; she'll do anything you want in time."

As we walked away I apologised to Tulip for hitting her on her beautiful nose, and, in my thoughts, for much else besides. In the light of Miss Canvey's interpretation, how infinitely more hideous that abject struggle in the last vet's surgery now seemed, how heroic her conduct, how mean and contemptible mine. I had apologized for her devotion, and then betrayed it. I recollected, with a shudder, how I had held her head still for the approaching trap. I felt very tender towards her.

After this, we may be said almost to have lived in the surgery of dear Miss Canvey, that Florence Nightingale of the animal world. I walked Tulip over to see her on any pretext, however trifling, and such was the confidence she inspired that very soon I no longer bothered to make special appointments, but dropped in during surgery hours and sat with Tulip in the crowded room awaiting our turn and watching wonderful Miss Canvey at work upon a miscellaneous assortment of sick dogs, cats, rabbits, and poultry. It was an enthralling and uplifting spectacle, and though her white overalls became less and less white and her bobbed hair more and more disordered, she never lost that air of calm authority which it was a positive tonic to breathe. That Tulip ever enjoyed these visits as much as I did, I cannot pretend; but my own freedom from anxiety no doubt affected her too; what resistance she put up seemed more perfunctory, and once inside, she sat by my knee quietly, except for an occasional mew of impatience, until her turn came. Then, of course, when the solid little figure of Miss Canvey approached us, she put on her act, though with less of the old conviction; with a genial word of welcome, Miss Canvey simply took the lead and towed her from the room.

One day I observed among the other pilgrims to this shrine a young working man with his Collie dog, which was muzzled. Miss Canvey was busily engaged in extracting a tintack from the anus of a hen, and it was some time before she noticed him. Then she called across the room:

"Why is your dog muzzled?"

"I don't trust 'im, Miss," said the young man, blushing.

"Take it off," said Miss Canvey.

She always spoke quietly, though sometimes, as now, rather abruptly; no one ever thought of disobeying her, and the young man complied. When his turn came she examined his dog with her usual coolness and thoroughness; then she took the young man aside and spoke earnestly to him in a corner. I could not catch what she said, but at the end of it he smiled and murmured "Thank you, Miss." Then he went off with his dog, carrying the muzzle in his hand.

While this little scene was being enacted, I happened to be sitting near the desk where Miss Canvey's kennel-maid was writing out prescriptions, and leaning over, I whispered to her:

"Has Miss Canvey ever been bitten?"

The kennel-maid looked cautiously round before replying; then she said, in a low, hesitant voice:

"Well, she has once, to my knowledge; but I don't think she'd like it known."

"Please tell me."

"I didn't actually see it happen," said the girl, "because I was busy with something else; but I heard a sort of scuffle—it was another Collie she was treating, too—and saw her go quickly out of the room holding her hand. When she returned she had a bandage on her wrist, but she went back to finish what she'd been doing. I asked, 'Did he bite you?' but all she said, rather shortly, was 'It was my fault. I was clumsy.' And though I offered to take over the case from her, and so did Mr. Mather when he got to hear of it, she would never let anyone else handle the dog all the time he was ill. He never hurt her again, and they became very good friends in the end."

"Sublime woman!" I said.

The kennel-maid smiled:

"She's fond of animals, and so they like and trust her. All animals, but specially horses. They're what she likes best."

Gary Allen Sledge

MY FATHER'S WAY

Pooch was my father's dog, a big, happy, flop-eared mongrel. She wore clown patches of tan and brown on her coat of short, white hair, and was tall enough to meet me nose to wet nose. My father loved Pooch for some improbable promise he saw in her. I saw only trouble.

Pooch was clumsy as an ox and exuberantly affectionate. I had to dodge and weave to avoid her kisses. She outweighed me by ten pounds, and sometimes she knocked me down. As an eight-year-old, I found such behavior unseemly.

That summer it was my job to take care of Pooch, since Dad was away during the week at "the Mountain," his sawmill on 200 acres of redwood and pine above the Russian River on the northern California coast. Mom and I stayed in Antioch in the San Joaquin delta because she didn't want me "growing up lonely and wild in the forest."

Dad wore an old, brown Stetson, and with one side of the oily brim cocked over his eye, he had the sharp, don't-talk-back-to-me look of Humphrey Bogart in *High Sierra*. I was not a little afraid of him.

"You mind your mother," he'd warn me before leaving for the Mountain every Monday morning.

"Yes, sir."

"You water the lawn, hear, every day. Cut it on Wednesday."

"Yes, sir."

"And knock them little almond trees in the back. And Pooch needs good scraps, some of them dog biscuits for her teeth and a good run morning and night." And good run with Pooch was like being dragged by a runaway steamroller.

"You're the man of the house, understand?" I said I did, but I didn't quite see how spending valuable summer hours picking up almonds and feeding his dish-faced, loose-boweled dog meant I was the man of the house.

Pooch always made the most of Dad's leave-takings, dancing around his legs, tail beating like a thick rope against a flagpole in her eager, woeful good-by. Dad would kneel to receive her kisses while he scratched her ears. I thought it was disgusting to be kissed by a sloppy dog.

My father and I regarded each other across a gulf in those days—that awkward, silent space males put between themselves about matters as soul-simple as love and fear. Dad had grown up quick and tough, making his own way in the world, never asking a penny from anyone. He worked his way from Dust Bowl Oklahoma to California, met and married my mother when he was 18 and then was called up to war.

I was born a few months after he shipped out to Saipan, and I grew accustomed to being spoiled by a tight maternal clan of mother, grandmother and a half-dozen aunts. My father's return when I was almost three disrupted that.

In some ways, we failed to live up to one another's expectations. He wanted a rough-and-tumble son who could fish and hunt, while I was a bookworm who wanted a father to hold me in his lap and read to me. Taking care of Pooch was his attempt to toughen me up and teach me responsibility. I resented the task.

Dad claimed that someday when he had time, he was going to train her. But the one time he took Pooch duck hunting, she came back with her tail drooping and a look of mortal humiliation on her sad-eyed face. It seemed that at the blast of the shotgun Pooch had hunkered down and begun to whine and shake. Still, Dad did not give up on her. "That dog has *ex-cep-tion-al* intelligence," he was fond of saying. "All I got to do is teach her discipline and self-control."

Pooch lived in a big doghouse that Dad had built of scrap wood behind a chicken-wire fence in our back yard. I hated going into those dung-marked grounds to feed that dog. Every morning I'd try to sneak in and get her water dish while she was sleeping. Only she was never sleeping. Out she'd jump, tail thumping, foot in the dish, paws on my chest.

Inevitably she'd bound for the gate before I could close it, for Pooch loved freedom more than anything. Then it was at least a ten-minute chase around the yard. Boy, could she run! Sometimes Pooch would vault over our five-foot-tall wooden fence, reverse gears and come bouncing back. She'd keep that up—tongue flopping and tail stretched arrow-straight—until she was out of breath. It was hard to have much respect for that dumb dog.

When Dad was home, he looked tired and anxious. I had some hazy idea that money was the problem, and the mill was not making much of it. Late Sunday nights, after a full week-end of work around the house, Mom and Dad would sit at the dining-room table with worried looks on their faces, a stack of yellow bills and a black checkbook in front of them. Monday morning early, Dad would pack up his duffel bag, kiss Mom and start back for the sawmill.

Late in August Dad took Mom and me up to the Mountain for a couple of weeks' vacation. Because there was no way to take Pooch that far in our car, Dad asked one of his hunting buddies, a man with some country-sounding name like Claggert, to care for Pooch.

Claggert's house looked like something out of a Ma and Pa

Kettle movie: unpainted, a ramshackle porch, an old car up on blocks, and a bunch of kids running around barefoot. The youngest child was about a year and a half, and there was something wrong with his legs. He lay on the porch in a box while the other kids played around him. I tried not to look at him, yet I couldn't keep from sneaking a glance.

Claggert tied Pooch's leash to a clothesline so she could run, and Dad and I left. It was hard to listen to her sorrowful howling as we drove away.

Unexpectedly, I didn't have a good time on the Mountain. Dad was too busy to take me swimming or fishing, and late at night, lying under heavy quilts, I could hear my parents whisper about "never-ending expenses" and the Forest Service demanding "cutbacks" and "fire precautions" and a "chip burner."

During the day, I'd perch on a knobby redwood burl and toss pieces of bark into a bucket. I missed my friends, and I even began to wish that Pooch was with me. At least then I could run up and down the dirt roads with someone, and we could chase squirrels and stalk deer together. At the end of two weeks, I was ready to go home.

WHEN Dad and I drove back to the Claggerts', the whole family came out on the porch. Mrs. Claggert was holding the baby with the shriveled legs. Mr. Claggert stepped forward with one of his sons about my age. The boy had Pooch on a leash.

"Hi, Bill," Claggert said. He seemed jovial, but his eyes avoided ours. While he traded stories with my dad, I went over and patted Pooch on the head. Her big tail beat the ground, and she licked my hand. But in uncharacteristic fashion she sat politely still, as if they had taught her some manners. The kid holding her gave me a funny look.

"That dog's something," Claggert was saying. "The kids just love her. Smart! Fetch and all. Bobbie here taught Pooch to pull the little one around in a wagon."

"Yeah," Dad said, "be a good hunting dog soon as I get around to learnin' her."

Claggert cleared his throat. "You ever think of selling her, Bill?"

"No, can't say as I have."

"I give you $50 for her."

I gasped. Fifty dollars was an unheard-of amount. Suddenly I was worried that Dad might take it, considering the bad times at the mill. Pooch was part of our family. You don't sell family.

"Nah," my dad said, "she's just a mongrel bitch."

"A hundred bucks."

Where would this dirt-poor Claggert get a hundred dollars? Something was wrong here. I saw a strange expression grow on Dad's face. "I don't want anything for her," he said, flat and hard. "I just want my dog."

"Give her here, Bobbie," Claggert said and shooed his son back to the porch. When my father tried to take the rope, Claggert held on.

"I'll fight you for her if I have to, Bill, but I gotta keep this dog."

My father regarded Claggert the way I'd seen him size up a snake that he'd kick or walk around. His hands clenched. "I told you she's not for sale. Period."

"I can't give her to you, Bill," Claggert pleaded. "My wife and kids won't let me." His face was twisted with pain.

"You know my littlest got bad legs. The missus puts him out on a blanket in the front yard there, and the kids are supposed to watch him. The other day, though, the kids were playing, and the baby crawled out in the road. The missus looks out the kitchen window and sees the baby laying in a rut with a car roaring down on him. She screams. Then Pooch jumps over the fence, runs up and grabs the baby by the seat of his pants and pulls him out of the road. Sure enough, it's some drunk that skids right over where the baby was."

Claggert cleared his throat. "Pooch saved his life."

Claggert looked at my father with pleading eyes. "We love that dog. My wife makes her up a bed in the baby's room every night. We'll take care of her till the day she dies. I'll pay you any amount, Bill."

My father waited in silence, then let go of the leash. "Well, I told you I ain't selling her." He bent down and scratched Pooch behind both ears and ran his hand gently down her smooth muzzle. "So I'll give her to you."

Claggert let out an explosion of breath, took Dad's hand and pumped it up and down. He looked back at his family on the porch and, with a big smile, nodded.

"Come on," Dad said to me, and he started back down the rutted dirt road to the car.

"Why'd you give her away?" I cried, tears springing shamelessly to my eyes. "She's yours!" But I was thinking. *She's mine! I feed and water her. I take her running.*

Dad picked me up and put me on the bumper of the Ford. "Listen, son. There ain't a living thing a man can hold on to in this world unless he loves it and works for it. Those folks love Pooch better than me. By rights she belongs to them."

They don't love her better than me, my heart cried, now that it was too late.

"Come on, be big. I know what you're feeling."

He opened the car door and put me inside, up front with him.

"Yes, sir," I said, coughing back tears.

Dad got in, started the engine and then did something he rarely did. He put his arm around my shoulder, drew me close and kept me by his side all the way home.

That fall, to support his family, my father finally had to forfeit his timberland and take a job he detested in a pulp mill. But I had learned something important from him—something more important than a lesson in loss. He showed me, in a world marred by misfortune, what effort and sacrifice and generosity it takes to be a man—to hold onto the essential things and to keep safe the ones you love.

James Thurber

A SNAPSHOT OF REX

I ran across a dim photograph of him the other day, going through some old things. He's been dead about forty years. His name was Rex (my two brothers and I named him when we were in our early teens) and he was a bull terrier. "An American bull terrier," we used to say, proudly; none of your English bulls. He had one brindle eye that sometimes made him look like a clown and sometimes reminded you of a politician with derby hat and cigar. The rest of him was white except for a brindle saddle that always seemed to be slipping off and a brindle stocking on a hind leg. Nevertheless, there was a nobility about him. He was big and muscular and beautifully made. He never lost his dignity even when trying to accomplish the extravagant tasks my brothers and I used to set for him. One of these was the bringing of a ten-foot wooden rail into the yard through the back gate. We would throw it out into the alley and tell him to go get it. Rex was as powerful as a wrestler, and there were not many things that he couldn't manage somehow to get hold of with his great jaws and lift or drag to wherever he wanted to put them, or wherever we wanted them put. He would catch the rail at the balance and lift it clear of the ground and trot with great confidence toward the gate. Of course, since the gate was only four feet wide or so, he couldn't bring the rail in broadside. He found that out when he got a few terrific jolts, but he wouldn't give up. He finally figured out how to do it, by dragging the rail, holding on to one end, growling. He got a great, wagging satisfaction out of his work. We used to bet kids who had never seen Rex in action that he could catch a baseball thrown as high as they could throw it. He almost never let us down. Rex could hold a baseball with ease in his mouth, in one cheek, as if it were a chew of tobacco.

He was a tremendous fighter, but he never started fights. I don't believe he liked to get into them, despite the fact that he came from a line of fighters. He never went for another dog's throat but for one of its ears (that teaches a dog a lesson), and he would get his grip, close his eyes, and hold on. He could hold on for hours. His longest fight lasted from dusk until almost pitch-dark, one Sunday. It was fought in East Main Street in Columbus with a large, snarly nondescript that belonged to a big colored man. When Rex finally got his ear grip, the brief whirlwind of snarling turned to screeching. It was frightening to listen to and to watch. The Negro boldly picked the dogs up somehow and began swinging them around his head, and finally let them fly like a hammer in a hammer throw, but although they landed ten feet away with a great plump, Rex still held on.

The two dogs eventually worked their way to the middle of the car tracks, and after a while two or three streetcars were held up by the fight. A motorman tried to pry Rex's jaws open with a switch rod; somebody lighted a fire and made a torch of a stick and held that to Rex's tail, but he paid no attention. In the end, all the residents and storekeepers in the neighborhood were on hand, shouting this, suggesting that. Rex's joy of battle, when battle was joined, was almost tranquil. He had a kind of pleasant expression during fights, not a vicious one, his eyes closed in what would have seemed to be sleep had it not been for the turmoil of the struggle. The Oak Street Fire Department finally had to be sent for—I don't know why nobody thought of it sooner. Five or six pieces of apparatus arrived, followed by a battalion chief. A hose was attached and a powerful stream of water was turned on the dogs. Rex held on for several moments more while the torrent buffeted him about like a log in a freshet. He was a hundred yards away from where the fight started when he finally let go.

THE story of that Homeric fight got all around town, and some of our relatives looked upon the incident as a blot on the family name. They insisted that we get rid of Rex, but we were very happy with him, and nobody could have made us give him up. We would have left town with him first, along any road there was to go. It would have been different, perhaps, if he had ever started fights, or looked for trouble. But he had a gentle disposition. He never bit a person in the ten strenuous years that he lived, nor ever growled at anyone except prowlers. He killed cats, that is true, but quickly and neatly and without especial malice, the way men kill certain animals. It was the only thing he did that we could never cure him of doing. He never killed or even chased a squirrel. I don't know why. He had his own philosophy about such things. He never ran barking after wagons or automobiles. He didn't seem to see the idea in pursuing something you couldn't catch, or something you couldn't do anything with, even if you did catch it. A wagon was one of the things he couldn't tug along with his mighty jaws, and he knew it. Wagons, therefore, were not a part of his world.

Swimming was his favorite recreation. The first time he ever saw a body of water (Alum Creek), he trotted nervously along the steep bank for a while, fell to barking wildly, and finally plunged in from a height of eight feet or more. I shall always remember that shining, virgin dive. Then he swam upstream and back just for the pleasure of it, like a man. It was fun to see him battle upstream against a stiff current, struggling and growling every foot of the way. He had as much fun in the water as any person I have known. You didn't have to throw a stick in the water to get him to go in. Of course, he would bring back a stick to you if you did throw one in. He would even have brought back a piano if you had thrown one in.

That reminds me of the night, way after midnight, when he went a-roving in the light of the moon and brought back a small chest of drawers that he had found somewhere—how far from the house nobody ever knew; since it was Rex, it could easily have been half a mile. There were no drawers in the chest when he got it home, and it wasn't a good one—he hadn't taken it out of anybody's house; it was just an old cheap piece that somebody had abandoned on a trash heap. Still, it was something he wanted, probably because it presented a nice problem in transportation. It tested his mettle. We first knew about his achievement when, deep in the night, we heard him trying to get the chest up onto the porch. It sounded as if two or three people were trying to tear the house down. We came downstairs and turned on the porch light. Rex was on the top step trying to pull the thing up, but it had caught somehow and he was just holding his own. I suppose he would have held his own till dawn if we hadn't helped him. The next day we carted the chest miles away and threw it out. If we had thrown it out in a near-by alley, he would have brought it home again, as a small token of his integrity in such matters. After all, he had been taught to carry heavy wooden objects about, and he was proud of his prowess.

I am glad Rex never saw a trained police dog jump. He was just an amateur jumper himself, but the most daring and tenacious I have ever seen. He would take on any fence we pointed out to him. Six feet was easy for him, and he could do eight by making a tremendous leap and hauling himself over finally by his paws, grunting and straining; but he lived and died without knowing that twelve-and sixteen-foot walls were too much for him. Frequently, after letting him try to go over one for a while, we would have to carry him home. He would never have given up trying.

There was in his world no such thing as the impossible. Even death couldn't beat him down. He died, it is true, but only as one of his admirers said, after "straight-arming the death angel" for more than an hour. Late one afternoon he wandered home, too slowly and too uncertainly to be the Rex that had trotted briskly homeward up our avenue for ten years. I think we all knew when he came through the gate that he was dying. He had apparently taken a terrible beating, probably from the owner of some dog that he had got into a fight with. His head and body were scarred. His heavy collar with the teeth marks of many a battle on it was awry; some of the big brass studs in it were sprung loose from the leather. He licked at our hands and, staggering, fell, but got up again. We could see that he was looking for someone. One of his three masters was not home. He did not get home for an hour. During that hour the bull terrier fought against death as he had fought against the cold, strong current of Alum Creek, as he had fought to climb twelve-foot walls. When the person he was waiting for did come through the gate, whistling, ceasing to whistle, Rex walked a few wabbly paces toward him, touched his hand with his muzzle, and fell down again. This time he didn't get up.

Rudyard Kipling

GARM—A HOSTAGE

One night, a very long time ago, I drove to an Indian military cantonment called Mian Mir to see amateur theatricals. At the back of the Infantry barracks a soldier, his cap over one eye, rushed in front of the horses and shouted that he was a dangerous highway robber. As a matter of fact, he was a friend of mine, so I told him to go home before any one caught him; but he fell under the pole, and I heard voices of a military guard in search of some one.

The driver and I coaxed him into the carriage, drove home swiftly, undressed him and put him to bed, where he waked next morning with a sore headache, very much ashamed. When his uniform was cleaned and dried, and he had been shaved and washed and made neat, I drove him back to barracks with his arm in a fine white sling, and reported that I had accidentally run over him. I did not tell this story to my friend's sergeant, who was a hostile and unbelieving person, but to his lieutenant, who did not know us quite so well.

Three days later my friend came to call, and at his heels slobbered and fawned one of the finest bull-terriers—of the old-fashioned breed, two parts bull and one terrier—that I had ever set eyes on. He was pure white, with a fawn-coloured saddle just behind his neck, and a fawn diamond at the root of his thin whippy tail. I had admired him distantly for more than a year; and Vixen, my own fox-terrier, knew him too, but did not approve.

" 'E's for you," said my friend; but he did not look as though he liked parting with him.

"Nonsense! That dog's worth more than most men, Stanley," I said.

" 'E's that and more. 'Tention!"

The dog rose on his hind legs, and stood upright for a full minute.

"Eyes right!"

He sat on his haunches and turned his head sharp to the right. At a sign he rose and barked thrice. Then he shook hands with his right paw and bounded lightly to my shoulder. Here he made himself into a necktie, limp and lifeless, hanging down on either side of my neck. I was told to pick him up and throw him in the air. He fell with a howl, and held up one leg.

"Part o' the trick," said his owner. "You're going to die now. Dig yourself your little grave an' shut your little eye."

Still limping, the dog hobbled to the garden-edge, dug a hole and lay down in it. When told that he was cured, he jumped out, wagging his tail, and whining for applause. He was put through half a dozen other tricks, such as showing how he would hold a man safe (I was that man, and he sat down before me, his teeth bared, ready to spring), and how he would stop eating at the word of command. I had no more than finished praising him when my friend made a gesture that stopped the dog as though he had been shot, took a piece of blue-ruled canteen-paper from his helmet, handed it to me and ran away, while the dog looked after him and howled. I read:

Sir—I give you the dog because of what you got me out of. He is the best I know, for I made him myself, and he is as good as a man. Please do not give him too much to eat, and please do not give him back to me, for I'm not going to take him, if you will keep him. So please do not try to give him back any more. I have kept his name back, so you can call him anything and he will answer, but please do not give him back. He can kill a man as easy as anything, but please do not give him too much meat. He knows more than a man.

Vixen sympathetically joined her shrill little yap to the bull-terrier's despairing cry, and I was annoyed, for I knew that a man who cares for dogs is one thing, but a man who loves one dog is quite another. Dogs are at the best no more than verminous vagrants, self-scratchers, foul feeders, and unclean by the law of Moses and Mohammed; but a dog with whom one lives alone for at least six months in the year; a free thing, tied to you so strictly by love that without you he will not stir or exercise; a patient, temperate, humorous, wise soul, who knows your moods before you know them yourself, is not a dog under any ruling.

I had Vixen, who was all my dog to me; and I felt what my friend must have felt, at tearing out his heart in this style and leaving it in my garden. However, the dog understood clearly enough that I was his master, and did not follow the soldier. As soon as he drew breath I made much of him, and Vixen, yelling with jealousy, flew at him. Had she been of his own sex, he might have cheered himself with a fight, but he only looked worriedly when she nipped his deep iron sides, laid his heavy head on my knee, and howled anew. I meant to dine at the Club that night, but as darkness drew in, and the dog snuffed through the empty house like a child trying to recover from a fit of sobbing, I felt that I could not leave him to suffer his first evening alone. So we fed at home, Vixen on one side, and the stranger-dog on the other; she watching his every mouthful, and saying explicitly what she thought of his table manners, which were much better than hers.

It was Vixen's custom, till the weather grew hot, to sleep in my bed, her head on the pillow like a Christian; and when morning came I would always find that the little thing had braced her feet against the wall and pushed me to the very edge of the cot. This night she hurried to bed purposefully, every hair up, one eye on the stranger, who had dropped on a mat in a helpless, hopeless sort of way, all four feet spread out, sighing heavily. She settled her head on the pillow several times, to show her little airs and graces, and struck up her usual whiney sing-song before slumber. The stranger-dog softly edged towards me. I put out my hand and he licked it. Instantly my wrist was between Vixen's teeth, and her warning *aaarh!* said as plainly as speech, that if I took any further notice of the stranger she would bite.

I caught her behind her fat neck with my left hand, shook her severely, and said:

"Vixen, if you do that again you'll be put into the veranda. Now, remember!"

She understood perfectly, but the minute I released her she mouthed my right wrist once more, and waited with her ears back and all her body flattened, ready to bite. The big dog's tail thumped the floor in a humble and peace-making way.

I grabbed Vixen a second time, lifted her out of bed like a rabbit (she hated that and yelled), and, as I had promised, set her out in the veranda with the bats and the moonlight. At this she howled. Then she used coarse language—not to me, but to the bull-terrier—till she coughed with exhaustion. Then she ran round the house trying every door. Then she went off to the stables and barked as though some one were stealing the horses, which was an old trick of hers. Last she returned, and her snuffing yelp said, "I'll be good! Let me in and I'll be good!"

She was admitted and flew to her pillow. When she was quieted I whispered to the other dog, "You can lie on the foot of the bed." The bull jumped up at once, and though I felt Vixen quiver with rage, she knew better than to protest. So we slept till the morning, and they had early breakfast with me, bite for bite, till the horse came round and we went for a ride. I don't think the bull had ever followed a horse before. He was wild with excitement, and Vixen, as usual, squealed and scuttered and scooted, and took charge of the procession.

There was one corner of a village near by, which we generally passed with caution, because all the yellow pariah-dogs of the place gathered about it. They were half-wild, starving beasts, and though utter cowards, yet where nine or ten of them get together they will mob and kill and eat an English dog. I kept a whip with a long lash for them. That morning they attacked Vixen, who, perhaps of design, had moved from beyond my horse's shadow.

The bull was ploughing along in the dust, fifty yards behind, rolling in his run, and smiling as bull-terriers will. I heard Vixen squeal; half a dozen of the curs closed in on her; a white streak came up behind me; a cloud of dust rose near Vixen, and, when it cleared, I saw one tall pariah with his back broken, and the bull wrenching another to earth. Vixen retreated to the protection of my whip, and the bull paddled back smiling more than ever, covered with the blood of his enemies. That decided me to call him "Garm of the Bloody Breast," who was a great person in his time, or "Garm" for short; so, leaning forward, I told him what his temporary name would be. He looked up while I repeated it, and then raced away. I shouted "Garm!" He stopped, raced back, and came up to ask my will.

Then I saw that my soldier friend was right, and that that dog knew and was worth more than a man. At the end of the ride I gave an order which Vixen knew and hated: "Go away and get washed!" I said. Garm understood some part of it, and Vixen interpreted the rest, and the two trotted off together soberly. When I went to the back veranda Vixen had been washed snowy-white, and was very proud of herself, but the dog-boy would not touch Garm on any account unless I stood by. So I waited while he was being scrubbed, and Garm, with the soap creaming on the top of his broad head, looked at me to make sure that this was what I expected him to endure. He knew perfectly that the dog-boy was only obeying orders.

"Another time," I said to the dog-boy, "you will wash the great dog with Vixen when I send them home."

"Does *he* know?" said the dog-boy, who understood the ways of dogs.

"Garm," I said, "another time you will be washed with Vixen."

I knew that Garm understood. Indeed, next washing-day, when Vixen as usual fled under my bed, Garm stared at the doubtful dog-boy in the veranda, stalked to the place where he had been washed last time, and stood rigid in the tub.

But the long days in my office tried him sorely. We three would drive off in the morning at half-past eight and come home at six or later. Vixen, knowing the routine of it, went to sleep under my table; but the confinement ate into Garm's soul. He generally sat on the veranda looking out on the Mall; and well I knew what he expected.

Sometimes a company of soldiers would move along on their way to the Fort, and Garm rolled forth to inspect them; or an officer in uniform entered into the office, and it was pitiful to see poor Garm's welcome to the cloth—not the man. He would leap at him, and sniff and bark joyously, then run to the door and back again. One afternoon I heard him bay with a full throat—a thing I had never heard before—and he disappeared. When I drove into my garden at the end of the day a soldier in white uniform scrambled over the wall at the far end, and the Garm that met me was a joyous dog. This happened twice or thrice a week for a month.

I pretended not to notice, but Garm knew and Vixen knew. He would glide homewards from the office about four o'clock, as though he were only going to look at the scenery, and this he did so quietly that but for Vixen I should not have noticed him. The jealous little dog under the table would give a sniff and a snort, just loud enough to call my attention to the flight. Garm might go out forty times in the day and Vixen would never stir, but when he slunk off to see his true master in my garden she told me in her own tongue. That was the one sign she made to prove that Garm did not altogether belong to the family. They were the best of friends at all times, *but,* Vixen explained that I was never to forget Garm did not love me as she loved me.

I never expected it. The dog was not my dog—could never be my dog—and I knew he was as miserable as his master who tramped eight miles a day to see him. So it seemed to me that the sooner the two were reunited the better for all. One afternoon I sent Vixen home alone in the dog-cart (Garm had gone before), and rode over to cantonments to find another friend of mine, who was an Irish soldier and a great friend of the dog's master.

I explained the whole case, and wound up with:

"And now Stanley's in my garden crying over his dog. Why doesn't he take him back? They're both unhappy."

"Unhappy! There's no sense in the little man any more. But 'tis his fit."

"What *is* his fit? He travels fifty miles a week to see the brute, and he pretends not to notice me when he sees me on the road; and I'm as unhappy as he is. Make him take the dog back."

"It's his penance he's set himself. I told him by way of a joke, afther you'd run over him so convenient that night, when he was drunk—I said if he was a Catholic he'd do penance. Off he went wid that fit in his little head *an'* a dose of fever, an' nothin' would suit but given' you the dog as a hostage."

"Hostage for what? I don't want hostages from Stanley."

"For his good behaviour. He's keepin' straight now, the way it's no pleasure to associate wid him."

"Has he taken the pledge?"

"If 'twas only that I need not care. Ye can take the pledge

for three months on an' off. He sez he'll never see the dog again, an' so mark you, he'll keep straight for evermore. Ye know his fits? Well, this is wan of them. How's the dog takin' it?"

"Like a man. He's the best dog in India. Can't you make Stanley take him back?"

"I can do no more than I have done. But ye know his fits. He's just doin' his penance. What will he do when he goes to the Hills? The docthor's put him on the list."

It is the custom in India to send a certain number of invalids from each regiment up to stations in the Himalayas for the hot weather; and though the men ought to enjoy the cool and the comfort, they miss the society of the barracks down below, and do their best to come back or to avoid going. I felt that this move would bring matters to a head, so I left Terence hopefully, though he called after me—

"He won't take the dog, sorr. You can lay your month's pay on that. Ye know his fits."

I never pretended to understand Private Ortheris; and so I did the next best thing—I left him alone.

That summer the invalids of the regiment to which my friend belonged were ordered off to the Hills early, because the doctors thought marching in the cool of the day would do them good. Their route lay south to a place called Umballa, a hundred and twenty miles or more. Then they would turn east and march up into the hills to Kasauli or Dugshai or Subathoo. I dined with the officers the night before they left—they were marching at five in the morning. It was midnight when I drove into my garden, and surprised a white figure flying over the wall.

"That man," said my butler, "has been here since nine, making talk to that dog. He is quite mad. I did not tell him to go away because he has been here many times before, and because the dog-boy told me that if I told him to go away, the great dog would immediately slay me. He did not wish to speak to the Protector of the Poor, and he did not ask for anything to eat or drink."

"Kadir Buksh," said I, "that was well done, for the dog would surely have killed thee. But I do not think the white soldier will come any more."

Garm slept ill that night and whimpered in his dreams. Once he sprang up with a clear, ringing bark, and I heard him wag his tail till it waked him and the bark died out in a howl. He had dreamed he was with his master again, and I nearly cried. It was all Stanley's silly fault.

The first halt which the detachment of invalids made was some miles from their barracks, on the Amritsar road, and ten miles distant from my house. By a mere chance one of the officers drove back for another good dinner at the Club (cooking on the line of march is always bad), and there I met him. He was a particular friend of mine, and I knew that he knew how to love a dog properly. His pet was a big fat retriever who was going up to the Hills for his health, and, though it was still April, the round, brown brute puffed and panted in the Club veranda as though he would burst.

"It's amazing," said the officer, "what excuses these invalids of mine make to get back to barracks. There's a man in my company now asked me for leave to go back to cantonments to pay a debt he'd forgotten. I was so taken by the idea I let him go, and he jingled off in an *ekka* as pleased as Punch. Ten miles to pay a debt! Wonder what it was really?"

"If you'll drive me home I think I can show you," I said.

So he went over to my house in his dog-cart with the retriever; and on the way I told him the story of Garm.

"I was wondering where that brute had gone to. He's the best dog in the regiment," said my friend. "I offered the little fellow twenty rupees for him a month ago. But he's a hostage, you say, for Stanley's good conduct. Stanley's one of the best men I have—when he chooses."

"That's the reason why," I said. "A second-rate man wouldn't have taken things to heart as he has done."

We drove in quietly at the far end of the garden, and crept round the house. There was a place close to the wall all grown about with tamarisk trees, where I knew Garm kept his bones. Even Vixen was not allowed to sit near it. In the full Indian moonlight I could see a white uniform bending over the dog.

"Good-bye, old man," we could not help hearing Stanley's voice. "For 'Eving's sake don't get bit and go mad by any measly pi-dog. But you can look after yourself, old man. *You* don't get drunk an' run about 'ittin' your friends'. You takes your bones an' you eats your biscuit, an' you kills your enemy like a gentleman. I'm goin' away—don't 'owl—I'm goin' off to Kasauli, where I won't see you no more."

I could hear him holding Garm's nose as the dog threw it up to the stars.

"You'll stay here an' be'ave, an'—an' I'll go away an' try to be'ave, an' I don't know 'ow to leave you. I don't know——"

"I think this is damn silly," said the officer, patting his foolish fubsy old retriever. He called to the private, who leaped to his feet, marched forward, and saluted.

"You here?" said the officer, turning away his head.

"Yes, sir, but I'm just goin' back."

"I shall be leaving here at eleven in my cart. You come with me. I can't have sick men running about all over the place. Report yourself at eleven, *here*."

We did not say much when we went indoors, but the officer muttered and pulled his retriever's ears.

He was a disgraceful, overfed doormat of a dog; and when he waddled off to my cookhouse to be fed, I had a brilliant idea.

At eleven o'clock that officer's dog was nowhere to be found, and you never heard such a fuss as his owner made. He called and shouted and grew angry, and hunted through my garden for half an hour.

Then I said:

"He's sure to turn up in the morning. Send a man in by rail, and I'll find the beast and return him."

"Beast?" said the officer. "I value that dog considerably more than I value any man I know. It's all very fine for you to talk—your dog's here."

So she was—under my feet—and, had she been missing, food and wages would have stopped in my house till her return. But some people grow fond of dogs not worth a cut of the whip. My friend had to drive away at last with Stanley in the back seat; and then the dog-boy said to me:

"What kind of animal is Bullen Sahib's dog? Look at him!"

I went to the boy's hut, and the fat old reprobate was lying on a mat carefully chained up. He must have heard his master calling for twenty minutes, but had not even attempted to join him.

"He has no face," said the dog-boy scornfully. "He is a *punniar-kooter* (a spaniel). He never tried to get that cloth off his jaws when his master called. Now Vixen-baba would have jumped through the window, and that Great Dog would have slain me with his muzzled mouth. It is true that there are many kinds of dogs."

Next evening who should turn up but Stanley. The officer had sent him back fourteen miles by rail with a note begging me to return the retriever if I had found him, and, if I had not, to offer huge rewards. The last train to camp left at half-past ten, and Stanley stayed till ten talking to Garm. I argued and entreated, and even threatened to shoot the bull-terrier, but the little man was as firm as a rock, though I gave him a good dinner and talked to him most severely. Garm knew as well as I that this was the last time he could hope to see his man, and followed Stanley like a shadow. The retriever said nothing, but licked his lips after his meal and waddled off without so much as saying "Thank you" to the disgusted dog-boy.

So that last meeting was over, and I felt as wretched as Garm, who moaned in his sleep all night. When we went to the office he found a place under the table close to Vixen, and dropped flat till it was time to go home. There was no more running out into the verandas, no slinking away for stolen talks with Stanley. As the weather grew warmer the dogs were forbidden to run beside the cart, but sat at my side on the seat, Vixen with her head under the crook of my left elbow, and Garm hugging the left handrail.

Here Vixen was ever in great form. She had to attend to all the moving traffic, such as bullock-carts that blocked the way, and camels, and led ponies; as well as to keep up her dignity when she passed low friends running in the dust. She never yapped for yapping's sake, but her shrill, high bark was known all along the Mall, and other men's terriers ki-yied in reply, and bullock-drivers looked over their shoulders and gave us the road with a grin.

But Garm cared for none of these things. His big eyes were on the horizon and his terrible mouth was shut. There was another dog in the office who belonged to my chief. We called him "Bob the Librarian," because he always imagined vain rats behind the bookshelves, and in hunting for them would drag out half the old newspaper files. Bob was a well-meaning idiot, but Garm did not encourage him. He would slide his head round the door panting, "Rats! Come along, Garm!" and Garm would shift one forepaw over the other, and curl himself round, leaving Bob to whine at a most uninterested back. The office was nearly as cheerful as a tomb in those days.

Once, and only once, did I see Garm at all contented with his surroundings. He had gone for an unauthorized walk with Vixen early one Sunday morning, and a very young and foolish artilleryman (his battery had just moved to that part of the world) tried to steal them both. Vixen, of course, knew better than to take food from soldiers, and, besides, she had just finished her breakfast. So she trotted back with a large piece of the mutton that they issue to our troops, laid it down on my veranda, and looked up to see what I thought. I asked her where Garm was, and she ran in front of the horse to show me the way.

About a mile up the road we came across our artilleryman sitting very stiffly on the edge of a culvert with a greasy handkerchief on his knees. Garm was in front of him, looking rather pleased. When the man moved leg or hand, Garm bared his teeth in silence. A broken string hung from his collar, and the other half of it lay, all warm, in the artilleryman's still hand. He explained to me, keeping his eyes straight in front of him, that he had met this dog (he called him awful names) walking alone, and was going to take him to the Fort to be killed for a masterless pariah.

I said that Garm did not seem to me much of a pariah, but that he had better take him to the Fort if he thought best. He said he did not care to do so. I told him to go to the Fort alone. He said he did not want to go at that hour, but would follow my advice as soon as I had called off the dog. I instructed Garm to take him to the Fort, and Garm marched him solemnly up to the gate, one mile and a half under a hot sun, and I told the quarter-guard what had happened; but the young artilleryman was more angry than was at all necessary when they began to laugh. Several regiments, he was told, had tried to steal Garm in their time.

That month the hot weather shut down in earnest, and the dogs slept in the bathroom on the cool wet bricks where the bath is placed. Every morning, as soon as the man filled my bath, the two jumped in, and every morning the man filled the bath a second time. I said to him that he might as well fill a small tub specially for the dogs. "Nay," said he smiling, "it is not their custom. They would not understand. Besides, the big bath gives them more space."

The punkah-coolies who pull the punkahs day and night came to know Garm intimately. He noticed that when the swaying fan stopped I would call out to the coolie and bid him pull with a long stroke. If the man still slept I would wake him up. He discovered, too, that it was a good thing to lie in the wave of air under the punkah. Maybe Stanley had taught him all about this in barracks. At any rate, when the punkah stopped, Garm would first growl and cock his eye at the rope, and if that did not wake the man—it nearly always did—he would tiptoe forth and talk in the sleeper's ear. Vixen was a clever little dog, but she could never connect the punkah and the coolie; so Garm gave me grateful hours of cool sleep. But he was utterly wretched—as miserable as a human being; and in his misery he clung so closely to me that other men noticed it, and were envious. If I moved from one room to another Garm followed; if my pen stopped scratching, Garm's head was thrust into my hand; if I turned, half awake, on the pillow, Garm was up and at my side, for he knew that I was his only link with his master, and day and night, and night and day, his eyes asked one question—"When is this going to end?"

Living with the dog as I did, I never noticed that he was more than ordinarily upset by the hot weather, till one day at the Club a man said: "That dog of yours will die in a week or two. He's a shadow." Then I dosed Garm with iron and quinine, which he hated; and I felt very anxious. He lost his appetite, and Vixen was allowed to eat his dinner under his eyes. Even that did not make him swallow, and we held a consultation on him, of the best man-doctor in the place; a lady-doctor, who cured the sick wives of kings; and the Deputy Inspector-General of the veterinary service of all India. They pronounced upon his symptoms, and I told them his story, and Garm lay on a sofa licking my hand.

"He's dying of a broken heart," said the lady-doctor suddenly.

" 'Pon my word," said the Deputy Inspector-General, "I believe Mrs. Macrae is perfectly right—as usual."

The best man-doctor in the place wrote a prescription, and the veterinary Deputy Inspector-General went over it afterwards to be sure that the drugs were in the proper dog-proportions; and that was the first time in his life that our doctor ever allowed his prescriptions to be edited. It was a strong tonic, and it put the dear boy on his feet for a week or two;

then he lost flesh again. I asked a man I knew to take him up to the Hills with him when he went, and the man came to the door with his kit packed on the top of the carriage. Garm took in the situation at one red glance. The hair rose along his back; he sat down in front of me, and delivered the most awful growl I have ever heard in the jaws of a dog. I shouted to my friend to get away at once, and as soon as the carriage was out of the garden Garm laid his head on my knee and whined. So I knew his answer, and devoted myself to getting Stanley's address in the Hills.

My turn to go to the cool came late in August. We were allowed thirty days' holiday in a year, if no one fell sick, and we took it as we could be spared. My chief and Bob the Librarian had their holiday first, and when they were gone I made a calendar, as I always did, and hung it up at the head of my cot, tearing off one day at a time till they returned. Vixen had gone up to the Hills with me five times before; and she appreciated the cold and the damp and the beautiful wood fires there as much as I did.

"Garm," I said, "we are going back to Stanley at Kasauli. Kasauli—Stanley; Stanley—Kasauli." And I repeated it twenty times. It was not Kasauli really, but another place. Still I remembered what Stanley had said in my garden on the last night, and I dared not change the name. Then Garm began to tremble; then he barked; and then he leaped up at me, frisking and wagging his tail.

"Not now," I said, holding up my hand. "When I say 'Go,' we'll go, Garm." I pulled out the little blanket coat and spiked collar that Vixen always wore up in the Hills to protect her against sudden chills and thieving leopards, and I let the two smell them and talk it over. What they said of course I do not know, but it made a new dog of Garm. His eyes were bright; and he barked joyfully when I spoke to him. He ate his food, and he killed his rats for the next three weeks, and when he began to whine I had only to say "Stanley—Kasauli;

Kasauli—Stanley," to wake him up. I wish I had thought of it before.

My chief came back, all brown with living in the open air, and very angry at finding it so hot in the Plains. That same afternoon we three and Kadir Buksh began to pack for our month's holiday, Vixen rolling in and out of the bullock-trunk twenty times a minute, and Garm grinning all over and thumping on the floor with his tail. Vixen knew the routine of travelling as well as she knew my office-work. She went to the station, singing songs, on the front seat of the carriage, while Garm sat with me. She hurried into the railway carriage, saw Kadir Buksh make up my bed for the night, got her drink of water, and curled up with her black-patch eye on the tumult of the platform. Garm followed her (the crowd gave him a lane all to himself) and sat down on the pillows with his eyes blazing, and his tail a haze behind him.

We came to Umballa in the hot misty dawn, four or five men, who had been working hard for eleven months, shouting for our dâks—the two-horse travelling carriages that were to take us up to Kalka at the foot of the Hills. It was all new to Garm. He did not understand carriages where you lay at full length on your bedding, but Vixen knew and hopped into her place at once; Garm following. The Kalka Road, before the railway was built, was about forty-seven miles long, and the horses were changed every eight miles. Most of them jibbed, and kicked, and plunged, but they had to go, and they went rather better than usual for Garm's deep bay in their rear.

There was a river to be forded, and four bullocks pulled the carriage, and Vixen stuck her head out of the sliding-door and nearly fell into the water while she gave directions. Garm was silent and curious, and rather needed reassuring about Stanley and Kasauli. So we rolled, barking and yelping, into Kalka for lunch, and Garm ate enough for two.

After Kalka the road wound among the hills, and we took a curricle with half-broken ponies, which were changed every six miles. No one dreamed of a railroad to Simla in those days, for it was seven thousand feet up in the air. The road was more than fifty miles long, and the regulation pace was just as fast as the ponies could go. Here, again, Vixen led Garm from one carriage to the other; jumped into the back seat, and shouted. A cool breath from the snows met us about five miles out of Kalka, and she whined for her coat, wisely fearing a chill on the liver. I had had one made for Garm too, and, as we climbed to the fresh breezes, I put it on, and Garm chewed it uncomprehendingly, but I think he was grateful.

"Hi-yi-yi-yi!" sang Vixen as we shot round the curves; "Toot-toot-toot!" went the driver's bugle at the dangerous places, and "Yow! yow! yow!" bayed Garm. Kadir Buksh sat on the front seat and smiled. Even he was glad to get away from the heat of the Plains that stewed in the haze behind us. Now and then we would meet a man we knew going down to his work again, and he would say: "What's it like below?" and I would shout: "Hotter than cinders. What's it like up above?" and he would shout back: "Just perfect!" and away we would go.

Suddenly Kadir Buksh said, over his shoulder: "Here is Solon"; and Garm snored where he lay with his head on my knee. Solon is an unpleasant little cantonment, but it has the advantage of being cool and healthy. It is all bare and windy, and one generally stops at a rest-house near by for something to eat. I got out and took both dogs with me, while Kadir Buksh made tea. A soldier told us we should find Stanley "out there," nodding his head towards a bare, bleak hill.

When we climbed to the top we spied that very Stanley, who had given me all this trouble, sitting on a rock with his face in his hands, and his overcoat hanging loose about him. I never saw anything so lonely and dejected in my life as this one little man, crumpled up and thinking, on the great gray hillside.

Here Garm left me.

He departed without a word, and, so far as I could see, without moving his legs. He flew through the air bodily, and

I heard the whack of him as he flung himself at Stanley, knocking the little man clean over. They rolled on the ground together, shouting, and yelping, and hugging. I could not see which was dog and which was man, till Stanley got up and whimpered.

He told me that he had been suffering from fever at intervals, and was very weak. He looked all he said, but even while I watched, both man and dog plumped out to their natural sizes, precisely as dried apples swell in water. Garm was on his shoulder, and his breast and feet all at the same time, so that Stanley spoke all through a cloud of Garm—gulping, sobbing, slavering Garm. He did not say anything that I could understand, except that he had fancied he was going to die, but that now he was quite well, and that he was not going to give up Garm any more to anybody under the rank of Beelzebub.

Then he said he felt hungry, and thirsty, and happy.

We went down to tea at the rest-house, where Stanley stuffed himself with sardines and raspberry jam, and beer, and cold mutton and pickles, when Garm wasn't climbing over him; and then Vixen and I went on.

Garm saw how it was at once. He said good-bye to me three times, giving me both paws one after another, and leaping on to my shoulder. He further escorted us, singing Hosannas at the top of his voice, a mile down the road. Then he raced back to his own master.

Vixen never opened her mouth, but when the cold twilight came, and we could see the lights of Simla across the hills, she snuffled with her nose at the breast of my ulster. I unbuttoned it, and tucked her inside. Then she gave a contented little sniff, and fell fast asleep, her head on my breast, till we bundled out at Simla, two of the four happiest people in all the world that night.

Anton Chekhov

GRIEF

I t is twilight. A thick wet snow is slowly twirling around the newly lighted street-lamps, and lying in soft thin layers on the roofs, the horses' backs, people's shoulders and hats. The cab-driver, Iona Potapov, is quite white, and looks like a phantom; he is bent double as far as a human body can bend double; he is seated on his box, and never makes a move. If a whole snowdrift fell on him, it seems as if he would not find it necessary to shake it off. His little horse is also quite white, and remains motionless; its immobility, its angularity, and its straight wooden-looking legs, even close by give it the appearance of a ginger-bread horse worth a kopeck. It is, no doubt, plunged in deep thought. If you were snatched from the plough, from your usual grey surroundings, and were thrown into this slough full of monstrous lights, unceasing noise and hurrying people, you too would find it difficult not to think.

Iona and his little horse have not moved from their place for a long while. They left their yard before dinner, and up to now, not a "fare." The evening mist is descending over the town, the white lights of the lamps are replacing brighter rays, and the hubbub of the street is getting louder. "Cabby, for Viborg way!" suddenly hears Iona. "Cabby!"

Iona jumps, and through his snow-covered eyelashes, sees an officer in a greatcoat, with his hood over his head.

"Viborg way!" the officer repeats. "Are you asleep, eh? Viborg way!"

With a nod of assent Iona picks up the reins, in consequence of which layers of snow slip off the horse's back and neck. The officer seats himself in the sleigh, the cab-driver smacks his lips to encourage his horse, stretches out his neck like a swan, sits up, and, more from habit than necessity, brandishes his whip. The little horse also stretches his neck, bends his wooden-looking legs, and makes a move undecidedly.

"What are you doing, were-wolf!" is the exclamation Iona hears, from the dark mass moving to and fro as soon as they started.

"Where the devil are you going? To the r-r-right!"

"You do not know how to drive. Keep to the right!" calls the officer angrily.

A coachman from a private carriage swears at him; a passer-by, who has run across the road and rubbed his shoulder against the horse's nose, looks at him furiously as he sweeps the snow from his sleeve. Iona shifts about on his seat as if he were on needles, moves his elbows as if he were trying to keep his equilibrium, and gapes about like someone suffocating, and who does not understand why and wherefore he is there.

"What scoundrels they all are!" jokes the officer; "one would think they had all entered into an agreement to jostle you or fall under your horse."

Iona looks round at the officer, and moves his lips. He evidently wants to say something, but the only sound that issues is a snuffle.

"What?" asks the officer.

Iona twists his mouth into a smile, and with an effort says hoarsely:

"My son, barin, died this week."

"Hm! What did he die of?"

Iona turns with his whole body towards his fare, and says:

"And who knows! They say high fever. He was three days in hospital, and then died. . . . God's will be done."

"Turn around! The devil!" sounded from the darkness. "Have you popped off, old doggie, eh? Use your eyes!"

"Go on, go on," said the officer, "otherwise we shall not get there by to-morrow. Hurry a bit!"

The cab-driver again stretches his neck, sits up, and, with a bad grace, brandishes his whip. Several times again he turns to look at his fare, but the latter had closed his eyes, and apparently is not disposed to listen. Having deposited the officer in the Viborg, he stops by the tavern, doubles himself up on his seat, and again remains motionless, while the snow once more begins to cover him and his horse. An hour, and another. . . . Then, along the footpath, with a squeak of goloshes, and quarreling, came three young men, two of them tall and lanky, the third one short and hump-backed.

"Cabby, to the Police Bridge!" in a cracked voice calls the hump-back. "The three of us for two griveniks!" (20 kopecks).

Iona picks up his reins, and smacks his lips. Two griveniks is not a fair price, but he does not mind if it is a rouble or five kopecks—to him it is all the same now, so long as they are wayfarers. The young men, jostling each other and using bad language, approach the sleigh, and all three at once try to get on to the seat; then begins a discussion which two shall sit and who shall be the one to stand. After wrangling, abusing each other, and much petulance, it was at last decided that the hump-back should stand, as he was the smallest.

"Now then, hurry up!" says the hump-back in a twanging voice, as he takes his place, and breathes in Iona's neck. "Old furry. Here, mate, what a cap you have got, there is not a worse one to be found in all Petersburg! . . ."

"Hi—hi,—hi—hi," giggles Iona. "Such a . . ."

"Now you, 'such a,' hurry up, are you going the whole way at this pace? Are you? . . . Do you want it in the neck?"

"My head feels like bursting," says one of the lanky ones. "Last night at the Donkmasovs, Vaska and I drank the whole of four bottles of cognac."

"I don't understand what you lie for," said the other lanky one angrily; "you lie like a brute."

"God strike me, it's the truth!"

"It's as much a truth as that a louse coughs!"

"Hi, hi," grins Iona, "what gay young gentlemen!"

"Pshaw, go to the devil!" indignantly says the hump-back.

"Are you going to get on or not, you old pest? Is that the way to drive? Use the whip a bit! Go on, devil, go on, give it him well!"

Iona feels at his back the little man wriggling, and the tremble in his voice. He listens to the insults hurled at him, sees the people, and little by little the feeling of loneliness leaves him. The hump-back goes on swearing until he gets mixed up in some elaborate six-foot oath, or chokes with coughing. The lankies begin to talk about a certain Nadejda Petrovna. Iona looks round at them several times; he waits for a temporary silence, then, turning round again, he murmurs:

"My son—died this week."

"We must all die," sighed the hump-back, wiping his lips after an attack of coughing. "Now, hurry up, hurry up! Gentlemen, I really cannot go any farther like this! When will he get us there?"

"Well, just you stimulate him a little in the neck!"

"You old pest, do you hear, I'll bone your neck for you! If one treated the like of you with ceremony one would have to go on foot! Do you hear, old serpent Gorinytch! Or do you not care a spit?"

Iona hears rather than feels the blows they deal him.

"Hi, hi," he laughs. "They are gay young gentlemen, God bless 'em!"

"Cabby, are you married?" asks a lanky one.

"I? Hi, hi, gay young gentlemen! Now I have only a wife: the moist ground. . . . Hi, ho, ho . . . that is to say, the grave! My son has died, and I am alive. . . . A wonderful thing, death mistook the door . . . instead of coming to me, it went to my son. . . ."

Iona turns round to tell them how his son died, but at this moment the hump-back, giving a little sigh, announces, "Thank God, they have at last reached their destination," and Iona watches them disappear through the dark entrance. Once more he is alone, and again surrounded by silence. . . . His grief, which had abated for a short while, returns and rends his heart with greater force. With an anxious and a hurried look, he searches among the crowds passing on either side of the street to find if there is just one person who will listen to him. But the crowds hurry by without noticing him or his trouble. Yet it is such an immense, illimitable grief. Should his heart break and the grief pour out, it would flow over the whole earth it seems, and yet, no one sees it. It has managed to conceal itself in such an insignificant shell that no one can see it even by day and with a light.

Iona sees a hall-porter with some sacking, and decides to talk to him.

"Friend, what sort of time is it?" he asks.

"Past nine. What are you standing here for? Move on."

Iona moves on a few steps, doubles himself up, and abandons himself to his grief. He sees it is useless to turn to people for help. In less than five minutes he straightens himself, holds up his head as if he felt some sharp pain, and gives a tug at the reins: he can bear it no longer, "The stables," he thinks, and the little horse, as if he understood, starts off at a trot.

About an hour and a half later Iona is seated by a large dirty stove. Around the stove, on the floor, on the benches, people are snoring; the air is thick and suffocatingly hot. Iona looks at the sleepers, scratches himself, and regrets having returned so early.

"I have not even earned my fodder," he thinks. "That's what's my trouble. A man who knows his job, who has had enough to eat, and his horse too, can always sleep peacefully."

A young cab-driver in one of the corners half gets up, grunts sleepily and stretches toward a bucket of water.

"Do you want a drink?" Iona asks him.

"Don't I want a drink!"

"That's so? Your good health! But listen, mate—you know, my son is dead. . . . Did you hear? This week, in hospital. . . . It's a long story."

Iona looks to see what effect his words have, but sees none—the young man has hidden his face, and is fast asleep again. The old man sighs, and scratches his head. Just as much as the young one wanted to drink, the old man wanted to talk. It will soon be a week since his son died, and he has not been able to speak about it properly to anyone. One must tell it slowly and carefully; how his son fell ill, how he suffered, what he said before he died, how he died. One must describe every detail of the funeral, and the journey to the hospital to fetch the defunct's clothes. His daughter Anissia remained in the village—one must talk about her too. Was it nothing he had to tell? Surely the listener would gasp and sigh, and sympathise with him? It is better, too, to talk to women; although they are stupid, two words are enough to make them sob.

"I'll go and look at my horse," thinks Iona; "there's always time to sleep. No fear of that."

He puts on his coat, and goes to the stables to his horse; he thinks of the corn, the hay, the weather. When he is alone, he dare not think of his son; he could speak about him to anyone, but think of him, and picture him to himself, is unbearably painful.

"Are you tucking in?" Iona asks his horse, looking at his bright eyes. "Go on, tuck in, though we've not earned our corn, we can eat hay. Yes! I am too old to drive—my son could have, not I. He was a first-rate cab-driver. If only he had lived!"

Iona is silent for a moment, then continues:

"That's how it is, my old horse. There's no more Kuzma Ionitch. He has left us to live, and he went off pop. Now let's say, you had a foal, you were that foal's mother, and suddenly, let's say, that foal went and left you to live after him. It would be sad, wouldn't it?"

The little horse munches, listens, and breathes over his master's hand. . . .

Iona's feelings are too much for him, and he tells the little horse the whole story.

Robert Graves

IN THE WILDERNESS

He, of his gentleness,
Thirsting and hungering
Walked in the wilderness;
Soft words of grace he spoke
Unto lost desert-folk
That listened wondering.
He heard the bitten call
From ruined palace-wall,
Answered him brotherly;
He held communion
With the she-pelican
Of lonely piety.
Basilisk, cockatrice,
Flocked to his homilies,
With mail of dread device,
With monstrous barbèd stings,
With eager dragon-eyes;
Great bats on leathern wings
And old, blind, broken things

Mean in their miseries.
Then ever with him went,
Of all his wanderings
Comrade, with ragged coat,
Gaunt ribs—poor innocent—
Bleeding foot, burning throat,
The guileless young scapegoat:
For forty nights and days
Followed in Jesus' ways,
Sure guard behind him kept,
Tears like a lover wept.

Two

PARTNERS

Willie Morris

MY DOG SKIP

I came across a photograph of him not long ago, his black face with the long snout sniffing at something in the air, his tail straight and pointing, his eyes flashing in some momentary excitement. Looking at a faded photograph taken more than forty years before, even as a grown man, I would admit I still missed him.

It was 1943. I was nine years old and in the third grade when I saw him for the very first time. I had known we were getting him. My father had ordered him from a dog breeder he had heard about in Springfield, Missouri. Daddy had picked him up at the Illinois Central train depot, and when I came home that day from school he had just put the wire portable kennel on our back porch. I opened the door to the box and looked inside. I saw a little puppy drinking water from a container attached to the bottom. He glanced up at me.

"Come here, boy," I said.

He walked on unsteady legs toward me. I was sitting on the floor of the porch when he came out. He jumped into my lap and began nuzzling my hand with his nose. When I leaned toward him, he gave me a moist lick on my chin. Then he hugged me.

I led him into the house and gave him some puppy food in a dish. Then I followed him as he gingerly explored every room in the house. That night he jumped into my bed and stared at me, as if he were looking me over. Then, perhaps because he missed his mother in Missouri, he went to sleep in my arms. I was an only child, and he now was an only dog.

This was the first of our many days and years together. We named him Skipper for the lively way he walked, but he was always just Skip to me.

We had had a whole string of dogs before. When I was a very little boy we had big bird dogs, and then two purebred English smooth-haired fox terriers like this one, and I got to know all about dogs, a most precocious expert—their funny or crazy moods, how they looked when they were hungry or sick, when they were ready to bite and when their growling meant nothing, what they might be trying to say when they moaned and made strange human noises deep in their throats.

None of those other dogs ever came up to this one. You could talk to him as well as you could to many human beings, and *much* better than you could to some. He would sit down and look you straight in the eye, a long mesmerizing gaze, and when he understood what you were saying he would turn his head sideways, back and forth, oscillating his whole body like the pendulum on a clock. Before going to sleep at night, with him sitting next to my face on the bed as he always did in such hours, I would say, "First thing tomorrow I want you to get your leash and then come get me up, because we're gonna get in the car and go out to the woods and get some *squirrels*," and the next morning sure enough he would get his leash, wake up both my father and me, walk nervously around the house with the leash in his mouth while we ate breakfast, and then lead us out to the car. Or I could say, "How about a little *swim*?" and his face would light up and he would push open the back door with his paws and escort me the quarter of a mile down the back alleyway to the swimming hole under the cypress near the bayou. Or, "Bubba's comin' over here today, and we're gonna play some *football*," and he would listen closely to this, and go out and wait around in front of the house and pick up Bubba's scent a block down the street and come tell me he was on his way. Or, "Skip, how about some *catch*?" and he would get up and walk into the front room, open a door in the antique cabinet with his improbable nose, and bring me his tennis ball.

I watched him grow up from the puppy who came to us from Missouri to the sleek, dexterous, affectionate creature who could do all these things, and more. He knew my father by the name of Big Boss. My mother was Bossie, and I was Little Boss or, interchangeably, Willie. (I called *him*, depending on the mood, Skip, Old Skip, and Boy. I have learned that when you love somebody, you will address him or her by different names.) Sometimes my father would hide in a closet and I would ask, "Skip, where's Big Boss?" and he would search the whole house, looking on every bed and under every chair and table until he arrived at the right closet, and began scratching it with his paws.

THE town where Old Skip and I grew up together was an unhurried and isolated place then. About ten thousand people lived there, of all races and origins, and it sat there crazily, half on steep hills and half on the flat Delta. Some of the streets were not paved, and the main street, stretching its several blocks from the Dixie Theater down to the bend in the river, was narrow and plain, but down along the quiet, shady streets, with their magnolia and pecan and elm and locust trees, were the stately old houses that had been built long before the Civil War, slightly dark and decaying until the descendants became prosperous enough to have them "restored," which usually meant one coat of white enamel.

All this was before the big supermarkets and shopping centers and affluent subdivisions with no sidewalks and the monster highways and the innocence lost. It was even before there was television, and people would not close their doors and shut their curtains to watch the quiz games or the comedy hours or the talk shows where everybody talks at once. We would sit out on our front porches in the hot, serene nights and say hello to everyone who walked by. If the fire truck came past, we all got in our cars to follow it, and Skip was always the first to want to go. The houses were set out in a line under the soft green trees, their leaves rustling gently with the breeze. From the river sometimes came the melancholy echo of a boat's horn.

I knew the place then better than I did my own heart—every bend in every road, every house and every field, the exact spot where the robin went for her first crocus. It was not in my soul then, only in my pores, as familiar to me as rain or grass or sunlight. The town was poor one year and rich the next; everything in it pertained to cotton, and hence to usury and mortgage, debenture and labor. We lived and died by nature and followed the whims of the timeless clouds. Our people played seven-card stud against God.

It was a sly and silent town then, and Skip and my friends and I absorbed its every rhythm and heartbeat and the slightest sounds from far away. I loved those funny silences. The whole town was also abundant with alleys behind the paved thoroughfares inherited from an earlier day, little vagrant pathways running with scant design or reason behind the houses and stores and barns and chicken yards and gardens. You could get away with anything in those alleys. How Skip adored the freedom of them!

It was a lazy town, all stretched out on its hills and its flat streets, and over the years Skip also grew to know almost every house, tree, street, and alley. Occasionally he wandered around the town by himself, and everybody of any consequence knew who he was. Unbelievable as this may seem, Skip had the most curious and spooky ways of sensing—don't ask me how—where I might be at any given moment, what a later day called ESP.

Our neighborhood was on one of the broad thoroughfares. In our side yard was a row of immense pecan trees shaped at the top like witches' caps, and in the back a huge field, vined and bosky. On the front lawn was a full, towering oak, one of Skip's favorite trees in the entire town.

Every time I shouted "*Squirrel!*" Skip would charge on the oak tree and try to climb it, sometimes getting as high as five or six feet with his spectacular leaps. This would stop traffic on the street in front of the house. People in cars would see him trying to shinny up the tree and would pull up to the curb and watch. They would signal to other passersby and point toward Skip, and these people would pull over too. They would gaze up into the tree to see what he was looking for, and, after a respectable pause, ask me, "What's he got up there?" and I would say, "Somethin' small and mean." They seldom recognized that Skip was just practicing.

This exercise was nothing to compare with football games, however. I cut the lace on a football and taught Old Skip how to carry it in his mouth, and how to hold it so he could avoid fumbles when he was tackled. I instructed him how to move on a quarterback's signals, to take a snap from center on the first bounce, and to follow me down the field. Ten or twelve of my comrades and I would organize a game of tackle in my front yard. Our side would go into a huddle, Skip included, and we would put our arms around one another's shoulders the way they did in real huddles at Ole Miss or Tennessee, and the dog would stand up on his hind legs and, with me kneeling, drape a leg around *my* shoulder. Then I would say, "Skip, pattern thirty-nine, off on three"; we would break out of the huddle with Skip dropping into the tailback position as I had taught him. Muttonhead or Peewee or Henjie or Bubba or Big Boy or Ralph would be the center, and I would station myself at quarterback and say, "Ready, set, one . . . two . . . *three*"; then the center would snap the ball on a hop to Skip, who would get it by the lace and follow me downfield, dodging would-be tacklers with no effort at all, weaving behind his blockers, spinning loose when he was cornered, sometimes balancing just inside the sidelines until he made it into the end zone. We would slap him on the back and say, nonchalantly, "Good run, boy," or when we had an audience: "Did you see my block back there?" Occasionally he would get tackled, but he seldom lost his grip on the ball, and he would always get up from the bottom of the pile and head straight for the huddle. He was an ideal safety man when the other side punted, and would get a grip on the second or third hop and gallop the length of the field for a touchdown. After considerable practice, I succeeded in teaching him the "Statue of Liberty" play, always shouting "*Statue of Liberty*" to him and our teammates before the play unfolded. I would take the snap from center and fade back in a low crouch, less a crouch than a forty-five-degree list, holding the ball behind my shoulder as if I were about to pass, all the while making sure the loosened lace was at a convenient angle. Skip, stationed at the left-end position, would circle around behind me, taking the lace of the pigskin between his teeth, then moving with deft assurance toward the right side of the line of scrimmage, where I was leading interference, whereupon he would follow his usual phalanx of blockers to the enemy's end zone for another spectacular score. *"Look at that dog playin' football!"* someone passing by would shout, and before the game was over we would have an incredulous crowd watching from cars or sitting on the sidelines, just as they did when he was after squirrels. The older men especially enjoyed this stunning spectacle. Walking down the sidewalk in front of the house, they would stop and let go with great whoops of astonishment: "Man, that's *some* dog. Can he catch a pass?"

For simple gratification, however, I believe Skip enjoyed our most imaginative intrigue above any other, and there are people still living in the town who will testify to it.

• • •

IN that place and time, we began driving our parents' cars when we were thirteen years old; this was common practice then, and the town was so small that the policemen knew who you were, and your family, although they of course expected you to be careful. When I started driving our old four-door green DeSoto, I always took Skip on my trips around town. He rode with his snout extended far out the window, and if he caught the scent of one of the boys we knew, he would bark and point toward him, and we would stop and give that person a free ride. Skip would shake hands with our mutual friend, and lick him on the face and sit on the front seat between us. Cruising through the fringes of town, I would spot a group of old men standing around up the road. I would get Skip to prop himself against the steering wheel, his black head peering out of the windshield, while I crouched out of sight under the dashboard. Slowing the car to ten or fifteen, I would guide the steering wheel with my right hand while Skip, with his paws, kept it steady. As we drove by the Blue Front Café, I could hear one of the men shout: *"Look at that ol' dog drivin' a car!"*

Later we would ride out into the countryside, past the cotton fields and pecan groves and winding little creeks on the dark flat land toward some somnolent hamlet consisting of three or four unpainted stores, a minuscule wooden post office with its porch stacked with firewood in the wintertime, and a little graveyard nearby. Here the old men in overalls would be sitting on the gallery of the general store with patent-medicine posters on its sides, whittling wood or dipping snuff or swatting flies. When we slowly came past with Skip behind the steering wheel I heard one of them yell, *"A dog! A dog drivin'!"* and when I glanced slightly above the dashboard I sighted him falling out of his chair over the side of the porch into the privet hedge. One afternoon not long after that Henjie and Skip and I were out and about in the same country vicinity when far up the gravel road we saw a substantial congregation of humanity emerging from a backwoods church after a revival meeting. A number of the people, in fact, were still shouting and wailing as they approached their dusty parked cars and pickup trucks. I stopped the car and placed Skip at his familiar spot behind the steering wheel; then we slowly continued up the road. As we passed the church, in the midst of the avid cacophony a woman exclaimed: *"Is that a dog drivin' that car?"* The ensuing silence as we progressed on by was most horrendously swift and pervasive, and that sudden bucolic hush and quell remained unforgettable for me, as if the very spectacle of Old Skip driving that green DeSoto were inscrutable, celestial, and preordained . . .

———

Why, in childhood and youth, do we wish time to pass quickly? We want to grow up—and yet again we do not. This is the way people are, and have always been, even before the telephone, television, electricity, jet airplanes, and fax machines. You want to grow older, and yet you don't. Can anyone explain it?

As my high school years began to close, Skip remained constant in his companionship. Rivers Applewhite and I, too, were a steady pair. When we double-dated with Big Boy and Daisye, or Muttonhead and Janie Sue, riding around town on Saturday nights along the streets of our childhood, Skip rode around with us, until we let him off at my house and went on to the midnight movie at the Dixie. Our baseball team won the state championship that year, and in the parade down Main Street, with the crepe paper decorating the lampposts and the marching band playing our fight song, he rode in the back of a flatbed truck with my teammates and me. They gave the team shiny read-and-white jackets with *State Champs, 1952,* on the back, and he loved that jacket so much that when I spread it out for him on the floor or the bed he would go to sleep on it, and on chilly nights I would wrap it around him with only the top of his head above it. At the graduation ceremonies in the school gymnasium that June, when my friends and I marched down the aisle in our mortarboards and gowns to the strains of *Tannhäuser*, he tried to go inside but was mindlessly turned away. Afterwards, however, he attended the midnight-to-dawn dance, a tradition at graduation among all the boys and girls in all the Delta towns of that day, with its black jazz bands and matronly chaperones and exhilarating air of ceremony and frolic, and Skip stayed up all night with the rest of us.

I went to college in another state far away. For our first paper in English composition the professor assigned us a two-thousand-word autobiography; I began with a description of the fading lonely sunlight outside my dormitory window, went back through the years with Skip, and concluded with much rhetoric in the same dormitory six hours later. One sentence read: "My dog and I wandered the woods and swamplands of our home shooting squirrels." To which the teacher appended the comment: "Who was the better shot, you or the dog?" When I telephoned my parents from college, they got Skip to bark at me from the other end. When I came home in the summers we did the same old things, but it was different—not that I was not as close to him as I had been, but that I was not a boy anymore, and that the whole outside world was beckoning to me.

And that Skip himself had somehow grown old. He was eleven when I graduated from college, and feeble, with arthritis in his legs. Sometimes he still had the devilish look of eye, but he did not retrieve sticks anymore, and preferred lying in the shade of the trees, or under the steps to the back door, and he did not want to ride in the car, and he never woke me up in the mornings; it was I who had to wake *him* up.

> In a wonderland they lie,
> Dreaming as the days go by
> Dreaming as the summers die.

Ever drifting down the stream—
Lingering in the golden gleam—
Life, what is it but a dream?

I won a scholarship to England to complete my studies; I would be away three years. The day came when my parents had to drive me to meet the train East, where I would take an oceanliner. I knew I would never see Skip again.

My parents were waiting in front of the house when I went to the backyard to say good-bye to him. He was lying under our elm tree, the one in which he had trapped Bubba and me years before, with the same old tree house up there, a little forlorn and neglected now. I sat beside him not far from the grave of the little kitten we had buried those years ago and rubbed the back of his neck, in the spot he had always wanted to be rubbed. He lifted his head and looked at me, then put his head in my lap, nuzzling me with his nose as he had done the first time I had seen him as a puppy. I told him I had to go and that I would miss him. He looked at me again, and licked my cheek. "Thank you, boy," I whispered. Then I left without looking back.

But as the car pulled away from the house, I looked back. Skip was walking along the front lawn, and then sat down and gazed at me. I watched him until he was just a tiny speck.

A month later there was a transatlantic call for me at Oxford University. I went to the front lodge of my college to take it. "Skip died," Daddy said. He and my mother had wrapped him in my baseball jacket and put him in the ground, close to the grave of the little kitten.

I wandered alone among the landmarks of the gray medieval town. A dozen chimes were ringing among the ancient spires and cupolas and quadrangles, all this so far in miles and in spirit from the small place he and I had once dwelled. Walking alone in the teasing rain, I remembered our days together on this earth. The dog of your boyhood teaches you a great deal about friendship, and love, and death: Old Skip was my brother.

They had buried him under our elm tree, they said—yet this was not totally true. For he really lay buried in my heart.

MacKinlay Kantor

THE HORSE LOOKED AT HIM

Jameson thought he saw something stirring on the burnt sullenness of the desert's face. He thought he saw a quiver among slopes of brown and red.

He opened his dry, cracked mouth; his mouth had been open for a long time, but he opened it wider. He tried to say, weakly, "Posse."

It wasn't a posse. Jameson never thought he'd see the day when he'd be glad to have a posse come smoking up to him; but he reckoned that if a man lived long enough, he saw different days from those he had expected to see.

No quiver in the blue, no twisting and dividing in the brown. . . . Jameson turned his head and felt the vast, round flame of sky searing his eyeballs. He managed to lift his hand, and in the scant shade granted by swollen fingers, he tried to find some buzzards. He couldn't find any buzzards. Nothing lived on this dry pan of desertion—nothing lived here but Jameson and Poco.

The man twisted the upper part of his body, and sighed. Poco's head lay against the burning shale a few feet away;

when Jameson stirred, the little horse moved his neck with the agony of a movement five hundred times repeated. There were flies eating slowly away at Poco's ears. His ears twitched them off now and again, but the flies came back.

"How you doing?" Jameson wanted to ask his horse.

Poco wasn't doing so well. He had done well, for the five years Jameson had ridden him. He had taken Jameson bustling out of towns, slapping along narrow mountain roads when the bullets squealed around them. And there was that night in Dundee when the wise little horse waited silently beside a dark doorway, aloof from the stampede of pursuing hoofs, and finally carried Jameson away with two bullets in his arm.

There were marks on Poco, too: there was a dark streak along his sorrel shoulder, where lead had branded him with the only brand he wore. There was a knobby place on one hock, and the contour of one inquisitive ear had been mis-shapen long before the flies ever sat there.

Jameson said to the horse, "Reckon you'd like a drink. So would I."

He stole Poco from the Maxwell ranch, clear over south of the Estella Plata range, when Poco was only a colt. Jameson had raised Poco on a bottle, so to speak—taught him to blow his nose and keep his clothes buttoned. He was the only kid Jameson had ever had.

Now the heat-warped fingers of the man's hand stole down to find his revolver butt, as they had stolen a dozen times before. He thought, Nothing in this country. Nothing for fifty miles. I ought to have known better than try to ride across. But we made it, other times. No water.

His hand trembled as he exposed the cylinder and saw the solitary undented cartridge cap which reposed on the surface of powder-grimed steel. One chamber was vacant; Jameson never kept a shell under his hammer. There were five shiny little wafers looking at him; the rims of four were marred by hammer strokes.

He put the gun back in its holster again, and felt around his cartridge belt. His raw fingers rubbed across empty sockets. Jameson had known men who wore two cartridge belts but he had never worn more than one. He had never expected that posse to cling upon his trail with such wolfish tenacity.

The blue sky came down and struck him across the face. It was a red sky—now it was yellow—now white. "Sky," he wanted to ask, "do you see any posses? I sure would like to see one."

Poco's ears fluttered again, and he tried to whinny. Still there was moisture in his muzzle, and one bubble formed there, and then it went away. It was mighty strange that there could be any moisture in either of them, after the hot day and the cold night, and the day before that.

Jameson said, "One of us went wrong. That was a bad slide. I reckon you might have seen that crack in the rocks, but I ain't blaming you. You seen plenty I've never seen."

His mind went away from him for a while, and came speeding back amid the hearty hoofs of phantom horses. There were men in this fantasy: enemies who came to gather him in, and all the time they laughed at him.

The mystic enemies said, "Why did you do it, Jimmy Jameson? You ain't never killed anyone. Time was when you were mighty charitable with what you took off the road. You're a bad man; but a lot of people like you."

They said, in this parched dream that formed within his mind, "It wouldn't have been hanging. We're the Law. We know. We've burned powder and shoved lead at each other, but you ain't really got a bad name. Maybe you'd have spent a couple years behind bars, but that's all. You shouldn't have tried the Llano Diablo. No water in the Llano Diablo. Nobody goes there."

He thought that the posse circled him, and then dismounted to pat Poco's red-hot flank and to moisten Jameson's own lips with cool, wet salve from a canteen. "You're an awful idiot," said the posse. "Here you are: your horse has got a broken back, and it looks as if both of your legs is busted, too. Can't either of you move. Can't even crawl. Not even coyotes go out on the Llano Diablo."

Now he awoke from his dream, and he had the gun in his hand. Twice he put the muzzle against his own temple, and twice he fought successfully to keep his finger from tightening. His horse watched him with glazing eyes; again it tried to lift its head.

"No," Jameson thought. "By God, I can't! It's hell for me, but I reckon it's double hell for you."

Once more the desert became a pasture, and in it he saw a lush green place where Poco trotted toward him, stiff-legged, knobby-kneed, his eyes young and coltish. "Sugar?" said Jameson to his darling. "You don't get none. I ain't going to ruin your teeth. I got a piece of apple here . . ." and his hands played with the thick, wiry mane. "Reckon some day you'll be a fine horse."

The sky changed from white back into yellow and orange. The shadow of a steep stone ridge grew longer; it went past the two suffering shapes—the swollen mass of living horse-flesh—the dry-skinned, crippled man who lay beside it.

"Not another night," said Jameson. "I can't stand it. Pity there ain't two shells. I never realized I didn't have another loading for this gun."

Again the muzzle found his temple, but the horse still looked at him.

Jameson breathed softly. "O.K.," he croaked. He remembered something about the Bible and a merciful man being merciful to his beast, but Jameson would never in this life call Poco a beast.

He inched forward, suffering horrors until he felt the metal barrel sinking against Poco's ear cavity, soft and warm and silky despite all endurances.

"Be seeing you," he said, and pulled the trigger.

The gun jumped loose from his hand. His first thought was that the flies wouldn't be bothering Poco any longer.

He did not know how many dreams possessed him, but not many; the night came closer every second. And then his ears picked out a faint scrambling, a sound of sliding gravel. Hoof rims scraped the burnished gray rocks.

They rode up; they were angels in leather and flannel; they wore guns. They would carry Jimmy Jameson behind the bars, but still they were angels.

The sheriff was on his knees beside him.

"Can't understand it," Jameson whispered. "So late. Nobody comes to Llano Diablo."

The sheriff looked at the dead horse. He shook his head, even while his hands moved to his water bottle.

"One shell," said Jameson. "It was him or me. Poco needed a break."

The brown, lined face of the sheriff bent closer, and there were other faces behind. Water touched Jameson's lips.

"Guess you got a break yourself, that time," the sheriff said. "We hadn't come across your trail, and we agreed to ride back to Dundee. We were just turning our horses, behind that hill, when we heard you shoot."

Hector Chevigny

My Eyes Have a Cold Nose

I am going to tell the story of my training at Seeing Eye as though it happened in one period, but actually I had the opportunity of spending two months there and of being classmates with two groups of students. I mention this to show the care taken with each individual case. Before my first period of training was finished, Wizard became ill and I was assigned another dog. I didn't take to the second dog as I had taken to Wizard. Seeing Eye, deciding that the second dog was not proper for me, offered to let me return to resume my training when Wiz was himself again. That turned out to be the following month. However . . .

Seeing Eye comprises what was formerly a private estate on Whippany Road, a few miles south of Morristown. The central structure is the former residence of the estate, a three-storied wooden building of the cupola era, to which, at various times, wings have been added as the staff and the number of students increased. Snow lay on the ground on that February day when I enrolled with fifteen other blind. My first class included two servicemen and two girls. Of my second class, four were women, three servicemen, four were Negroes, and there was a Latin American. In this group, too, were three men returning for their second and third dogs. They came from many different walks of life; they were musicians, salesmen, newsstand operators, factory employees. One was a housewife with three children; she needed a dog to help her do her shopping. Another, an old-timer returning for his second dog, was a practicing attorney whose first dog had taken him through four years at Cornell. Still another was a masseur and our ranks also included a night-club entertainer. They came from all parts of the United States—from as far away as Austin, Texas, and Chehalis, Washington. Seeing Eye examines every application that comes to Morristown carefully. You pass quite a physical and mental scrutiny before admittance is granted, but none of its norms have anything to do with your social, religious, or economic standing. Your own desire for independence has a great deal to do with it, however; you have to show that your dog will be of use to you. When Seeing Eye admits you, its investment in you is heavy.

The system is to divide each class into two groups of eight students, each under the instructor who, during the previous three months, has been training the dogs with which the students will work.

Enrollment day had no ceremony in it. Everything was very casual. When I arrived I was taken upstairs, shown the comfortable room I would share with another, told where to hang my clothes, find the bathroom, shown the recreation room and the way to the dining hall. After that I was expected to find things for myself. If I lost a sock or a shoe, I was to discover I could ask an instructor or one of the chamber maids to help me find it, but I had to make my own search first. No one ever led me anywhere. On my first evening I got lost trying to locate the front door in the lobby; after a time Mr. Debataz came to my rescue but with the genial remark, "What are you trying to do, knock the house down?" You butter your own bread, cut your own meat; if you complain that you have never done these things before you are told it's about time you started. All this is part of the philosophy of Seeing Eye. Leave a man alone and he will re-find his independence. Every member of the staff, even the cooks in the kitchen and the waitresses in the dining hall, keeps in mind this philosophy when dealing with the students and never deviates from it.

I doubt if a single one of us students deemed any of it harsh or unkind. The atmosphere was reminiscent of a military boarding-school and we found it curiously refreshing. It might be more accurate to say the staff treated us as complete equals and it was good to feel that these people, so experienced in dealing with the blind, would so consider us, after the impression too often given us by relatives and friends alike that those who lose vision are in some way fundamentally changed. I had thought the rule a silly one that visitors, even our closest relatives, could see us for only two hours on Saturdays and Sundays during our month. I hadn't counted on going into retreat too. But the inept touch of the public which so often destroys self-confidence has to be excluded. For Seeing Eye trains not only dogs but people. This goes beyond the obvious necessity for inculcating confidence on sidewalks or road.

Elsewhere in this book I have dwelt on the tendency of the blind to acquire bad habits of posture and carriage, the result, sometimes, of anxieties of walking alone—more often the result of never having been allowed to walk alone. In every case these physical idiosyncrasies are deep-seated, difficult to correct. They must be corrected, however, or the dog cannot be properly walked with. Also it is the exception rather than the rule for a blind man who comes to Seeing Eye for the first time to remember what it is to walk fast. The dogs walk at slightly faster than a man's normal pace; for many, here is another new habit that must be acquired. Even the student's voice sometimes needs training, for it is the medium of communication between dog and master; habitual gruffness, too much variation of mood expressed in tone, must be corrected. All this is a job to do in one month; it requires the utmost concentration on the part of the student and outside interference cannot be allowed to disturb it. The student is told that Seeing Eye wants him to learn not merely how to walk in confidence with the dog but to walk freely, rapidly, and with grace and strength—and he does not have to hear this twice to make him desire it.

Of course we received instruction, but the method of giving it was such that we were made to feel that each of us worked out his own problem for himself. Carefully following their philosophy, the staff never intruded on our leisure hours. There was complete absence of "supervised" recreation—for which those among us who had been in blind centers of another kind were inordinately grateful. The kind of recreation we devised in those evenings at Seeing Eye would have amazed those who think of the blind as helpless. We played bridge (with Braille cards). We danced. We composed a song and did a great deal of listening to the radio. Once we nailed up the door in the instructor's room. We held innumerable bull sessions in which we respectfully listened to those who were returning for their second or third dogs tell of their adventures with their canine companions. Woollcott would have listened with real interest.

"Well, I'll tell you just how smart that dog of mine was. We had quite a time breakin' 'er of tryin' to sleep on the sofa and the beds. She preferred 'em to the floor and it took a long time to convince 'er that that rug on the floor was her place. You new fellers'll learn that you've got to be consistent with your dogs; you can't let 'em get on the furniture sometimes and make 'em get off at other times when they happen to be all wet and dirty. Anyway, Nelly took to sneakin' quick naps on the bed when she thought I wouldn't know about it. Tried to catch 'er at it but she always jumped off before I could do it. One day I decided to correct 'er on the strength of the fact that I could feel the warm place on the bed where she'd just been. Well, sir, do you know what she was doin' the next time I came in that bedroom? She was blowin' on the warm spot she'd made to cool it off."

I can't remember when the conversation at Seeing Eye didn't sooner or later turn to dogs.

I began to understand some of the reason for the unanimity of purpose among the personnel at Seeing Eye when I learned that every important member of the staff has himself not only dealt extensively with dogs but has spent at least one month living the life of a blind person, his vision cut off by a close-fitting black mask, until he is only too thoroughly convinced he knows what it is to be without sight. Sympathy, therefore, is not excluded at Seeing Eye, for its work rests upon it. But pity is; the essence of its philosophy being that pity is the luxury of the giver and the destroyer of the recipient.

THE drama that has touched my life has been mostly contrived; I have but seldom been close in reality to the perfectly fashioned drama of the theater and more seldom still has it ever happened to me. But that day on which the seven members of my group and I were assigned our dogs was as perfectly fashioned a piece of drama as any I have ever heard devised.

We had come to this place, many of us from great distances and not a few of us on our first journey of any length away from home. We'd come because we had hope and some of us were a little afraid to trust that hope. We were possessed of one ambition; to be free men. We had spent two days at Seeing Eye, had listened to our preliminary lectures, and had been shown the equipment that we would use. Now, at breakfast on the morning of the third day, Mr. Debetaz said in his strong Swiss accent, "You will go to your rooms. Please remain there until each of you is called. Then you will go to the recreation room, and there your instructors will introduce you to your dogs. I hope you will be satisfied with them."

I shall never forget the next two hours; my roommate and I were the last of our group to be called. We paced up and down our room, we smoked too many cigarettes, we exhaustively speculated on the kind of dog each of us would get. No doubt some of us prayed. We knew in a general way that the staff's estimate of our personalities would determine the choice of the dog selected for each of us. The hint had been dropped that as a rule an effort was made to give you a dog opposite to you in temperament. If you were phlegmatic you got a venturesome dog and the more excitable among us could count on getting the quieter, more even-tempered animals. But that didn't tell us much, it only whetted our curiosity and it didn't answer the question: would our dogs like us?

We were profoundly uneasy on that point because our success or failure here at Seeing Eye depended entirely on the rapport which would be effected between our dogs and ourselves. We knew we had a month in which to bring it about, and we had been warned that it was unlikely that the bond would be set up immediately, but we also wanted our first impressions on our dogs to be of the best. To those among us who had never had dogs, to whom arousing affection in one was an unknown art, waiting to find out if their new eyes would like them was an ordeal indeed.

Finally there came that knock for which my roommate and I were waiting. His name was called.

"Wish me luck," he said, and left me alone to my own thoughts. Ten minutes later he was back, bursting through the door like a tornado and yelling like an Indian, "Holy smoke—look what I got! Meet Deedee." The friendly German Shepherd bitch at the end of the leash he held was jumping all over me. But I had no time to get acquainted with Deedee just then. The instructor, laughing at the door, said, "You're next"—meaning me.

All the blood in my legs as far up as my hips turned to water on the way to the recreation room; how that happened I don't know, I just know it did. "Chair to your right hand," came the instructor's quiet voice. I put out my hand and sank into the chair. Then the instructor said, "This is Wizard." And that big male Boxer was suddenly all over me, snuffling and whiffling and licking my face—the creature who would be my almost inseparable companion for presumably the next decade of years.

I cannot remember when I felt a relief of tension and anxiety so complete and overwhelming as I felt at that moment. I didn't know, and it was just as well at the time, that Wizard went for me with that demonstration at the instructor's command. Even at that, however, I wouldn't have been inclined to look gift demonstrations in the mouth and probably would have accepted it on any terms. Only as I was leading Wiz to my room by his leash did it occur to me that none of my worry had been whether *I* would take to the dog. Also there was a minute's rueful reflection over a statement by the instructor to the effect that Wiz is an unusually friendly and obedient animal. I wondered if they figured that was the opposite of me, temperamentally speaking.

We spent the rest of the day in our rooms, getting acquainted with our dogs and playing with them. Our floor sounded like a house full of canaries; everybody was whistling. The first disagreement developed that afternoon between my roommate and myself; he maintained that German Shepherds are the world's greatest dogs, flying in the face of the plain evidence of Wizard that the Boxer is the world's greatest breed.

It didn't take much consultation with the rest of the class to discover that each man was firmly convinced that he'd been given the pick of Seeing Eye's kennels. The conviction was unanimous though our ways of expressing what we felt varied with our temperaments and experience with dogs. Some petted and praised their dogs extravagantly, others were more reserved.

The dogs responded with equally varied reactions. Some were bewildered by all the unaccustomed attention, some received it with apparently complete indifference. Others took to it at once. Wizard was one of the indifferent ones. Oh, he took my caresses patiently enough, and even obligingly wagged his stump of tail when I brought him his food, but he was full of the dignity peculiar to a Boxer and his entire attitude expressed the feeling that in accepting any attentions from me at all he was only doing what his real master, the instructor, wanted.

Not until the fourth day did we try it in harness on the streets of Morristown. Wizard allowed me to put on the light equipment and trotted beside me amiably enough, responding to the ten words used in command when I gave them. But it soon became apparent that he was co-operating because ordered to do so by the instructor. Wizard and the other seven dogs of our class had just gone through some three months' training with the instructor who was our mentor as well. It was during these three months that he had learned to walk in the light harness with the U-shaped handle, pause at up and down curbs, stop for passing automobiles, and pay no attention to lampposts. In that period he had also conceived a passionate adoration for the instructor. As if I hadn't enough to do, it now developed I also had to show this dog that I was the more desirable master; I had to win him over, in other words. It didn't seem at all probable, for Wizard was obviously a one-boss dog and the instructor held his job partly because he was the kind whom dogs instinctively like. Not that dogs dislike me, but it did make things look tough. The instructor assured me, though, that there would come a day, a definite day and even an observable moment—if things went well, that is—when Wizard would show himself my dog. The instructor would recognize that moment because Wizard would no longer be doing by rote what he had been trained to do, but would be actively on guard for my safety, leading me around puddles, keeping me from hitting lampposts, and finding a way to get me up on the curb without running me up against a mailbox, which he did not yet seem willing to do. In answer to my anxious question, I was told that although this rapport had been seen to take place between student and dog in as few as four days, it usually takes about three weeks. Sometimes it never takes place, and then the student has failed.

For the work of Seeing Eye is based on this simple principle: The dogs are not "trained" to work for the blind, they are persuaded. And for all their professional lives as guide dogs thereafter they have to be kept persuaded. Seeing Eye knows this and in its rigid examinations of candidates for entrance into the school, the cruel, the warped, and those who secretly hate dogs are usually denied admittance. Occasionally such a person gets by the examinations and becomes a student, but he seldom graduates. The reason: The dogs cannot be fooled. Seeing Eye can be patient and try him with dog after dog; the animals will work obediently enough with him for weeks on end, but they will never give those signs which in the experience of the instructors indicate that any of them has adopted the man.

LIFE was strenuous. I understood now the reason for that careful physical examination at the hands of a physician before I entered. We got up at 5:45 A.M. to take the dogs outdoors for curbing. That isn't heat they have around Morristown in February at that hour. The hearty breakfast served at seven was welcome. By eight we were on the Morristown streets practicing, our instructors taking us in pairs with our dogs. Staff and students took all meals together at the same tables. Sometimes at lunch board members and others directly interested in the work would be our guests. We always took our dogs to table with us, that was part of their training. They were supposed to lie perfectly still on command. But with sixteen dogs in one dining hall, sudden eruptions under the table were excitingly frequent. At one, we were back on the streets. Our day ended with the last visit of the dogs outdoors at 8 P.M.

It might have been fine if we could have gotten some sleep. But with each man's dog under his bed, things happened at night too. A couple of the dogs had the notion they were on some kind of guard duty and had to be cured of barking every time anyone moved within the county. The instructor, whose room was in our wing, got even less sleep than we did. There was always some student waking him with the news that (a) his dog was no longer under his bed and couldn't be found, (b) his dog was on the bed and wouldn't let him get back into it, and (c) another job of housebreaking had to be done. Tempers shortened and sometimes flared. In short, it wasn't very much fun for the students at first, but it was even less for the dogs.

I began to wonder what went on in Wizard's mind as we went about our practice rounds or he received my attentions in our room with his usual indifference. Having been at Seeing Eye, I can never subscribe to the belief that dogs don't think. The old question of canine thinking too often becomes involved in a struggle over definitions, but if thought means the power to form judgments, harbor options, and retain memories, certain dogs do have it. Although, clearly, the nature of their concepts and the process by which they arrive at them may well be quite different from man's. Dogs, however, can became aware of responsibility, as we will see, and reason with this awareness as a basis. Had Mrs. Eustis and all those associated with her not believed that dogs think and have reasoning powers, the work at Seeing Eye might never have been begun.

However, there seems to be a great variance of mental powers in dogs, and the mind as well as the body is characteristic of the breed. Certain breeds, with the exception of rare individuals within them, cannot, as a rule, be trained for Seeing Eye work. The Poodle is one. He can be taught everything a guide dog must know except one thing; responsibility for the master. He will turn left, right, go forward, or halt with neatness and celerity, but let him be brought to the brink of an open sidewalk elevator by his blind master who, of course, knows nothing of the danger before him, and he will not disobey the order to go forward, or attempt to lead his master around the danger, but will take the order literally and jump it.

Nor do all dogs among the breeds considered suitable for guide dog work pass the rigid specifications of Seeing Eye before entering training. Pure blood, incidentally, is not one of Seeing Eye's norms; many a dog with a questionable grandfather makes the grade. The Shepherd breed, both German and Belgian, is still the mainstay, but several other breeds have been found very suitable. In the first group with which I trained, in addition to my Boxer, there were two Labrador Retrievers. My second group included two Boxers and four Labrador Retrievers, in each case the remainder of the complement being made up of Shepherds. Originally, only females were much used in the work but it has been found that the male can be trained to full effectiveness. The female still predominates among the dogs as a sex but that is merely because more females than males are available at Seeing Eye.

Intelligence, of course, ranks high among the specifications. But, curiously, some dogs turn out to have altogether too much intelligence for Seeing Eye work. After a week or two of training with the instructor, such a dog sometimes evidently decides that this is too much like work and spends more time devising ways of getting out of his contract than of fulfilling it. Obviously, a dog like this would be quite unfit to turn over to anyone who is blind. And the animal gets what he wants— his release. The dogs who achieve the highest ratings at Seeing Eye are those with intelligence tempered with a dog's version of social consciousness.

I am quite certain that at first Wizard felt little but profound contempt for me. I think if he had realized I was going to become his permanent master he would have quit very early in the game. He probably wondered why he had been turned over to this jerk who held the harness so ineptly and who kept veering to the left against him and stepping on his toes. The fact that I fed and watered him didn't fool him a bit— he knew the instructor brought the food pans to the recreation room and handed them to the students to take to their rooms where the dogs waited. I knew he knew because I made a test: I brought a pan to the room one day. Wizard just yawned— he hadn't heard the instructor come up the stairs beforehand.

I knew then that if I ever won Wizard it was going to be on the rebound. I began to count on the fact that he obviously felt a deep and tragic hurt because his adored instructor would turn him over to anybody like me. I figured that if I could just paint the instructor in black enough colors to him, he might then start taking up with me as a bad second choice. But he wouldn't listen to anything against his beloved. Apparently he kept hoping that if he just went along beside me and obeyed orders, I'd go away or drop down a manhole or something.

Then suddenly his attitude changed from indifference to something worse. It has often been asked if Seeing Eye dogs actually realize their masters cannot see. Whether dogs grasp the full implication of the fact of blindness is something that probably never can be determined but, as the staff well know, the dogs recognize the difference between the blind and the visioned. As they lie sprawled in attitudes of comfort in the recreation room or dining hall, they don't change position when a sighted person steps close to them. But let one of the students approach and they pull their paws to safety or silently find another position. At any rate, Wizard certainly made the discovery that I could not see. That meant that all kinds of tricks could be played on me. He observed that I didn't seem to know when I was at the end of a street until I touched the curb. If he just succeeded in turning me ever so neatly at a corner before taking me to the curb, he could deflect me to the warmth of the bus station or toward the automobile in which we had come from the school, thus saving himself an hour's practice with me. He found, too, that because the ground was frozen I didn't know it when he took me off the sidewalk and so he devised a shortcut to the park when we visited it for curbing at 5:45 A.M.

This beginning to play tricks on Wizard's part marked a crucial point in my own training. My classmates began having the same trouble, although of course with some of them it came much earlier and with others later. We were disappointed and gloomy. For the first time in our evening bull sessions in each other's rooms, we stopped bragging about our dogs and complained of their behavior. It seemed ungrateful of them, after the care and affection we constantly lavished on them, to respond like this. It seemed that far from achieving increased safety on the streets we were running into lampposts and fire hydrants more often than before and we bitterly anticipated getting run over as the next adventure. We beefed about the instructor. We wondered what he had been up to during the three months he was supposed to have been training our dogs.

The instructor knew what was happening, however, with both dogs and men. The time had come to teach us how to administer discipline. Until then, we had not been allowed to use more than a mild, verbal reproof, although we were expected to give loud and extravagant praise when the dog did his job correctly. Now we were taught the word—"pfui"—which is used in dog training as the sign of disapproval, and to give it authority, if necessary, by an expert tug on the leash. This was not punishment, we were taught. Dogs are never punished; they are corrected. The correction must come instantly upon the realization by the master that the dog is doing something wrong, and when the dog resumes doing things the correct way the praise must be unmistakable. Obviously, the principle is one of identification in the dog's mind of correction with what he does wrong and praise for the right. Just as obviously, correction mistakenly given, when the master is unsure of just what the dog is up to, or given too late, leads to confusion in the dog's mind as to what the master wants. Exact timing and complete certainty on the master's part, therefore, are essential or the guide dog can be made unfit, temporarily, at least, for his job.

Awareness that the human being who had been so clumsily walking beside him the past two or three weeks, as well as feeding, watering, and grooming him, might be his permanent master instead of a temporary nuisance, seems to dawn in the dog's mind about the time that attempts at disciplining him begin. Here is someone who certainly has to be reckoned with and who seems to know what he wants, if only those wants can be fathomed. He notices the alternation of tone and words between the terms of correction and the extravagant praises heaped on him. He determines to avoid the correction and strive for the praise, finding that both easier and more pleasant.

The class begins to relax. We are not hitting nearly so many lampposts or running down so many street signs. Our dogs have learned that quick, sharp reproof will follow either mistake, and that the only reward for playing tricks is to be brought back to position to perform the task over again. But this is still rote. We haven't yet been truly adopted by our dogs. True, they now return our caresses with real affection, they sometimes growl when others approach our possessions, and they may whine when they think themselves deserted. But they aren't aware of their responsibility. They still can't be trusted entirely alone with their masters in crossing a busy street.

What makes the dog decide to assume this responsibility seems to be beyond human understanding. The dog will go to sleep under his master's bed at Seeing Eye one night without it and the next morning awaken with it. From that point on the master is safe. He can cross any street that any sighted person would ordinarily brave. He can proceed up the most crowded sidewalk with assurance. His period of training, except for a few further technical pointers and a few more lectures on such subjects as the ordinary diseases of the dog, is over. He is ready to go home.

From that day until the dog's death he is seldom separated from his master. He looks upon the master as the source of all his comfort, as the center of his universe. He sleeps beside his master's bed. His ears are so accustomed to his master's tones that he can distinguish soft spoken commands amid the roar of traffic.

What is the dog's reward for this lifetime of devotion? What does he get out of it? I am often asked this question, especially by those who are under the impression that the dog is forced to his task or that his training has been based on coercion. The food, shelter, and care the dog receives would not, even in human terms, seem to be enough to account for it and they aren't. The dog's true reward is affection. In human terms this seems quite ridiculous, but in a dog's terms it is anything but that. I know of no explanation why, in the dawn of history, the dog has sought out man and has been willing to work for him. Certainly the status of the dog has always been different from that of the ox and the horse, which are truly in servitude. Escape from man has always been possible for the dog. Yet dogs have been known to remain by man when food and shelter both were quite meager, provided they received affection. This would seem to be the dog's peculiar craving. The relation between the blind man and his dog is the closest rapport of its kind ever achieved. The very privilege of this closeness is the dog's reward.

Graduation at Seeing Eye is as casual as matriculation. The staff, busy preparing for the class which is coming in the next day, seems mildly surprised at our hearty handshakes and enthusiastic promises to write. There are no diplomas, no certificates. We merely go to the Executive Offices to pay our bill or to arrange for credit if we haven't all of that $150 which covers everything.

Next we are in our rooms packing, all final arrangements to go home having been made. The bell rings for our last meal; in ten seconds we have our dogs harnessed. We bound from our rooms, banging the doors behind us—the first day we dared to quit our rooms, we felt our way along the walls.

We dash across the recreation room, run downstairs—strictly against the rules—burst into the dining hall and find our places. Time: thirty seconds. On our first day it took us an average of twelve minutes.

But however great the change the past month has effected in us, it is no less great in our dogs. There is a tautness about them as they stand beside us in harness, a concentration on their jobs. There is a new pride in their carriage. They hold their heads high, ears cocked for every suspicious sound. They are creatures with an important office and they know it.

That afternoon my wife came to Seeing Eye. We greeted each other for the first time since we'd parted at the Santa Fe station in Los Angeles five months before. It might have been a meeting harrowing in the extreme but for the presence of one creature—by name, Wizard. For I went to the meeting walking like anyone else, and when we took the bus for New York an hour later it was with the confidence of one very accustomed to getting into such things as busses without assistance. Our family had acquired another member—that was all.

Paul Gallico

HONORABLE CAT

This is my chair.
Go away and sit somewhere else.
This one is all my own.
It is the only thing in your house that I possess,
And insist upon possessing.
Everything else therein is yours.
My dish,
My toys,
My basket,
My scratching post and my Ping-Pong ball;
You provided them for me.
This chair I selected for myself.
I like it,
It suits me.
You have the sofa,
The stuffed chair
And the footstool.
I don't go and sit on them do I?

Then why cannot you leave me mine,
And let us have no further argument?

———————

I have loved my cats with a curious kind of affection unlike
that of any other emotion that I have experienced for man
or beast and one which I have never, up to this point, tried
to analyze, dissect, or understand. And now that I try to do
so I think that it is compounded of admiration, sympathy,
and amusement. To this I add a slight and curious tincture of
pity plus a wholly unpredictable and irrational feeling which
comes welling up out of depths indefinable.

Somewhere, sometime, this extraordinary thing happened
between humans and felines.

Looking backward, our original association was simply mu-
tually and practically rewarding and wholly unsentimental.
When first man learned to store his grain he found that mice
got into it. The cat was a hunter and small rodents his natural
prey. Clever man therefore engaged a cat to help him save his
food by putting it where it could hunt to its heart's content
and serve man by doing so.

We know that this situation obtained in Egypt so long ago
because this is the first record in painting and writing that we
have of this relationship. It is most curious. Primitive man was
beginning to save up food long before the Pharaohs. Dog
helped him to hunt, but there is no record of cat assisting him
to store.

On the banks of the Nile then, where originally was estab-
lished this perfect mutual arrangement and balance, one day
or one millennium something inexplicable happened; the fero-
cious guardian of the granaries became a cold, distant, high-
placed and worshipped god in the temples.

The cat in those times was even further involved with hu-
mans in that it performed the service eventually usurped by the
bird dog and accompanied its owner on the hunt as testified by

wall paintings showing a definitely striped tabby lurking in the reeds of the swamps to put up a bird. And not only that but the animal was further willing to act as retriever after the hunter had brought down the quarry with an arrow, spear, or throwing-stick. It didn't take it too long to discover it was being conned.

All in all, for an animal which up to that time appeared not to have been heard of, or noticed, it accomplished the neatest trick of the ages of which the most astonishing and enduring was the manner in which it crept into the hearts and minds of men, women, and children and established itself in the home, and there inspired not only awe, worship, and respect, but above everything else that mattered—love. The paintings and the written records show that the ancient Egyptians pampered and spoiled their house cats, treated them as honored guests, and loved them. But did the cats love the Egyptians, and when and how did that love come about in the breast of that feral creature, or wherever the seat of that emotion might be, and does my cat love me?

I raise the question, because whereas it is easy for those of us so constituted to be drawn toward those soft, beautiful, and admirable animals, if I were of their species, I think I would find man very difficult to love.

In fact, taking my cat's point of view, it ought to regard me as something of an unstable and capricious lunatic, stupid, unpredictable, tyrannical, and utterly selfish; satisfactory for board and lodging and an occasional caress, but for the rest utterly useless.

Well, admitted that uselessness is no bar to affection as many men have discovered, what, besides food and shelter, have I to offer my four-footed companion except that human type of possessive love that even humans eventually find cloying and my cat certainly does?

By and large they will take just so much of it. When we love members of our own species we take them in our arms and press them to our hearts. Cats don't like to be squeezed.

For that matter they do not care for any manner of confinement and will only rest quiescent in one's grasp for a period they consider polite before starting a scramble for the floor.

They will take only so much petting, tickling, rubbing, or mauling before, smothering a yawn, they will walk away with a firmness that is unmistakable. And if still you fail to get the message, they will either leave the room entirely, or produce a toy from where it has been stashed beneath the bureau and start a game.

A gentleman cat who loves a lady cat embraces her right enough in what is a combination of a football charge and an all-in wrestling match at the climax of which the object of his amour gets a severe bite in her neck. But we are not considering that kind of love. And besides, when our cat does give it to us, that is to say, when in play we sometimes unwittingly stimulate it sexually and it digs the claws of all four feet into our arm and gives our hand a nip as well, we yell blue murder and accuse the animal of being false, sly, and treacherous.

It is a human fallacy, the belief that love must engender love and the like, in intensity, to that bestowed. This illusion has been getting men into trouble with women and themselves ever since the emotion was discovered and classified. "But I love you so," pleads the unhappy and idiot swain. "How can you possibly not love me in return?" And even when there exists a mutuality of affection, people lovers want to make it quantitative. "Do you love me as much as I love you?" They wish to put it onto a scale and see whether it balances or which way it tips. We at least can find out linguistically or lie decently to one another. But my wise, dumb animal isn't saying.

And so I wonder whether it has the mechanism of love, the kind of which I am thinking; unphysical, abstract, yet deeply felt, surging and impelling, the kind which is not "made" but which simply happens when the object thereof comes within range.

For there is always the lurking suspicion in all of us of the power of the cupboard. Was there in bygone days a real cat deity, a supercat who one moment, smitten with a stroke of genius, discovered and imparted to all that followed it that man is the eternal sucker who can be flattered or conned into anything with the right approach? When ofttimes we are compelled to the same doubts as to the sincerity of the fervent declarations of undying passion from members of our own kind, what is so strange in suspecting that our cat maybe is putting on the act of the ages? In fact, one would have to be wholly besotted with one's own worth *not* to wonder, knowing the cat's reserve and independence. Suspicion is further an outgrowth of the fact that they can turn it on and they can turn it off. And if, for the most part, you seem to remember that they turn it on when there would appear to be something in it for them, then you suddenly remember that day when you sat depressed in a chair, suffering from a hurt concealed, a worry, a disappointment, or a crisis, and suddenly there was someone soft and furry in your lap and a body pressed close to yours in warmth and comfort.

Or there is the presentation mouse which would come wrapped in white tissue and tied with a golden ribbon if a cat could. Or the waiting by the gate or door for you to come home or some other strange mark of unselfish feeling. Everyone who has ever kept a cat has a story to tell in proof.

I wrote earlier of the element of pity that was a part of the emotion I feel and sometimes I wonder whether it is not upon this level that mutuality is established and that my wise and well-adjusted cat is feeling sorry for me and would like to help me to be more like its quiet and contented self.

The true animal lover will understand my use of the word pity, not in the sense of patronizing, for in that there is nothing akin to love, but rather a sympathy with and for them, for their lot, which is not an easy one anymore than is ours. It will be then just as easy to love a hippopotamus as much as a prize Persian, or a jackal, dingo, or hyena as much as a Seal

Point Siamese or a silver tabby. More so, perhaps, since the former haven't got it so good and need it so much more.

No, this compassion, I think, stems from the fact that in one way or another, we are all in the same trap of life cycle and in the short time allotted us we are trying to make out the best we can. And the cat more often than not has a hard row to hoe.

This creature is also the least insistent upon pity, which in itself is attractive and breeds the respect that is often the backbone of love. While it is constantly demanding the best, we have seen that it will also do without. The cat can be spoiled rotten, but basically life has taught it to expect little. It is a master of survival on its own terms. It may be an expert at panhandling you or tugging at your heart, but it is always to be remembered that essentially it promises nothing in return, and then suddenly, at the most surprising and unexpected of moments, gives freely.

Well, there you are, and as the saying goes, we have come a "fur piece" from the beginning of the journey without getting any forrader. One starts out by reflecting upon one's house pet and winds up with a self-analysis that is not too flattering with genuine communication reduced to a few signals affording only rare and actually reliable glimpses into the mind and heart of one's cat. And if out of this one is able to salvage something at least slightly admirable in oneself as voluntary associates of this creature, it is the fact that one, in some measure, is able to bear to love something or someone without expecting a return.

I am Cat.
I am honorable.
I have pride.
I have dignity.
And I have memory.
For I am older than you.
I am older than your gods; the Tree Gods, the Stone
    Gods,
The Thunder and Lightning and the Sun Gods
And your God of Love.
I too can love
But with only half a heart
And that I offer you.
Accept what I am able to give
For were I to give you all
I could not bear your inevitable treachery.
Let us remain honorable friends.

John Steinbeck

TRAVELS WITH CHARLEY

Although it was only mid-morning, I cooked a sumptuous dinner for myself, but I don't remember what it was. And Charley, who still had vestiges of his Chicago grooming, waded in the water and became his old dirty self again.

After the comfort and the company of Chicago I had had to learn to be alone again. It takes a little time. But there on the Maple River, not far from Alice, the gift of it was coming back. Charley had forgiven me in a nauseatingly superior way, but now he had settled down to business also. The pullover place beside the water was pleasant. I brought out my garbage-can washing machine and rinsed clothes that had been jiggling in detergent for two days. And then, because a pleasant breeze was blowing, I spread my sheets to dry on some low bushes. I don't know what kind of bushes they were, but the leaves had a rich smell like sandalwood, and there's nothing I like better than scented sheets. And I made some notes on a sheet of yellow paper on the nature and quality of being alone. These notes would in the normal course of events have been lost as notes are always lost, but these particular notes turned up long afterward wrapped around a bottle of ketchup and secured with a rubber band. The first note says, "Relationship Time to Aloneness." And I remember about that. Having a companion fixes you in time and that the present, but when the quality of aloneness settles down, past, present and future all flow together. A memory, a present event, and a forecast all equally present.

The second note lies obscurely under a streak of ketchup, or catsup, but the third is electric. It says: "Reversion to pleasure-pain basis," and this is from some observation of another time.

A number of years ago I had some experience with being alone. For two succeeding years I was alone each winter for eight months at a stretch in the Sierra Nevada mountains on Lake Tahoe. I was a caretaker on a summer estate during the winter months when it was snowed in. And I made some observations then. As the time went on I found that my reactions thickened. Ordinarily I am a whistler. I stopped whistling. I stopped conversing with my dogs, and I believe that subtleties of feeling began to disappear until finally I was on a pleasure-pain basis. Then it occurred to me that the delicate shades of feeling, of reaction, are the result of communication, and without such communication they tend to disappear. A man with nothing to say has no words. Can its reverse be true—a man who has no one to say anything to has no words as he has no need for words? Now and then there appear accounts of babies raised by animals—wolves and such. It is usually reported that the youngster crawls on all fours, makes those sounds learned from his foster parents, and perhaps even thinks like a wolf. Only through imitation do we develop toward originality. Take Charley, for example. He has always associated with the learned, the gentle, the literate, and the reasonable both in France and in America. And Charley is no more like a dog dog than he is like a cat. His perceptions are sharp and delicate and he is a mind-reader. I don't know that he can read the thoughts of other dogs, but he can read mine.

Before a plan is half formed in my mind, Charley knows about it, and he also knows whether he is to be included in it. There's no question about this. I know too well his look of despair and disapproval when I have just thought that he must be left at home. And so much for the three notes below the red stain on the ketchup bottle.

Soon Charley moved downstream and found some discarded bags of garbage, which he went through with discrimination. He nosed over an empty bean can, sniffed in its opening, and rejected it. Then he took up the paper bag in his teeth and gently shook it so that more treasures rolled out, among them a balled-up piece of heavy white paper.

I opened it and smoothed the angry creases from its surface. It was a court order addressed to Jack So-and-so informing him that if he didn't pay his back alimony he would be in contempt and punishable. The court sat in an eastern state, and this was North Dakota. Some poor guy on the lam. He shouldn't have left this spoor around, in case anyone was looking for him. I snapped my Zippo lighter and burned the evidence with full knowledge that I compounded the contempt. Good Lord, the trails we leave! Suppose someone, finding the ketchup bottle, tried to reconstruct me from my notes. I helped Charley sort over the garbage, but there was no other written material, only the containers of prepared foods. The man was no cook. He lived out of cans, but then perhaps his former wife did also.

It was only shortly after noon but I was so relaxed and comfortable that I hated to move. "Should we stay the night, Charley?" He inspected me and wagged his tail as a professor wags a pencil—once to the left, once to the right, and return to center. I sat on the bank, took off socks and boots, and dipped my feet in water so cold it burned until the freezing went deep and deadened feeling. My mother believed that cold water on the feet forced the blood to your head so that you thought better. "Time for examination, *mon vieux Chamal*," I said aloud, "which is another way of saying I feel comfortingly lazy. I came out on this trip to try to learn something of America. Am I learning anything? If I am, I don't know what it is. So far can I go back with a bag full of conclusions, a cluster of answers to riddles? I doubt it, but maybe. When I go to Europe, when I am asked what America is like, what will I say? I don't know. Well, using your olfactory method of investigations, what have you learned, my friend?"

Two complete wags. At least he didn't leave the question open.

"Does all America so far smell alike? Or are there sectional smells?" Charley began to turn around and around to the left, and then he reversed and turned eight times to the right before he finally settled and put his nose on his paws and his head within reach of my hand. He has a hard time getting down. When he was young a car hit him and broke his hip. He wore a cast for a long time. Now in his golden age his hip troubles him when he is tired. After too long a run he limps on his right hind leg. But because of his long turning before lying down, we sometimes call him a whirl poodle—much to our shame. If my mother's rule was right I was thinking pretty well. But she also said, "Cold feet—warm heart." And that's a different matter.

I had parked well away from the road and from any traffic for my time of rest and recount. I am serious about this. I did not put aside my sloth for the sake of a few amusing anecdotes. I came with the wish to learn what America is like. And I wasn't sure I was learning anything. I found I was talking aloud to Charley. He likes the idea but the practice makes him sleepy.

"Just for ducks, let's try a little of what my boys should call this generality jazz. Under heads and subheads. Let's take food as we have found it. It is more than possible that in the cities we have passed through, traffic-harried, there are good and distinguished restaurants with menus of delight. But in the eating places along the roads the food has been clean, tasteless, colorless, and of a complete sameness. It is almost as though the customers had no interest in what they ate as long as it had no character to embarrass them. This is true of all but the breakfasts, which are uniformly wonderful if you stick to bacon and eggs and pan-fried potatoes. At the road-sides I never had a really good dinner or a really bad breakfast. The bacon or sausage was good and packaged at the factory, the eggs fresh or kept fresh by refrigeration, and refrigeration was universal." I might even say roadside America is the paradise of breakfast except for one thing. Now and then I would see a sign that said "home-made sausage" or "home-smoked bacons and hams" or "new-laid eggs" and I would stop and lay in supplies. Then, cooking my own breakfast and making my own coffee, I found that the difference was instantly apparent. A freshly laid egg does not taste remotely like the pale, battery-produced refrigerated egg. The sausage would be sweet and sharp and pungent with spices, and my coffee a wine-dark happiness. Can I then say that the America I saw has put cleanliness first, at the expense of taste? And—since all our perceptive nerve trunks including that of taste are not only perfectible but also capable of trauma—that the sense of taste tends to disappear and that strong, pungent, or exotic flavors arouse suspicion and dislike and so are eliminated?

"Let's go a little farther into other fields, Charley. Let's take the books, magazines, and papers we have seen displayed where we have stopped. The dominant publication has been the comic book. There have been local papers and I've bought and read them. There have been racks of paperbacks with some great and good titles but overwhelmingly outnumbered by the volumes of sex, sadism, and homicide. The big-city papers cast their shadows over large areas around them, the *New York Times* as far as the Great Lakes, the *Chicago Tribune* all the way here to North Dakota. Here, Charley, I give you a warning, should you be drawn to generalities. If this people has so atrophied its taste buds as to find tasteless food not only acceptable but desirable, what of the emotional life of the nation? Do they find their emotional fare so bland that it must be spiced with sex and sadism through the medium of the paperback? And if this is so, why are there no condiments save ketchup and mustard to enhance their foods?

"We've listened to local radio all across the country. And apart from a few reportings of football games, the mental fare has been as generalized, as packaged, and as undistinguished as the food." I stirred Charley with my foot to keep him awake.

I had been keen to hear what people thought politically. Those whom I had met did not talk about the subject, didn't seem to want to talk about it. It seemed to me partly caution and partly a lack of interest, but strong opinions were just not stated. One storekeeper did admit to me that he had to do business with both sides and could not permit himself the luxury of an opinion. He was a graying man in a little gray store, a crossroads place where I stopped for a box of dog biscuits and a can of pipe tobacco. This man, this store might have been anywhere in this nation, but actually it was back in Minnesota. The man had a kind of gray wistful twinkle in his eyes as though he remembered humor when it was not against the law, so that I dared to go out on a limb. I said, "It looks then as though the natural contentiousness of people had died. But I don't believe that. It'll just take another channel. Can you think, sir, of what that channel might be?"

"You mean where will they bust out?"

"Where do they bust out?"

I was not wrong, the twinkle was there, the precious, humorous twinkle. "Well, sir," he said, "we've got a murder now and then, or we can read about them. Then we've got the World Series. You can raise a wind any time over the Pirates or the Yankees, but I guess the best of all is we've got the Russians."

"Feelings pretty strong there?"

"Oh, sure! Hardly a day goes by somebody doesn't take a belt at the Russians." For some reason he was getting a little easier, even permitted himself a chuckle that could have turned to throat-clearing if he saw a bad reaction from me.

I asked, "Anybody know any Russians around here?"

And now he went all out and laughed. "Course not. That's why they're valuable. Nobody can find fault with you if you take out after the Russians."

"Because we're not doing business with them?"

He picked up a cheese knife from the counter and carefully ran his thumb along the edge and laid the knife down. "Maybe that's it. By George, maybe that's it. We're not doing business."

"You think then we might be using the Russians as an outlet for something else, for other things."

"I didn't think that at all, sir, but I bet I'm going to. Why, I remember when people took everything out on Mr. Roosevelt. Andy Larsen got red in the face about Roosevelt one time when his hens got the croup. Yes, sir," he said with growing enthusiasm, "those Russians got quite a load to carry. Man has a fight with his wife, he belts the Russians."

"Maybe everybody needs Russians. I'll bet even in Russia they need Russia. Maybe they call it Americans."

He cut a sliver of cheese from a wheel and held it out to me on the knife blade. "You've given me something to think about in a sneaking kind of way."

"I thought you gave it to me."

"How?"

"About business and opinions."

"Well, maybe so. Know what I'm going to do? Next time Andy Larsen comes in red in the face, I'm going to see if the Russians are bothering his hens. It was a great loss to Andy when Mr. Roosevelt died."

Now, there is not any question that Charley was rapidly becoming a tree expert of enormous background. He could probably get a job as a consultant with the Davies people. But from the first I had withheld from him any information about the giant redwoods. It seemed to me that a Long Island poodle who had made his devoirs to *Sequoia sempervirens* or *Sequoia gigantia* might be set apart from other dogs—might even be like that Galahad who saw the Grail. The concept is staggering. After this experience he might be translated mystically to another plane of existence, to another dimension, just as the redwoods seem to be out of time and out of our ordinary thinking. The experience might even drive him mad. I had thought of that. On the other hand, it might make of him a consummate bore. A dog with an experience like that could become a pariah in the truest sense of the word.

The redwoods, once seen, leave a mark or create a vision that stays with you always. No one has ever successfully painted or photographed a redwood tree. The feeling they produce is not transferable. From them comes silence and awe. It's not only their unbelievable stature, nor the color which seems to shift and vary under your eyes, no, they are not like any trees we know, they are ambassadors from another time. They have the mystery of ferns that disappeared a million years ago into the coal of the carboniferous era. They carry their own light and shade. The vainest, most slap-happy and irreverent of men, in the presence of redwoods, goes under a spell of wonder and respect. Respect—that's the word. One feels the need to bow to unquestioned sovereigns. I have known these great ones since my earliest childhood, have lived among them, camped and slept against their warm monster bodies, and no amount of association has bred contempt in me. And the feeling is not limited to me.

A number of years ago, a newcomer, a stranger, moved to my country near Monterey. His senses must have been blunted and atrophied with money and the getting of it. He bought a grove of sempervirens in a deep valley near the coast, and then, as was his right by ownership, he cut them down and sold the lumber, and left on the ground the wreckage of his slaughter. Shock and numb outrage filled the town. This was not only murder but sacrilege. We looked on that man with loathing and he was marked to the day of his death.

Of course, many of the ancient groves have been lumbered off, but many of the stately monuments remain and will remain, for a good and interesting reason. States and governments could not buy and protect these holy trees. This being so, clubs, organizations, even individuals, bought them and dedicated them to the future. I don't know any other similar case. Such is the impact of the sequoias on the human mind. But what would it be on Charley?

Approaching the redwood country, in southern Oregon, I kept him in the back of Rocinante, hooded as it were. I passed several groves and let them go as not quite adequate—and then on a level meadow by a stream we saw the grandfather, standing alone, three hundred feet high and with the girth of a small apartment house. The branches with their flat, bright green leaves did not start below a hundred and fifty feet up. Under that was the straight, slightly tapering column with its red to purple to blue. Its top was noble and lightning-riven by some ancient storm. I coasted off the road and pulled to within fifty feet of the godlike thing, so close that I had to throw back my head and raise my eyes to vertical to see its branches. This was the time I had waited for. I opened the back door and let Charley out and stood silently watching, for this could be dog's dream of heaven in the highest.

Charley sniffed and shook his collar. He sauntered to a weed, collaborated with a sapling, went to the stream and drank, then looked about for new things to do.

"Charley," I called. "Look!" I pointed at the grandfather. He wagged his tail and took another drink. I said, "Of course. He doesn't raise his head high enough to see the branches to prove it's a tree." I strolled to him and raised his muzzle straight up. "Look, Charley. It's the tree of all trees. It's the end of the Quest."

Charley got a sneezing fit, as all dogs do when the nose is elevated too high. I felt the rage and hatred one has toward non-appreciators, toward those who through ignorance destroy a treasured plan. I dragged him to the trunk and rubbed his nose against it. He looked coldly at me and forgave me and sauntered away to a hazelnut bush.

"If I thought he did it out of spite or to make a joke," I said to myself, "I'd kill him out of hand. I can't live without knowing." I opened my pocket knife and moved to the creekside, where I cut a branch from a small willow tree, a Y-branch well tufted with leaves. I trimmed the branch ends neatly and finally sharpened the butt end, then went to the serene grandfather of Titans and stuck the little willow in the earth so that its greenery rested against the shaggy redwood bark. Then I whistled to Charley and he responded amiably enough. I pointedly did not look at him. He cruised casually about until he saw the willow with a start of surprise. He sniffed its new-cut leaves delicately and then, after turning this way and that to get range and trajectory, he fired.

Three

NEIGHBORS

Floyd Skloot

DAYBREAK

The shapes that moved outside
our door tonight were four deer
come to feed on the last winter
weeds. The riot of their flight
seemed to echo through the dark
when I left my bed to see them.

Now the valley sends its voices
up through morning mist. Cows low,
the sheep farmer's old border
collie barks as she herds strays,
and the southbound freight is
an hour late. Where our hillside
plummets, a fringe of feathery
wild grasses webbed with frost
bends as though lost in prayer.

My wife built this house round
because a clear loop of moonlight

found the space for her early
on a morning like this. She woke
in her down sleeping bag under
a canopy of second growth to hear
great horned owls call from oaks
creaking in a sudden surge of wind.
When she sat up, there was a deer
standing exactly where a dowser
had told her the well should go.

Hope Ryden

LILY POND

While I was laboring to deliver food to two incarcerated beavers in the New Pond lodge, the colony at Lily Pond wintered well, gorging on lily rhizomes in such excess that by spring the shoreline was littered with partially eaten roots, each one bearing witness to the beavers' profligacy. Many appeared to have been hardly nibbled before being cast away. Such behavior on the part of wild animals is not unusual and of small importance, though human critics often think otherwise. In actual fact, little if anything in a natural system is lost. What food is not consumed by the animal that harvests it will be discovered by another or will be returned to the earth in the form of nutrients. On the other hand, human activities do indeed contribute to the permanent degradation of natural systems; for example, the loss of valuable topsoil by strip mining, the pollution of water tables by chemical dumpers, the destruction of entire forests by acid rain. By contrast, even when animals overharvest the very resource that is vital to their survival, the effect simply hastens their departure from the site, thus insuring that plant food a period of recovery. Realizing this, I eyed the plethora of partly eaten roots that had washed ashore not judgmentally, but with regret. I did not want to lose my Lily Pond colony. At the same time, I was happy that all six beavers had fared so well over winter, for they emerged from the lodge fatter than ever and in robust health.

Huckleberry and Buttercup, who had entered the winter as babies, appeared so grown in spring that I had difficulty distinguishing them from their older siblings, Blossom and Lotus. From any distance, all four looked the same size. Moreover, the lighter beavers in each age class had become darker, just to confuse me further. I saw no recourse but to lure the entire family to the cove and inspect them all anew. So once again I placed aspen branches in the water and retired to my viewing rock to await the beavers' evening appearance.

At close range I was able to detect some previously unnoticed characteristics. Blossom, for example, had at some time over winter incurred a minor injury, a split on the left side of his tail tip. Since beavers frequently hold their tails aloft while feeding, this gave me a long-distance marker by which to distinguish him from my other dark beaver, Huckleberry. I expected that Lotus would soon turn blond, as she had done the previous spring; meanwhile, I discovered that she and Buttercup carried an indelible marker for the predisposition to fade, namely, pink claws. In contrast, the claws of the other beavers were either dark gray or yellowish gray. Identifying the Inspector General was no trick. No beaver came close to him in size. And Lily, wondrous creature, retained that quality of expression that was uniquely hers and that never failed to incite in me the urge to reach out and touch her. Her muzzle had become more grizzled over the winter, and now I wondered how old she might be.

Few wild beavers live even as long as a decade, but in 1966 one female whose teeth and eye lenses suggested to researchers that she had attained twenty and one half years was trapped in Maryland. Though captive beavers have been known to surpass even that great age, this does seem to be the record for beavers living wild; the Maryland study found no other animal that had survived beyond twelve. Lily, I suspected, had already lived well past the norm.

Once I had scrutinized the Lily Pond colony at close range, I was again able to pick up individual characteristics at a distance through binoculars. Though all age classes interacted with each other, littermates, I noticed, preferred one another's company to that of older or younger family members. After being apart for a time, same-age siblings would approach and greet with loud vocalization and by touching noses. Sometimes they would swim apart, one traveling clockwise, the other counterclockwise, each tracing a perfect semi-circle until they met again. Sometimes they would engage in a round of play or dive alongside one another while traveling the pond.

On rare occasions these water games got out of hand and led to shoving matches. Like Japanese wrestlers, the contenders would square off, grip one another's loose ruff with their black satiny hands, and then drive forward with all their might until the stronger one propelled the weaker backward into deep water. Breast-to-breast, cheek-to-cheek, heads tilted skyward, eyes rolled upward so that only membranes showed, their resemblance to Samurai warriors was uncanny, both in bodily shape and in the martial strategies they employed. They inflicted no wounds; theirs was a contest of strength, not an outlet for vengeance. Nor was the animal who was momentarily being bested automatically defeated. As the prevailing beaver tired, the receding one summoned strength to halt his ignominious retreat. Then he or she would drive forward, forcing the other to backpaddle. Thus locked together, the grunting beavers advanced and retreated, advanced and retreated, advanced and retreated until at last one gave up. Giving up was always necessary to satisfy the victor. The vanquished animal was required to grovel or make a show of his submission, as does a defeated wolf. No blood was shed, no grudges festered as an outcome of these beaver contests.

Afterward the combatants swam together and behaved as if nothing untoward had occurred.

I watched these matches many times and thought a lot about them. Any species that possesses sharp teeth with which to chew food must avoid using those hazardous tools against its kind, as doing so would bring about its extinction. Moreover, it is certainly not in the interest of an individual animal to kill a close relative whose hereditary make-up (being similar to his own) offers a biological means by which his own genetic material may be propagated. Finally, only a colony that is able to live in peace is assured the work of many hands and jaws in the creation and maintenance of its waterworks. Thus it is not surprising that the beaver has even strong inhibitions against biting, together with a ritualistic way by which to safely settle disputes.

That is not to say, however, that push matches never escalate into out-and-out warfare. Though biting is under strong inhibition, this restraint can be overruled—especially when the animals that come into conflict are not of the same family. Although strangers are, as a rule, ignored by resident animals and allowed to travel through already claimed territory, should any transient linger too long, he may find his hindquarters under attack. And if the trespasser then stands his ground, a wrestling match will erupt and can rapidly intensify into serious combat. Lars Wilsson describes the process as follows:

> When on land, both animals rise on their hind legs, using the tail for support and balance, grasp each other's skin with both hands and try to push each other backwards. . . . The nearer the animals are to the lodge of the territory, the fiercer is the fight, and finally the incisors are used as weapons. The bites are mainly directed against the opponent's hindquarters, and the trespasser may be killed by having its spine bitten off just above the root of the tail.

I never saw any of my beavers engage in that kind of fight. All their push matches ended peaceably, and many appeared to be mere expressions of playfulness. Like dogs, who employ the same stereotypical moves in a mock fight as when they truly join in battle, beavers appear to indulge in ritualized wrestling just for sport. Dorothy Richards interpreted every match she witnessed as nothing other than play. She recorded the behavior in two five-day-old kits whom she was rearing, between a mated pair, and by some half-grown residents of her pond. In *Beaversprite* she describes how a group of youngsters once paired off and put on a wrestling performance that reminded her of dancers doing the old-fashioned Bunny Hug.

I often failed to see what triggered the eruption of a wrestling match, but once I clearly did. The whole thing started when two beavers attempted to snitch a branch from a third one, who was blithely feeding on it in the water. They approached stealthily, like two submarines, and attacked from two directions at once. In a microsecond, one had seized the prize and was off with it by underwater route. The startled victim, upon realizing his branch was gone, turned on the luckless raider who had failed to obtain any part of the booty, and after a short tussle in the water, the two engaged in serious wrestling that lasted a full two minutes. Afterward peace was restored.

That spring Huckleberry and Buttercup seemed to grow before my eyes, and at any distance appeared to be big beavers, even though they had barely achieved yearling status. I attributed their large size to the colony's out-of-the-ordinary winter fare; bite-for-bite, the caloric content of lily rhizomes likely exceeds that of cambium-lined bark.

Now the two refused to give up dining on that food. Long after the crispy, stalk-like roots had given rise to equally edible pads and flowers, Huckleberry and Buttercup continued to dredge and eat them. In so doing, they not only depleted the beavers' winter staple, they eroded the colony's summer mainstay as well, for each rhizome they unearthed supported numerous long-stemmed leaves and flowers, which the youngsters let go to waste. For that matter, they rarely consumed an entire root. After taking a few bites from one they cast it aside and mined the muck for another. As I saw it, their addiction to this food threatened the colony's most reliable resource. Already I had observed a significant change in the nature of the pond. Two years earlier, its entire surface had been blanketed by lilies; now those plants lay in matted patches here and there, scattered islands of jade and white surrounded by expanses of water. And while this altered condition allowed me to spot beavers with greater ease than ever before, I had to wonder what they would use for food, come winter.

Of course, I had expected something like this to happen. Beavers do "eat themselves out of lodge and pond" and then muster elsewhere. Such is the fate of a creature whose way of life is profoundly bound up with biotic succession. Even so, I harbored a private hope that the colony would not prove equal to their uprooting a crop of water lilies that had reached such proportions. If indeed it did, such ability deserved recognition and ought to be put to use by those who clear lakes and ponds of the hard-to-destroy water lily. I remembered reading that a South American relative of the beaver, the nutria, was introduced into waterways in the South during the 1930s in the hope that it would perform the task. Now I suspected a home-grown animal would have been a better candidate for the job.

By June the fat yearlings, Huckleberry and Buttercup, were performing work appropriate to youngsters of their age. Huckleberry became obsessive about adding material to the dam; no matter that the structure was in absolutely no need of repair. So absorbed did he become in diving for muck and transporting sticks to the structure's overbuilt crest that he seemed oblivious to all else, including my presence at three feet.

As for Lotus and Blossom, their interest in one another was

hard for me to interpret. Were they engaged in a dominance contest of some kind? When not feeding—which is what beavers mostly do in spring—they converged on the pond to greet, nudge, dive, talk, and wrestle. I suspected that they, like the Skipper and Laurel, had become a bonded pair and might any day slip off together to found their own colony.

Meanwhile the Inspector General was actively harvesting grass and carrying it into the lodge—a pretty good sign that newborn kits were inside; Lily was conspicuous by her frequent absences from the pond—a pretty good sign that she was spending time with infants; and try as I would, I could count but five beavers out of the lodge at any one time—a pretty good sign that one or another of the six was remaining behind to baby-sit.

Then disaster struck. It was June 20, the eve of the summer solstice. The weekend was to have been a special one. In all the year, no twilight lasts so long, no opportunity for beaver-viewing is so extended. John and I arranged to be at the pond by midafternoon on Friday so we could examine the upper waterworks before the animals woke up. Afterward we planned to spend most of that night observing the beavers.

After parking, we followed a short trail that led to the northwest corner of the dam; but even before we came to an elevated section along that footpath, at which point the pond becomes visible, we both knew something was terribly amiss. A menacing sound, the steady drone of fast-flowing water, galvanized us, and we broke into a run.

"It's the dam," I shouted.

As the pond loomed into view, we both stopped, stunned by what we saw. Water was spewing forth through a break in the five-foot-high dam with stupendous force, carving an ever-deepening, ever-widening crater in the structure. The pond was sinking before our eyes.

I raced downhill toward the broken dam, falling twice in panic, and then edged across a still intact part of it to the very brink of the catapulting water. There I stood, helpless in the presence of such awesome power. Like an oil gusher, like a broken water machine, like a torrential flash flood, water surged past me with astonishing force. Below the dam, the land naturally fell away, allowing the released water to gain ever more momentum as it searched wildly for the shortest possible route to the sea. A fish, caught in the span, swept by. And wood, large pieces of the dam, wood that the beavers had cut, years of their cuttings, washed past me and cascaded downhill.

I stood without moving, stupefied, rendered impotent by what was happening. Then I became aware of John moving toward the breach, struggling to carry a small boulder. Oh, he will staunch this flow, I thought. My spirits momentarily brightened. But the heavy stone he tossed catapulted past me, riding the torrent as if it were a beach ball.

We stared after it, tracked its swift course downhill with our eyes. What energy had been unleashed here. John spoke, and his words were barely audible above the roar.

"This pond will be gone in two hours."

He hadn't meant for me to hear.

"Oh, why? Why? Why has this happened?"

I expected no response. My question was a lament, a protestation against the irreversibility of such an event—the cry of Job railing against an act of God. Yet my words alerted John to look for an answer, to take note of the ground. A man's track was evident everywhere around the break.

"Why, this is the work of a vandal! See here? The dam has been pried apart with a tool of some kind."

There it was. The evidence that we had almost neglected to look for.

Now, having connected the disaster to human perniciousness, rage acted as a catalyst in us, unleashing our power to act. It was quickly decided that I would drive seven miles to the nearest phone to notify park police, while John would remain behind to await their arrival, for should a radio car be dispatched from a nearby point, it likely would reach the pond before my return. Meanwhile John would try to implement an idea he had.

"The pond is sinking fast," he explained. "Obviously, I can't place rocks directly in the breach, the water has too much force just there. What I will try to do is tie the severed dam together with an underwater stone wall that bows out into the pond. With luck the gathering force of the water, as it nears the drop-off, will tighten the stones, rather than wash them away."

Then seeing hope in my face, he hastened to add:

"You understand that such an underwater wall will be so full of chinks it could not possibly stop the pond from draining. Still, if it slows down the process, we might buy some time. Then maybe the park rangers can figure out a way to drive in here and dump a load of rocks in the breach—or some such thing. Anyway, I can't think of anything else to try."

I didn't question the soundness of John's plan. Taking action, however futile, seemed better than standing by. I struggled to pick up a massive rock to assist in his ambitious scheme, but he chased me away.

"Go get the police," he ordered.

Halfway up the path, however, I thought of something I should do first and turned back. Quickly, I photographed the break, shot a few pictures of John heaving stones into it, and documented on film the incriminating tracks we had discovered on the dam. I wanted evidence to convict whoever was responsible for this heinous crime. On behalf of the legion of wild creatures who would soon die or be set adrift because of a deliberately vicious act of man, I would seek vindication. . . .

By the time I got back, two police officers were already on the scene, standing beside John on what remained of the dam and shaking their heads over what they were seeing and hearing. As I approached, I overheard them conclude that nothing would stop the inexorable flow of water from the pond, that the huge break in the dam had been deliberately created by a vandal, and that the pond would be history by morning. So much for man's technology, I thought. We have the means at our command to make the planet uninhabitable with the press of a button, but we aren't able to save a beaver pond.

After introducing myself, I answered routine questions about the incident, then added a few facts about the value of beaver ponds and described the colony's current status.

"There are kits in the lodge," I said, "and they must remain there, because they are too young to maneuver about in water. But babies or not, once the beaver house is high and dry it will be abandoned. The colony must be assured a covering of water over its entryways as protection against predators. Where the family will go and what will become of the kits is anybody's guess."

Both men seemed moved by the beavers' predicament and expressed a desire to see whoever was responsible brought to justice. But they quickly added that they did not hold out much hope of catching the guilty party.

"Even if we nabbed the guy, it wouldn't be easy to get a conviction. We would need an eyewitness, and you people didn't actually see who did this. While the footprints and toolmarks left little doubt in our minds that someone deliberately broke the dam for some sick reason or another, we'd have trouble making a case in court with that kind of circumstantial evidence."

The deed then would go unavenged. Worse, the vandal would remain at large and might at any time drain other beaver ponds in the park.

"Be careful when you work here at night," one of the officers warned me. "This doesn't look like teenage high jinks. The fact that a single individual was involved suggests it was done out of malice. Someone may have a grudge against the park. Or possibly it was the work of a deranged mind."

The two men assured me they would be on the lookout for anyone acting strangely, but added that they were understaffed to deal with all the problems that arise daily in such a large park. Even while they were speaking, a call came in over the walkie-talkies, and they had to rush off. A woman was being molested at a park campsite.

During all this time, John had made no mention of the underwater wall he had begun building before I left, and now I was eager to hear what had come of it. No rocks were visible above the surface of the pond, but it seemed to me that the torrent of water pouring through the break had lost some power.

"It's not moving as fast as it was," he conceded, "but the pond is still draining at a pretty impressive rate, and there's no way anybody's going to stop it. The pile of rocks I threw together over there is like a colander. It only serves as a break-water to slow down the current, that's all. Let's face it, you can't hold back Niagara Falls with a fish net."

I had to agree. I was as convinced as John that the beavers would only try to stop the noisy spill of water flowing over the top of his jerry-built breakwater. Everything we had ever seen, heard or read about beavers informed us that they would automatically act out this encoded response, however futile. Meanwhile, silent underwater leaks, such as those that were now inexorably draining the pond, would remain untended.

We climbed onto a big rock and studied the shoreline. High-water marks on bank boulders indicated that the water level had dropped by more than two feet since our arrival. Soon the lodge would stand on dry ground, like a tepee, with all directions open to passing predators. Already the tops of its entryway showed above the water line, like three dark moons rising. And considering the tremendous force at the point of spillage, we came to the conclusion that the beavers would not be able to repair the dam until the pond was completely drained. Should they try, the current would carry them over the falls.

During the next half hour the pond continued to sink, re-vealing the uppermost stones in John's wall. I was now able to understand how his makeshift jetty functioned. From the far stream side, I could see water gushing through chinks and holes in it, to say nothing of the torrent that poured over its top. But the bowed wall reconnected the severed dam and did indeed reduce the force and size of the outflow. John seemed surprised that the unmortared masonry was holding up at all. Privately, he had expected it to crumble under so much pressure.

Suddenly my heart began to pound. A beaver had emerged from the lodge and was swimming toward the dam at top speed. By the time I pointed, the animal had dipped underwater and didn't surface again until a few feet in front of us. It was the Inspector General and he appeared agitated. Ignoring our presence, he surveyed the broken dam with a wild eye, swam back and forth alongside the porous wall and took in the dreadful scene. Then he went off to the far shore, where he felled a large laurel shrub with all dispatch.

"He's going to try to do the impossible," John said.

"Yes, and he's going to wear himself out failing. It's too bad there are no fallen branches around here. I wish we'd thought to bring some from across the road before he woke up. (Illegal clearing had picked the banks of Lily Pond clean of firewood.)

As we watched, the big beaver hauled a six-foot shrub into he water and began transporting it to the break. The scene reminded me of the witches' prophecy in *Macbeth*. "Here comes Birnam Woods," I said, for the bush was in full bloom and traveling without a sign of the beaver beneath its dense foliage. At John's submarine wall, the apparition idled for a moment, then its voluminous branches rose into the air and tipped over the rim of that rockpile. For a moment, I thought the huge cutting would be carried downstream by the torrent of water cascading over, under, and through it. But the beaver held on to its short stem with his teeth and, using front hand-like paws, wedged its butt end in between two top stones, thus hanging it over the backside of the underwater wall.

"That's not going to do much good in this kind of flow," John commented.

The beaver must have come to the same conclusion, for he made only one more trip to the far shore to cut, tow, and anchor a second laurel branch before abandoning that tactic in favor of another. Now, to our amazement, he turned his attention to underwater leakage. To plug the myriad crannies in the rock pile through which enormous volumes of water were escaping, he uprooted whole plants, higgledy-piggledy to the right, left, back and front of the wall, and he used these as caulking material.

"He's going right to the heart of the problem!" John said. "I wouldn't have believed this if I hadn't seen it. According to theory, he should pile all that stuff on the crest of the dam to put out the noise, so to speak. Instead he's using it underwater where it's most needed, and it's a sure bet he can't hear water escape down there. So what goes?"

I was equally impressed by the Inspector's resourceful use of materials at hand. Normally, beavers do not build edible vegetation into their structures. Old dead wood, debarked food sticks resurrected from the pond bottom, muck, fallen leaves, and even human litter (bottles and plastic bags) are materials of choice. Now, however, time was of the essence. The pond had to be saved, and the long-stemmed, rubbery lily plants were pliable and could easily be packed into the interstices between the rocks. Moreover, they were readily at hand, and the Inspector General was working at a fanatical pace—diving, plucking, packing, diving, plucking, packing, diving, plucking, packing. Almost as soon as he disappeared underwater, he bobbed up again and swam for more aquatic vegetation. Nothing distracted him, neither our proximity nor the noise of water rolling over the top of the wall.

Soon we spotted three more beavers steaming toward the broken dam and recognized the two yearlings, Huckleberry and Buttercup, trailing in the wake of Blossom, who was still a few weeks shy of his second birthday. Within seconds, they were on-site, swimming back and forth and taking in information with all their senses. In short order, they followed the Inspector General's lead and went to work pulling up whole lily plants—stems, pads, blossoms, and even roots—and clutching these vegetative masses between their short arms and chin, they too disappeared underwater, where they remained for however long it took them to locate and plug up an underwater chink in the stone wall.

I had never before observed beavers behave like the busy workaholics they are reputed to be, but on this night they seemed to understand that their very existence depended on nonstop action. Trip after trip they made to shrinking lily patches to obtain more caulking material. Down and up the four of them bobbed, like a crew of scuba divers on a rescue mission. Watching them, I began to hope that what they were doing might actually save the pond, that the soft vegetation they were using might actually hold back a deluge.

Still the backside of the wall continued to spurt great volumes of water. And over the wall's irregular rim the pond continued to empty itself. And all that water converged on the far side to form a stream that gouged an ever deepening channel in its seaward rush.

So this is the awesome power of water, I thought to myself. Small wonder we harness it to our service. But who would dream that a quiet beaver-pond contained such energy?

I despaired that such a force could be checked. But the beavers continued to battle it with lilies, one handful at a time. Was there not some significance in this? And did not their perseverance imply that success was at least possible? After all, wild animals do not spend their precious energy reserves indiscriminately, with no real potential for return. Natural selection eliminates those individuals who squander hard-won calories pointlessly. So it is that wolves test many possible victims to determine how vigorous they are before running down the one they stand a chance of catching. So it is that wildcats make short, fast dashes at prey, but abandon the effort if they fail to catch their dinner at once. Would not beavers too possess a sense of what can and cannot be attained? Would not beavers too know when to quit?

Yet these four beavers continued to hustle. Once again the Inspector General made an attempt to buttress the downside of the unstable wall with hard, woody material. Once again he swam to the far shore and returned with an oversized laurel bush which he tipped over the crest and anchored between the stones. When this held, he returned for more and was soon joined in the endeavor by two of the younger beavers.

I was struck by how well the animals worked together. While their labors could not be described as coordinated (each performed tasks according to his own inner dictates), they did not seem to get in each other's way. Nor did any of them show signs of annoyance when his or her work was redone by another. The Inspector General, in particular, arranged sticks placed by the others. Was this some compulsive busywork on his part, or was he actually making improvements?

I recalled an experiment performed by two Swiss researchers, A. Aeschbacher and George Pilleri. Noting that lodge-building beavers frequently rearrange sticks that have already been put in place, the two men marked forty branches and returned hours later to see which of these had been moved and where. What they discovered was that beavers sort lumber according to size, shifting pieces around to meet specific building requirements. Long logs, for example, had been removed from the lodge's low-vantage entryway and worked into the high-vaulted main dome of the structure; by the same token, short sticks had been removed from the high-vaulted main structure and put to better use in the low entryway.

Whether or not the Inspector General was doing something practical, his efforts did seem to tighten the leaky structure. By contrast, Huckleberry's revisions were inadvertent. When inserting a contribution he had brought, he often dislodged work done by others, thus causing the sound of escaping water to augment sharply.

As the hours passed, I began to wonder when the four beavers would take time out to eat. It seemed extraordinary to me that they had not already done so. In two years of watching the colony, on no evening had I failed to make the notation: "Beavers spent first hour feeding." Like all plant eaters, *Castor canadensis* must devote a large part of its waking life to ingesting food. Yet on this night the work crew seemed perfectly able to ignore that need. Only Huckleberry took a brief lunch-break on a glob of lilies the Inspector General had packed onto the work-in-progress.

I wondered about Lotus and Lily. Where were they? Was it necessary for *two* beavers to remain in the lodge with the kits now that all its entryways were open to the world?

When darkness obscured the identities of the four individuals we were watching, we stayed on, straining to catch sight of their rotund shapes moving about in the water. Even after these vague forms could no longer be discerned, we lingered awhile longer to listen to the sound of diving. In the dark, the soft plopping of beaver bodies slipping underwater was as evocative as the dip-dip-dip of a canoe paddle. Just before giving up for the night, I shined my light along the curved jetty and discovered the Inspector General on its downstream side, hard at work plugging it from behind. This was a first observation for me. Until then, I had not questioned a widely held belief that beavers do not work from the backside of a dam.

Driving back to the cabin, I tried to elicit words from John to the effect that the beavers could and would save their pond, but without success, and his refusal to patronize me with false encouragement created tension between us. The most he could concede was that the animals' Herculean try was cause for wonder.

That night I slept poorly, haunted by the events of the day and night, and in the morning I prepared myself for the worst. Perhaps the stone wall had collapsed while we slept, releasing a surge of water that washed away all the work the beavers had done, together with what remained of the original dam. Perhaps, upon arriving, we would find a mud flat where Lily Pond had been.

As we approached the point on the path where all would be revealed, I lagged behind, keeping my eye on John's back for some warning of what lay ahead. For a moment after reaching the top of the hill, he kept me in suspense. Then he swung around and faced me with a wide grin.

"It's held!" he shouted.

"It's held?"

I raced to his side, and on that high vantage point we hugged each other and cheered the beavers—who by now had retired to their lodge for a well-earned rest. The pond was low, but the little connecting piece John had laid out and the beavers had buttressed and chinked had stood through the night and was doing the job. We ran downhill to inspect it. Though it was still leaking a good deal of water, the beavers had greatly strengthened it during our absence, thus reducing outflow by perhaps two thirds.

To say that that scrappy-looking insert appeared out of keeping with the original dam would be an understatement worthy of inclusion in the *Guinness Book of World Records*. Not only did it bulge into the pond in a most ungraceful and incongruous manner, its cover of fresh vegetation—leafy cuttings, pink and white blossoms, lily pads, and black roots—called to mind a homecoming float that didn't make it to the parade. By contrast, what remained of the original dam looked a sensible affair. Its neat backing of bleached branches, all set at the same vertical angle against the downstream face, resembled a tightly made picket fence. And a well trodden crest of hard-packed earth was almost indistinguishable from many other sections of the pond's natural shoreline.

"This thing you and the beavers have put together looks like what it is—a dam dreamed up by a committee," I told John. Then I gave him a big hug for the part he, as committee chairman, had played in designing it.

Of course the dam insert was a fragile affair and needed a great deal of reinforcing. So that morning we enlisted the help of three small boys who had come to the pond to fish, and the five of us toted load after load of badly needed sticks to the dam site and dumped these into the water. A good deal of what we brought was material from the original dam that had been washed one hundred and fifty yards downhill before getting hung up on stumps and brush.

"This represents years of beaver cutting," John remarked as he trudged uphill bearing a cumbersome load on his shoulder. "The colony couldn't make up for such a loss of material if they were to do nothing but fell trees for a month."

We worked all morning, recovering what seemed to be seven cords of thick sticks. But John remained convinced that more reinforcement would be needed and he worked for several more hours backing the jerry-built wall with sticks.

When at last he felt satisfied that the still leaky structure was somewhat more stable, we followed the example of our nocturnal beaver friends and returned to my cabin for a fast nap; for it was our intention to spend most of that midsummer's night at the pond, watching what the beavers would do next.

Dian Fossey

GORILLAS IN THE MIST

Often I am asked about the most rewarding experience I have ever had with gorillas. The question is extremely difficult to answer because each hour with the gorillas provides its own return and satisfaction. The first occasion when I felt I might have crossed an intangible barrier between human and ape occurred about ten months after beginning the research at Karisoke. Peanuts, Group 8's youngest male, was feeding about fifteen feet away when he suddenly stopped and turned to stare directly at me. The expression in his eyes was unfathomable. Spellbound, I returned his gaze—a gaze that seemed to combine elements of inquiry and of acceptance. Peanuts ended this unforgettable moment by sighing deeply, and slowly resumed feeding. Jubilant, I returned to camp and cabled Dr. Leakey I'VE FINALLY BEEN ACCEPTED BY A GORILLA.*

---

*Nine years after Dr. Leakey's death in 1972 I learned that he had carried the cable in his pocket for months, even taking it on a lecture tour to America. I was told that he read it proudly, much as he once spoke to me of Jane Goodall's outstanding success with chimpanzees.

Two years after our exchange of glances, Peanuts became the first gorilla ever to touch me. The day had started out as an ordinary one, if any day working from Karisoke might be considered ordinary. I felt unusually compelled to make this particular day outstanding because the following morning I had to leave for England for a seven-month period to work on my doctorate. Bob Campbell and I had gone out to contact Group 8 on the western-facing Visoke slopes. We found them feeding in the middle of a shallow ravine of densely growing herbaceous vegetation. Along the ridge leading into the ravine grew large *Hagenia* trees that had always served as good lookout spots for scanning the surrounding terrain. Bob and I had just settled down on a comfortable moss-cushioned *Hagenia* tree trunk when Peanuts, wearing his "I want to be entertained" expression, left his feeding group to meander inquisitively toward us. Slowly I left the tree and pretended to munch on vegetation to reassure Peanuts that I meant him no harm.

Peanuts' bright eyes peered at me through a latticework of vegetation as he began his strutting, swaggering approach. Suddenly he was at my side and sat down to watch my "feeding" techniques as if it were my turn to entertain him. When Peanuts seemed bored with the "feeding" routine, I scratched my head, and almost immediately, he began scratching his own. Since he appeared totally relaxed, I lay back in the foliage, slowly extended my hand, palm upward, then rested it on the leaves. After looking intently at my hand, Peanuts stood up and extended his hand to touch his fingers against my own for a brief instant. Thrilled at his own daring, he gave vent to his excitement by a quick chestbeat before going off to rejoin his group. Since that day, the spot has been called *Fasi Ya Mkoni,* "the Place of the Hands." The contact was among the most memorable of my life among the gorillas.

Habituation of Group 8 progressed far more rapidly than with other groups because of the consistency of Rafiki's tolerant nature and the important fact that the group had no infants to protect; thus they did not need to resort to highly defensive behavior. Their "youngster" was old Coco, who received solicitous attention from the others. Coco seemed to be even older than Rafiki and had a deeply wrinkled face, balding head and rump, graying muzzle, and flabby, hairless upper arms. She was also missing a number of teeth, causing her to gum her food rather than chew it. She often sat hunched over with one arm crossed over her chest while the other hand rapidly patted the top of her head in a seemingly involuntary motion. Sitting in this manner, with mucus draining from her eyes, her lower lip hanging down, Coco presented a pathetic picture. I suspected that her senses of hearing and seeing were considerably dulled by age.

The remarkable displays of affection between Coco, Rafiki, Samson, and Peanuts could be described as poignant, though this was not surprising when one considered the number of years the family had probably shared together. One day I was able to hide myself from the group feeding on a wide open slope 130 feet away from me. They were widely spread out with Rafiki at the top, moving uphill, and Coco far at the bottom, wandering erratically on a feeding course that led away from the rest of the group. Rafiki suddenly stopped eating, paused as if listening for something, and gave a sharp questioning type of vocalization. Coco obviously heard it, for she paused in her wanderings and turned in the general direction of the sound. Rafiki, out of sight from her, sat and gazed downhill. The other group members followed his example as though they were waiting for her to catch up. Coco began climbing slowly, stopping occasionally to determine their whereabouts before again meandering in the general direction of the patient males. Once within sight of Rafiki, the elderly female moved directly to him, exchanged a greeting series of soft belch vocalizations until reaching his side. They looked directly into each other's face and embraced. She placed her arm over his back and he did likewise over hers. Both walked uphill in this fashion, murmuring together like contented conspirators. The three young males followed the couple, feeding along the way, while the young silverback, Pugnacious, watched them intently from a farther, more discreet distance. He too then disappeared out of sight over the top of the hill. I did not let Group 8 know of my presence that day since I felt that to intrude upon them for an open contact would have been improper.

Working on Visoke's western slopes usually gave me the opportunity to contact Groups 4 and 8 on the same day within an area of nearly two square miles. Alternating contacts with Groups 4 and 8 provided almost daily knowledge of their respective range routes and locations. Thus, in December 1967, I was puzzled to hear a series of screams, *wraaghs,* and chestbeats coming from an unknown group located about halfway out in the five-mile-wide saddle area between Mts. Visoke and Mikeno, a region that only Group 8 had been known to frequent.

The search was started for the "ghost group," which, when finally found, was named Group 9. The dominant silverback, one in his prime, perhaps twenty-five to thirty years old, was named Geronimo. He was a most distinctive male, with a triangular red blaze of hair in the middle of his massive brow ridge and luxuriant blue-black body hair that framed bulging pectoral muscles resembling steel cables. Geronimo's supportive male, about eleven years old, was a blackback named Gabriel, because he was usually the first to spot my presence and inform the group with chestbeats or vocalizations. The degree of physical resemblance between the two adult males suggested they probably had a common sire. One young adult female was all too easy to identify because of a recent trap injury which had rendered her right hand useless. The hand, with its swollen pink fingers, hung limply from the wrist and was frequently cradled by the young female. Within two weeks the young female became adept at preparing food by using her right arm or foot to stabilize vegetation stalks and her mouth or left hand for the more intricate tasks, such as peeling or discarding unwanted parts of a plant. She was able to climb or descend trees by hooking her right arm around branches and tree trunks instead of using her injured hand. Within two months after first being observed, she was no longer seen with the group and was assumed dead. The dominant female among Geronimo's harem of four was named Maidenform because of her long pendulous breasts. Each of Group 9's four adult females had at least one dependent offspring, which indicated Geronimo's degree of reproductive success.

The addition of Group 9 to the study area provided a total of 48 individuals in four distinct groups, a population with both an adult male-to-female ratio and an adult-to-immature ratio of 1 : 1.1 at the start of 1968.

By this time Coco, the aged female of Group 8, could no longer be considered capable of reproduction. Peanuts, estimated as nearly six years of age, had probably been her last offspring. Group 8, therefore, had no breeding females, and Rafiki, the old but still potent silverback leader of the group, sought physical interactions with Group 4, which contained four females who were either approaching or had recently reached sexual maturity.

Encounters between distinct social units increase in frequency when range areas overlap, or if there is a disproportionate ratio of males to females, as was the case on Visoke's western slopes during the early years of the study. It was not long before Groups 4 and 8 met for a physical interaction instigated by Rafiki after following Group 4 for several days.

The two groups first met in a section of ridges separated by deep ravines at the edge of Group 8's range on the southwestern-facing slopes of Visoke. Climbing toward the loudly vocalizing animals, I looked ahead and saw what appeared to be an aerial act of five flying silverbacks: three from Group 4 and Rafiki and Pug of Group 8 leapt from tree to tree, charged parallel to one another, chestbeat, and broke branches along the ridge with crashing, splintering sounds. Their powerful muscular bodies varied in shades from white to tones of dull gray, and formed a vivid contrast to the green forest background. So engrossed were the displaying silverbacks that they seemed unconscious of my presence.

Hoping to remain unnoticed, I crept to a nearby *Hagenia* tree and found old Coco resignedly huddled against the tree trunk—one hand tapping the top of her head and the other arm crossed against her chest. She glanced at me calmly and heaved a big sigh as if expressing patient tolerance of the commotion going on around her. Occasionally Peanuts rushed down to her side to reassure himself that she was there. After brief embraces he would rejoin Group 8's second young adult male, Geezer, with chestbeats directed toward the three silverbacks of Group 4.

Excitement, rather than aggression, dominated this first observed physical interaction between Groups 4 and 8. While watching the discretion of the parallel displays between the two dominant silverbacks—Rafiki of Group 8 and Whinny of Group 4—I received the impression that both were equally experienced and were thus capable of avoiding overt combat because of mutual respect based on numerous previous interactions. Late that afternoon the two groups separated, though they continued to exchange hootseries and chestbeats for several hours, communications that seemed to become more taunting as the distance between the two familial units increased.

Two months later, in February 1968, Rafiki had ceased trying to interact with either Group 4 or Group 9, which were then also ranging on Visoke's western slopes. Old Coco had weakened, and because of her difficulty in keeping up with the group, Rafiki adjusted their travel and feeding pace to meet hers. On February 23 I found no sign of either Coco or Rafiki after contacting Group 8. Only the four males—Pug, Geezer, Samson, and Peanuts—were to be seen wrestling playfully together as carefree as boys at a summer camp. Backtracking the group's trail, I found that Coco and Rafiki had night-nested together in connecting nests for the past two nights, but I completely lost all trail sign after that. Two days later Rafiki returned to Group 8 alone. Coco's body was never found.

The old female's disappearance and assumed death resulted in a lack of cohesion among the five males. Their intragroup squabbles became more frequent and they resumed interactions with Groups 4 and 9, whose ranges overlapped their own.

Group 8's first encounter with Group 9 was held only days after Coco's disappearance and several ridges away from where she last had been seen. The tracker and I came upon Group 9 at unexpectedly close range, giving my assistant just time enough to dive under a large *Hagenia* tree before the gorillas became aware of us. Because of tall vegetation, I climbed into the same tree to gain a better view of Group 9. Within moments loud brush-breaking sounds were heard coming from below. Hiding myself in the tree's heavy vine growth, I was surprised to see Rafiki leading his bachelor band directly toward Group 9 without the chestbeats or hootseries that usually precede an intergroup encounter. The only obvious evidence of excitement at the initiation of the contact was the overpowering silverback odor, most of which was coming from Rafiki. Almost immediately Samson and Peanuts began mingling with three young adults in Group 9. Rafiki calmly made a day nest directly below me in the hollow bole of the *Hagenia,* unaware of the presence of myself or the tracker. Previously I had considered a gorilla's sense of smell superior to that of a human, but this observation did not support the supposition.

After nearly thirty minutes of quiet, my accidental breaking of a tree branch sounded like a pistol shot in the stillness of the resting period. Rafiki jumped from his nest and glared upward through the heavily vined skirts of the tree. Then the majestic silverback strutted deliberately around the trunk before posing stiffly some four feet below me. In an accusing manner he stared into my face nervously chewing his lips, one indication of his stress. Trying to act as innocent as possible and with anxiety only for the cramps in my legs, I gazed at the sky, yawned, and scratched myself while the old male indignantly displayed around the base of the tree unaware of the tracker huddled out of sight only several feet away from him.

Although curious about Rafiki's tolerance of a human's presence, the members of Group 9 eventually moved off to feed after contributing their own chestbeats and alarm vocalizations to this unexpected encounter. Rafiki instantly followed them, though I couldn't help but feel he had enjoyed being the intermediary between a gorilla-habituated human and a nonhuman-habituated group of gorillas.

THE northwestern slopes of Visoke offered several ridges of *Pygeum africanum* trees shared by both Groups 8 and 9. The fruits of this tree are highly favored by gorillas, though such site-specific food prompts competition and increases opportunities for interactions between distinct social units. Groups 8 and 9 often met along the ridges for prolonged interactions because of their interest in obtaining the fruits.

Rafiki, more dominant and experienced than Geronimo, usually established Group 8's claim to the most prolifically fruiting trees higher on the slopes and Geronimo's Group 9 raided the lower-ridge trees. It was an amazing sight to watch the 350-pound silverbacks climbing onto thin tree limbs about 60 feet above the ground and harvesting with mouth and hands as many fruits as they could collect before climbing down to sit close to the tree trunks to gorge on their yield.

On one occasion Peanuts and Geezer, bored with the long feeding period, playfully galloped downhill toward several of Group 9's immature youngsters. The two Group 8 males failed to see Geronimo bringing up the rear of his group. Giving harsh pig-grunts, Geronimo immediately charged uphill. This caused the two young males to brake to a stop and momentarily stand bipedally, their arms around one another, their expressions panic-stricken. Then both rapidly turned and ran back toward their group, all the while screaming fearfully. Geronimo pursued them to the top of the ridge, where he encountered Rafiki, who was running down to the defense of Peanuts and Geezer. Discretion prevailed when Geronimo turned heel and herded his group away from the bachelors.

The absence of Coco, coupled by frequent interactions with other groups, increased the unrest among the all-male Group 8. Pug and Geezer finally left their natal group to travel together on Visoke's northern slopes in a range area not too far removed from that of Group 8. Their departure left Rafiki only with his and Coco's presumed progeny, Samson and Peanuts. For nearly a year, however, squabbles continued between Rafiki and his oldest son. The friction occurred most often when the three males interacted with other groups and Samson's excitement grew beyond Rafiki's toleration. The old male had little difficulty in subduing Samson by either running or strutting directly toward his sexually maturing son, who would immediately assume a typical submissive posture by bowing down on his forearms, his gaze averted from his father and his rump upward. Rafiki needed only to maintain his stilted pose for a few seconds, his head hair erect, his gaze directed toward Samson, before temporary harmony was restored within the group.

Three and a half years after Coco's death Rafiki acquired two females, Macho and Maisie, from Group 4 during a violent physical interaction in June 1971. During the encounter Peanuts' right eye was permanently injured from a bite wound inflicted by Uncle Bert, the young silverback who had inherited the leadership of Group 4 three years previously following the death of his father, Whinny.

With the acquisition of the two new females Rafiki seemed invigorated. He staunchly defended his harem against Samson, thereby causing more friction between father and son. It was obvious that Samson was wasting breeding years by remaining in his natal group. He was prompted to leave just as Pugnacious and Geezer had done nearly a year before. Samson became a peripheral silverback, one who travels three hundred to six hundred feet from his natal group before setting out to establish his own range area and gain experience from interactions with other gorilla groups in order to acquire and retain his own females. Both peripheral and lone travel are usually necessary stages for any maturing male unless breeding opportunities are available within his natal group. Samson's departure left Rafiki with Maisie and Macho, the two young females taken from Group 4, and with young Peanuts.

Unexpectedly, Samson returned from his distant ranging area and managed to take Maisie away from Rafiki in September 1971. Fourteen months later Maisie and Samson were observed with a newly born infant. In June 1973 Rafiki proved his own virility when his only female, Macho, gave birth to a female infant named Thor.

Group 8 remained an oddly composed group, consisting of Rafiki, his young mate Macho, his eleven-year-old son Peanuts, and his newborn daughter Thor. Seemingly content with his little family, Rafiki no longer sought other groups. When Thor was about six months old Rafiki was observed in one last interaction with Group 4. I noticed that the regal old silverback's chestbeats and hootseries lacked resonance and strength, though his physical appearance seemed as impressive as ever. Possibly he had been avoiding other groups because he realized his physical limitations brought on by age.

Farley Mowat

NEVER CRY WOLF

B y mid-September the tundra plains burned somberly in the subdued glow of russet and umber where the early frosts had touched the ground cover of low shrubbery. The muskeg pastures about Wolf House Bay were fretted with fresh roads made by the southbound herds of caribou, and the pattern of the wolves' lives had changed again.

The pups had left the summer den and, though they could not keep up with Angeline and the two males on prolonged hunts, they could and did go along on shorter expeditions. They had begun to explore their world, and those autumnal months must have been among the happiest of their lives.

When Ootek and I returned to Wolf House Bay after our travels through the central plains, we found that our wolf family was ranging widely through its territory and spending the days wherever the hunt might take it.

Within the limits imposed upon me by my physical abilities and human needs, I tried to share that wandering life, and I too enjoyed it immensely. The flies were all gone. Though there were sometimes frosts at night, the days were usually warm under a clear sun.

ON one such warm and sunlit day I made my way north from the den esker, along the crest of a range of hills which overlooked a great valley, rich in forage, and much used by the caribou as a highway south.

A soot-flecking of black specks hung in the pallid sky above the valley—flocks of ravens following the deer herds. Families of ptarmigan cackled at me from clumps of dwarf shrub. Flocks of Old Squaw ducks, almost ready to be off for distant places, swirled in the tundra ponds.

Below me in the valley rolled a sluggish stream of caribou, herd after herd grazing toward the south, unconscious, yet directly driven by a knowledge that was old before we even knew what knowledge was.

Some miles from the den esker I found a niche at the top of a high cliff overlooking the valley, and here I settled myself in comfort, my back against the rough but sun-warmed rock, my knees drawn up under my chin, and my binoculars leveled at the living stream below me.

I was hoping to see the wolves and they did not disappoint me. Shortly before noon two of them came into sight on the crest of a transverse ridge some distance to the north. A few moments later two more adults and the four pups appeared. There was some frisking, much nose smelling and tail wagging, and then most of the wolves lay down and took their ease, while the others sat idly watching the caribou streaming by on either side only a few hundred feet away.

I easily recognized Angeline and George. One of the other two adults looked like Uncle Albert; but the fourth, a rangy dark-gray beast, was a total stranger to me. I never did learn who he was or where he came from, but for the rest of the time I was in the country he remained a member of the band.

Of all the wolves, indeed of all the animals in view including the caribou and myself, only George seemed to feel any desire to be active. While the rest of us sprawled blissfully in the sun, or grazed lethargically amongst the lichens, George began to wander restlessly back and forth along the top of the ridge. Once or twice he stopped in front of Angeline but she paid him no attention other than to flop her tail lazily a few times.

Drowsily I watched a doe caribou grazing her way up the ridge on which the wolves were resting. She had evidently found a rich patch of lichens and, though she must have seen the wolves, she continued to graze toward them until not twenty yards separated her from one of the pups. This pup watched her carefully until, to my delight, he got to his feet, stared uneasily over his shoulder to see what the rest of the family was doing, then turned and slunk toward them with his tail actually between his legs.

Not even the restless George, who now came slowly toward the doe, his nose outthrust as he tasted her scent, seemed to disturb her equanimity until the big male wolf, perhaps hurt in his dignity by her unconcern, made a quick feint in her direction. At that she flung her head high, spun on her ungainly legs and gallumphed back down the ridge apparently more indignant than afraid.

Time slipped past, the river of deer continued to flow, and I expected to observe nothing more exciting than this brief interlude between the doe and the wolves, for I guessed that the wolves had already fed, and that this was the usual after-dinner siesta. I was wrong, for George had something on his mind.

A third time he went over to Angeline, who was now stretched out on her side, and this time he would not take "no" for an answer. I have no idea what he said, but it must have been pertinent, for she scrambled to her feet, shook herself, and bounced amiably after him as he went to sniff at the slumbering forms of Uncle Albert and the Stranger. They too got the message and rose to their feet. The pups, never slow to join in something new, also roused and galloped over to join their elders. Standing in a rough circle, the whole group of wolves now raised their muzzles and began to howl, exactly as they used to do at the den esker before starting on a hunt.

I was surprised that they should be preparing for a hunt so early in the day, but I was more surprised by the lack of reaction to the wolf chorus on the part of the caribou. Hardly a deer within hearing even bothered to lift its head, and those few who did contented themselves with a brief, incurious look toward the ridge before returning to their placid grazing. I had no time to ponder the matter, for Angeline, Albert and the Stranger now started off, leaving the pups sitting disconsolately in a row on the crest, with George standing just ahead of them. When one of the youngsters made an attempt to follow the three adults, George turned on him, and the pup hurriedly rejoined his brothers and sisters.

What little wind there was blew from the south and the three wolves moved off upwind in a tight little group. As they reached the level tundra they broke into a trot, following one another in line, not hurrying, but trotting easily through the groups of caribou. As usual the deer were not alarmed and none took evasive action except when the wolves happened to be on a collision course with them.

The three wolves paid no attention to the caribou either, although they passed many small herds containing numbers of fawns. They made no test runs at any of these groups, but continued purposefully on their way until they were almost abreast the niche where I was sitting. At this point Angeline stopped and sat down while the other two joined her. There was more nose smelling, then Angeline got up and turned toward the ridge where George and the pups still sat.

There were at least two hundred deer between the two groups of wolves, and more were coming constantly into view around the eastern shoulder of the transverse ridge. Angeline's glance seemed to take them all in before she and her companions began to move off. Spreading out to form a line abreast, with intervals of a couple of hundred yards between them so that they almost spanned the whole width of the valley, they now began to run north.

They were not running hard, but there was a new purposefulness to their movements which the deer seemed to recognize; or perhaps it was just that the formation the wolves were using made it difficult for the herds to avoid them in the usual way by running off to one side. In any event herd after herd also began to turn about and move north, until most of the caribou in the valley were being driven back the way they had come.

The deer were clearly reluctant to be driven, and several herds made determined efforts to buck the line; but on each occasion the two nearest wolves converged toward the recalcitrant caribou and forced them to continue north. However, three wolves could not sweep the whole width of the valley; the deer soon began to discover that they could swing around the open wings and so resume their southerly progress. Nevertheless, by the time the wolves were nearing the ridge, they were herding at least a hundred deer ahead of them.

Now for the first time the deer showed real signs of nervousness. What had become an almost solid mass of a hundred or more animals broke up into its constituent small bands again, and each went galloping off on its own course. Group after group began to swerve aside, but the wolves no longer attempted to prevent them. As the wolves galloped past each of these small herds, the caribou stopped and turned to watch for a moment before resuming their interrupted journey south.

I was beginning to see what the wolves were up to. They were now concentrating their efforts on one band of a dozen does and seven fawns, and every attempt which this little herd made to turn either left or right was promptly foiled. The deer gave up after a while, and settled down to outrun their pursuers in the straightaway.

They would have done it, too, but as they swept past the clump of willows at the end of the ridge a perfect flood of wolves seemed to take them in the flank.

I could not follow events as well as I would have wished because of the distance, but I saw George racing toward a doe accompanied by two fawns. Then, just as he reached them, I saw him swerve away. He was passed by two pups going like gray bullets. These two went for the nearest of the two fawns, which promptly began jinking. One of the pups, attempting too sharp a turn, missed his footing and tumbled head over heels, but he was up on the instant and away again.

The other pups seemed to have become intermingled with the balance of the deer, and I could not see what they were up to; but as the herd drew away at full gallop the pups appeared in the rear, running hard, but losing ground.

A single fawn now began outdistancing its pursuers too. All four pups were still running flat out, although they no longer had a chance of overtaking any of the deer.

What of the adult wolves meanwhile? When I swung my glasses back to look for them I found George standing exactly where I had seen him last, his tail wagging slowly as he watched the progress of the chase. The other three wolves had by now returned to the crest of the ridge. Albert and the Stranger had lain down to rest, after their brief exertions, but Angeline was standing up and watching the rapidly re-treating caribou.

It was half an hour before the pups came back. They were so weary they could hardly climb the ridge to join their elders, all of whom were now lying down relaxing. The pups joined the group and flopped, panting heavily; but none of the adults paid them any heed.

School was over for the day.

Sterling North

RASCAL

Early in March the first signs of spring began to appear. My woodchucks came up from their holes under the barn to take a cautious look at the world and decided it would be wiser to sleep for a few more weeks. Meadow mice broke through the old snow crust to view the sky; and their big cousins, the muskrats, made similar forays from their ponds and streams to graze on any vegetation which showed a tint of green.

As the mating season approached, the tabby cats mewed and treaded to attract neighborhood toms. Cottontail rabbits thumped the ground, calling for mates. And skunks wandered for miles seeking the consolation that only another skunk can give.

Rascal was becoming restless and unreasonable. On one moonlit night I heard hair-raising screams of rage. Grabbing a flashlight, I went out to find Rascal and another undoubtedly male raccoon trying to get at each other through the chicken wire. I chased away the intruder and put iodine on Rascal's scratches. On another evening I heard very different sounds—

173

the tremolo crooning of an amorous female raccoon trying to reach Rascal for more romantic reasons.

I was only twelve, but not unaware of the meaning of spring. The sighing of the wind through the fur-tipped willows and the disturbing voices of the night made me almost as restless as the other young animals now awakening.

During a week of unseasonably warm weather we put the screens on the windows and doors. On the first night that we left the doors open, Rascal paid me a surprise visit. Evidently he had learned how to lift the hook from the eye on the door of his cage and he had not forgotten how to open the back screen door to the house. He came to my bedroom, chirring happily, and burrowed under the covers.

I could have padlocked the cage, but decided against it. That would have been a grossly unjust reward for Rascal's dexterity and his obvious delight in finding his way to freedom.

However, when on a subsequent night my raccoon raided Reverend Thurman's henhouse, I realized that time was fast running out on our year-long idyl.

Since Christmas I had spent many hours completing my canoe. The most difficult part was stretching and fastening the heavy canvas while the unwieldy fabric was soaking wet. This process did the living room rug a distinct disservice. But I was so pleased with the finished result that my father did not scold me unduly. I asked him to tap the canvas, which had shrunk as tight as a drum over the ribs as it dried. He could see for himself the advantages of nailing it on while wet.

I trimmed the pointed prow and stern with sheet copper, ran a molding around the gunwale, added covered compartments at each end for duffel, and screwed on an outer keel. Except for varnishing the inside and enameling the outside my canoe was ready for service.

"It might be wise to paint it in the barn," my father suggested.

"That seems reasonable," I agreed.

"The green you have chosen will look fine in the water," my father said, "but it doesn't go very well with the other colors in the rug."

The canoe was heavier than I thought it would be, so I asked two very good friends of mine—Art Cunningham, a fishing maniac like myself, and Royal Ladd, who owned a player piano—to help me carry the canoe to the barn, where we mounted it on sawhorses. We worked together on varnishing the smoothly sanded interior and enameling the outside with four coats of glossy green. It was a beautiful thing, that long, streamlined canoe.

The launching was on Saunder's Creek, which had risen many feet above its banks in the spring runoff. In some places the brown flood waters had spread more than a mile in width through the marshes. Art Cunningham and I gave the pencil-slim craft its first workout, skimming over pasture fences, circling into placid backwaters, and streaking down the main current with the ease of a fish or a water bird.

As on the Brule, Rascal rode the prow, fascinated as always by the speed and danger.

EXCEPT for the success of the canoe, there was little to be happy about as the season progressed. Reverend Thurman had his shotgun loaded, waiting for one more raid on his henhouse.

Almost as dismaying, Theo and Jessica had finally won their point. We were acquiring a full-time housekeeper whether we wanted one or not. Mrs. Quinn was said to be qualified in every respect: middle-aged, ugly, cranky-clean, and no non-sense. She examined our house minutely, ran her finger over the furniture to show us the dust, and demanded my bedroom for herself.

"That is, if I decide to take the position," Mrs. Quinn added. "I'll let you know in a couple of weeks."

It was sadly apparent that my father would be no match

for our new housekeeper. But since we were being allowed two blessed weeks in which to maneuver, I decided to build a second line of defense. The presently unoccupied back bedroom on the second floor was virtually impregnable after I fitted a strong lock on the door and pocketed the key. I explained to my father that I would make my own bed, clean my own room, and let Mrs. Quinn take care of the rest of the place in any way that suited her.

She had expressed herself quite firmly: "No pets in the house!"

I thought that perhaps I might circumvent this unreasonable ruling by preparing a new entrance to my quarters. Opening off the large and airy bedroom was a small study at the very rear of the house. This too would be safeguarded by the lock on the bedroom door. And the little back room furnished another advantage. One window at the end of the gable offered enticing possibilities.

Cutting neat cleats, each eighteen inches in length, I nailed them one above another at convenient intervals up the house to that back window. Now Rascal could climb to see me whenever he wished. I could also conveniently entertain some of my other more-or-less human friends—boys of twelve for the most part.

When I showed my father this new ladder, he merely sighed and suggested that I paint the cleats the same color as the house. I thought this was a brilliant idea since it made them practically invisible. My enemies would never be able to spy them out. In any case they wouldn't know the secret knock: Dum, de, de, dum, dum, DUM DUM, the easily remembered rhythm of "Shave and a Haircut, Six Bits."

With Rascal for my constant companion in all these preparations, I was exhilarated with my stratagems to foil Mrs. Quinn. But deep in my heart I knew that none of these plans would insure Rascal's life. He ran the constant peril of being shot.

Moreover, now that he had grown to young adulthood, he

was not entirely happy as a domesticated pet. I realized that I was being selfish and inconsiderate to keep him from his natural life in the woods.

In my prayers I always put Rascal first these days: "Bless Rascal and Daddy and Theo and Jessica and Herschel. And make me a good boy, God, Amen." I suppose I realized that no one needed more protection than my raccoon.

The fourteen days of grace sped by far too swiftly, and the awful moment approached when Mrs. Quinn would confirm her acceptance and move in, bag and baggage. I was certain that she would chase the cats with her broom, flap her apron at the crow, hurt Wowser's feelings by speaking to him sharply, and insist that I padlock Rascal's cage. She had been terrified of my raccoon on the day she had inspected us, and she might become his mortal enemy.

One warm and pleasant Saturday I made my decision. I can remember every detail of that day, hour by hour. Rascal and I had slept in my new bedroom. We came down the fifteen steps of the curved stairway, and ate as usual at the dining room table. Rascal was not behaving well that morning. He walked directly across the tablecloth to the sugar bowl, lifted the lid, and helped himself to two lumps. Thirteen pounds of raccoon on the dining room table is quite a centerpiece. But knowing in my heart what I was plotting, I couldn't scold or slap him.

I told my father that Rascal and I would be away all afternoon and evening on a long canoe ride. I think he knew what I was planning. He looked at us quite sympathetically.

Taking jelly sandwiches, strawberry pop, and more than a pound of soft-shelled pecans, I led Rascal to where my canoe was waiting near the edge of the flooded creek. In a moment it was launched upon the racing stream. All unknowing, my raccoon stood at the prow, occasionally coming back to me for another pecan. I remember thinking that it was sad that Herschel had not come home in time to see my handsome pet.

We floated down the creek, ducking to pass beneath the

bridges. Soon we sped out into Rock River, and turned up-stream toward Lake Koshkonong. Rascal fell asleep during the hours I labored against the current. He awoke toward sunset as we reached the quiet mirror of the lake itself, heading toward the dark, wild promontory named Koshkonong Point.

It was an evening of full moon, much like the one when I had found my little friend and carried him home in my cap. Rascal was a big, lusty fellow now, thirteen times the weight of the helpless creature to whom I had fed warm milk through a wheat straw. He was very capable in many ways—able to catch all the food he needed along a creek or in a marshy bay. He could climb, swim, and almost talk. As I thought over his accomplishments I was both proud and sad.

We entered the mouth of Koshkonong Creek by moonlight and paddled up this stream several hundred feet into the depths of this wet wilderness. It is a region rich in fish and crayfish, fresh-water clams, muskrats, and mallards—the many forms of life that love wildness and water. The peepers shrilled, and bullfrogs thrummed their bass fiddles, and a little screech owl trilled a note reminiscent of Rascal's when he was much younger.

I had decided to let my raccoon make his own decision. But I took off his collar and his leash and put them in a pocket of my corduroy jacket as something to remember him by if he should choose to leave me. We sat together in the canoe, listening to the night sounds all around us, but for *one* sound in particular.

It came at last, the sound I had been waiting for, almost exactly like the crooning tremolo we had heard when the ro-mantic female raccoon had tried to reach him through the chicken wire. Rascal became increasingly excited. Soon he an-swered with a slightly deeper crooning of his own. The female was now approaching along the edge of the stream, trilling a plaintive call, infinitely tender and questing. Rascal raced to the prow of the canoe, straining to see through the moonlight and shadow, sniffing the air, and asking questions.

"Do as you please, my little raccoon. It's your life," I told him.

He hesitated for a full minute, turned once to look back at me, then took the plunge and swam to the near shore. He had chosen to join that entrancing female somewhere in the shadows. I caught only one glimpse of them in a moonlit glade before they disappeared to begin their new life together.

I left the pecans on a stump near the waterline, hoping Rascal would find them. And I paddled swiftly and desperately away from the place where we had parted.

Four

ANIMALS AFAR

Jack London

WHITE FANG

He was different from his brothers and sisters. Their hair already betrayed the reddish hue inherited from their mother, the she-wolf; while he alone, in this particular, took after his father. He was the one little gray cub of the litter. He had bred true to the straight wolf-stock—in fact, he had bred true, physically, to old One Eye himself, with but a single exception, and that was that he had two eyes to his father's one.

The gray cub's eyes had not been open long, yet already he could see with steady clearness. And while his eyes were still closed, he had felt, tasted, and smelled. He knew his two brothers and his two sisters very well. He had begun to romp with them in a feeble, awkward way, and even to squabble, his little throat vibrating with a queer rasping noise (the fore-runner of the growl), as he worked himself into a passion. And long before his eyes had opened, he had learned by touch, taste, and smell to know his mother—a fount of warmth and liquid food and tenderness. She possessed a gentle, caressing tongue that soothed him when it passed over his soft little body, and that impelled him to snuggle close against her and to doze off to sleep.

Most of the first month of his life had been passed thus in sleeping; but now he could see quite well, and he stayed awake for longer periods of time, and he was coming to learn his world quite well. His world was gloomy; but he did not know that, for he knew no other world. It was dim-lighted; but his eyes had never had to adjust themselves to any other light. His world was very small. Its limits were the walls of the lair; but as he had no knowledge of the wide world outside, he was never oppressed by the narrow confines of his existence.

But he had early discovered that one wall of his world was different from the rest. This was the mouth of the cave and the source of light. He had discovered that it was different from the other walls long before he had any thoughts of his own, any conscious volitions. It had been an irresistible attraction before ever his eyes opened and looked upon it. The light from it had beat upon his sealed lids, and the eyes and the optic nerves had pulsated to little, sparklike flashes, warm-colored and strangely pleasing. The life of his body, and of every fibre of his body, the life that was the very substance of his body and that was apart from his own personal life, had yearned toward this light and urged his body toward it in the same way that the cunning chemistry of a plant urges it toward the sun.

Always, in the beginning, before his conscious life dawned, he had crawled toward the mouth of the cave. And in this his brothers and sisters were one with him. Never, in that period, did any of them crawl toward the dark corners of the back-wall. The light drew them as if they were plants; the chemistry of the life that composed them demanded the light as a necessity of being; and their little puppet-bodies crawled blindly and chemically, like the tendrils of a vine. Later on, when each developed individuality and became personally conscious of impulses and desires, the attraction of the light increased.

They were always crawling and sprawling toward it, and being driven back from it by their mother.

It was in this way that the gray cub learned other attributes of his mother than the soft, soothing tongue. In his insistent crawling toward the light, he discovered in her a nose that with a sharp nudge administered rebuke, and later, a paw, that crushed him down or rolled him over and over with swift, calculating stroke. Thus he learned hurt; and on top of it he learned to avoid hurt, first, by not incurring the risk of it; and second, when he had incurred the risk, by dodging and by retreating. These were conscious actions, and were the results of his first generalizations upon the world. Before that he had recoiled automatically from hurt, as he had crawled automatically toward the light. After that he recoiled from hurt because he *knew* that it was hurt.

He was a fierce little cub. So were his brothers and sisters. It was to be expected. He was a carnivorous animal. He came of a breed of meat-killers and meat-eaters. His father and mother lived wholly upon meat. The milk he had sucked with his first flickering life was milk transformed directly from meat, and now, at a month old, when his eyes had been open for but a week, he was beginning himself to eat meat—meat half-digested by the she-wolf and disgorged for the five growing cubs that already made too great demand upon her breast.

But he was, further, the fiercest of the litter. He could make a louder rasping growl than any of them. His tiny rages were much more terrible than theirs. It was he that first learned the trick of rolling a fellow-cub over with a cunning paw-stroke. And it was he that first gripped another cub by the ear and pulled and tugged and growled through jaws tight-clenched. And certainly it was he that caused the mother the most trouble in keeping her litter from the mouth of the cave.

The fascination of the light for the gray cub increased from day to day. He was perpetually departing on yard-long adventures toward the cave's entrance, and was perpetually being driven back. Only he did not know it for an entrance. He did not know anything about entrances—passages whereby one goes from one place to another place. He did not know any other place, much less of a way to get there. So to him the entrance of the cave was a wall—a wall of light. As the sun was to the outside dweller, this wall was to him the sun of his world. It attracted him as a candle attracts a moth. He was always striving to attain it. The life that was so swiftly expanding within him, urged him continually toward the wall of light. The life that was within him knew that it was the one way out, the way he was predestined to tread. But he himself did not know anything about it. He did not know there was any outside at all.

There was one strange thing about this wall of light. His father (he had already come to recognize his father as the one other dweller in the world, a creature like his mother, who slept near the light and was a bringer of meat)—his father had a way of walking right into the white far wall and disappearing. The gray cub could not understand this. Though never permitted by his mother to approach that wall, he had approached the other walls, and encountered hard obstruction on the end of his tender nose. This hurt. And after several such adventures, he left the walls alone. Without thinking about it, he accepted this disappearing into the wall as a peculiarity of his father, as milk and half-digested meat were peculiarities of his mother.

In fact, the gray cub was not given to thinking—at least, to the kind of thinking customary of men. His brain worked in dim ways. Yet his conclusions were as sharp and distinct as those achieved by men. He had a method of accepting things, without questioning the why and wherefore. In reality, this was the act of classification. He was never disturbed over *why* a thing happened. *How* it happened was sufficient for him. Thus, when he had bumped his nose on the backwall a few times he accepted that he would not disappear into walls. In the same way he accepted that his father could disappear into walls. But he was not in the least disturbed by desire to find out the reason for the difference between his father and himself. Logic and physics were no part of his mental make-up.

Like most creatures of the Wild, he early experienced famine. There came a time when not only did the meat-supply cease, but the milk no longer came from his mother's breast. At first, the cubs whimpered and cried, but for the most part they slept. It was not long before they were reduced to a coma of hunger. There were no more spats and squabbles, no more tiny rages nor attempts at growling; while the adventures toward the far white wall ceased altogether. The cubs slept, while the life that was in them flickered and died down.

One Eye was desperate. He ranged far and wide, and slept but little in the lair that had now become cheerless and miserable. The she-wolf, too, left her litter and went out in search of meat. In the first days after the birth of the cubs, One Eye had journeyed several times back to the Indian camp and robbed the rabbit snares; but, with the melting of the snow and the opening of the streams, the Indian camp had moved away, and that source of supply was closed to him.

When the gray cub came back to life and again took interest in the far white wall, he found that the population of his world had been reduced. Only one sister remained to him. The rest were gone. As he grew stronger, he found himself compelled to play alone, for the sister no longer lifted her head nor moved about. His little body rounded out with the meat he now ate; but the food had come too late for her. She slept continuously, a tiny skeleton flung round with skin in which the flame flickered lower and lower and at last went out.

Then there came a time when the gray cub no longer saw his father appearing and disappearing in the wall nor lying down asleep in the entrance. This had happened at the end of a second and less severe famine. The she-wolf knew why One Eye never came back, but there was no way by which she could tell what she had seen to the gray cub. Hunting herself for meat, up the left fork of the stream where lived the lynx, she had followed a day-old trail of One Eye. And she had found him, or what remained of him, at the end of the trail. There were many signs of the battle that had been fought, and of the lynx's withdrawal to her lair after having won the victory. Before she went away, the she-wolf had found this lair, but the signs told her that the lynx was inside, and she had not dared to venture in.

After that, the she-wolf in her hunting avoided the left fork. For she knew that in the lynx's lair was a litter of kittens, and she knew the lynx for a fierce, bad-tempered creature and a terrible fighter. It was all very well for half a dozen wolves to drive a lynx, spitting and bristling, up a tree; but it was quite a different matter for a lone wolf to encounter a lynx—especially when the lynx was known to have a litter of hungry kittens at her back.

But the Wild is the Wild, and motherhood is motherhood, at all times fiercely protective whether in the Wild or out of it; and the time was to come when the she-wolf, for her gray cub's sake, would venture the left fork, and the lair in the rocks, and the lynx's wrath.

———

By the time his mother began leaving the cave on hunting expeditions, the cub had learned well the law that forbade his approaching the entrance. Not only had this law been forcibly and many times impressed on him by his mother's nose and paw, but in him the instinct of fear was developing. Never, in his brief cave-life, had he encountered anything of which to be afraid. Yet fear was in him. It had come down to him from a remote ancestry through a thousand thousand lives. It was a heritage he had received directly from One Eye and the she-wolf; but to them, in turn, it had been passed down through all the generations of wolves that had gone before. Fear!—that legacy of the Wild which no animal may escape nor exchange for pottage.

So the gray cub knew fear, though he knew not the stuff of which fear was made. Possibly he accepted it as one of the restrictions of life. For he had already learned that there were such restrictions. Hunger he had known; and when he could not appease his hunger he had felt restriction The hard obstruction of the cave-wall, the sharp nudge of his mother's nose, the smashing stroke of her paw, the hunger unappeased of several famines, had borne in upon him that all was not freedom in the world, that to life there were limitations and restraints. These limitations and restraints were law. To be obedient to them was to escape hurt and make for happiness.

He did not reason the question out in this man-fashion. He merely classified the things that hurt and the things that did not hurt. And after such classification he avoided the things that hurt, the restrictions and restraints, in order to enjoy the satisfactions and the remunerations of life.

Thus it was that in obedience to the law laid down by his mother, and in obedience to the law of that unknown and nameless thing, fear, he kept away from the mouth of the cave. It remained to him a white wall of light. When his mother was absent, he slept most of the time, while during the intervals that he was awake he kept very quiet, suppressing the whimpering cries that tickled in his throat and strove for noise.

Once, lying awake, he heard a strange sound in the white wall. He did not know that it was a wolverine, standing outside, all a-tremble with its own daring, and cautiously scenting out the contents of the cave. The cub knew only that the sniff was strange, a something unclassified, therefore unknown and terrible—for the unknown was one of the chief elements that went into the making of fear.

The hair bristled up on the gray cub's back, but it bristled silently. How was he to know that this thing that sniffed was a thing at which to bristle? It was not born of any knowledge of his, yet it was the visible expression of the fear that was in him, and for which, in his own life, there was no accounting. But fear was accompanied by another instinct—that of concealment. The cub was in a frenzy of terror, yet he lay without movement or sound, frozen, petrified into immobility, to all appearances dead. His mother, coming home, growled as she smelt the wolverine's track, and bounded into the cave and licked and nozzled him with undue vehemence of affection. And the cub felt that somehow he had escaped a great hurt.

But there were other forces at work in the cub, the greatest of which was growth. Instinct and law demanded of him obedience. But growth demanded disobedience. His mother and fear impelled him to keep away from the white wall. Growth is life, and life is forever destined to make for light. So there was no damming up the tide of life that was rising within him—rising with every mouthful of meat he swallowed, with every breath he drew. In the end, one day, fear and obedience were swept away by the rush of life, and the cub straddled and sprawled toward the entrance.

Unlike any other wall with which he had had experience, this wall seemed to recede from him as he approached. No hard surface collided with the tender little nose he thrust out tentatively before him. The substance of the wall seemed as permeable and yielding as light. And as condition, in his eyes, had the seeming of form, so he entered into what had been wall to him and bathed in the substance that composed it.

It was bewildering. He was sprawling through solidity. And ever the light grew brighter. Fear urged him to go back, but growth drove him on. Suddenly he found himself at the mouth of the cave. The wall, inside which he had thought himself, as suddenly leaped back before him to an immeasurable distance. The light had become painfully bright. He was dazzled by it. Likewise he was made dizzy by this abrupt and tremendous extension of space. Automatically, his eyes were adjusting themselves to the brightness, focusing themselves to meet the increased distance of objects. At first, the wall had leaped beyond his vision. He now saw it again; but it had taken upon itself a remarkable remoteness. Also, its appearance had changed. It was now a variegated wall, composed of the trees that fringed the stream, the opposing mountain that towered above the trees, and the sky that out-towered the mountain.

A great fear came upon him. This was more of the terrible unknown. He crouched down on the lip of the cave and gazed out on the world. He was very much afraid. Because it was unknown, it was hostile to him. Therefore the hair stood up on end along his back and his lips wrinkled weakly in an attempt at a ferocious and intimidating snarl. Out of his puniness and fright he challenged and menaced the whole wide world.

Nothing happened. He continued to gaze, and in his interest he forgot to snarl. Also, he forgot to be afraid. For the time, fear had been routed by growth, while growth had assumed the guise of curiosity. He began to notice near objects—an open portion of the stream that flashed in the sun, the blasted pine tree that stood at the base of the slope, and the slope itself, that ran right up to him and ceased two feet beneath the lip of the cave on which he crouched.

Now the gray cub had lived all his days on a level floor. He had never experienced the hurt of a fall. He did not know what a fall was. So he stepped boldly out upon the air. His hind-legs still rested on the cave-lip, so he fell forward head downward. The earth struck him a harsh blow on the nose that made him yelp. Then he began rolling down the slope, over and over. He was in a panic of terror. The unknown had caught him at last. It had gripped savagely hold of him and was about to wreak upon him some terrific hurt. Growth was now routed by fear, and he ki-yi'd like any frightened puppy.

The unknown bore him on he knew not to what frightful hurt, and he yelped and ki-yi'd unceasingly. This was a different proposition from crouching in frozen fear while the unknown lurked just alongside. Now the unknown had caught tight hold of him. Silence would do no good. Besides, it was not fear, but terror, that convulsed him.

But the slope grew more gradual, and its base was grass-covered. Here the cub lost momentum. When at last he came to a stop, he gave one last agonized yelp and then a long, whimpering wail. Also, and quite as a matter of course, as though in his life he had already made a thousand toilets, he proceeded to lick away that dry clay that soiled him.

After that he sat up and gazed about him, as might the first man of the earth who landed upon Mars. The cub had broken through the wall of the world, the unknown had let go its hold of him, and here he was without hurt. But the first man on Mars would have experienced less unfamiliarity than did he. Without any antecedent knowledge, without any warning whatever that such existed, he found himself an explorer in a totally new world.

Now that the terrible unknown had let go of him, he forgot that the unknown had any terrors. He was aware only of curiosity in all the things about him. He inspected the grass beneath him, the mossberry plant just beyond, and the dead trunk of the blasted pine that stood on the edge of an open space among the trees. A squirrel, running around the base of the trunk, came full upon him, and gave him a great fright. He cowered down and snarled. But the squirrel was as badly scared. It ran up the tree, and from a point of safety chattered back savagely.

This helped the cub's courage, and though the woodpecker he next encountered gave him a start, he proceeded confidently on his way. Such was his confidence, that when a moose-bird impudently hopped up to him, he reached out at it with a playful paw. The result was a sharp peck on the end of his nose that made him cower down and ki-yi. The noise he made was too much for the moose-bird, who sought safety in flight.

But the cub was learning. His misty little mind had already made an unconscious classification. There were live things and things not alive. Also, he must watch out for the live things.

The things not alive remained always in one place; but the live things moved about, and there was no telling what they might do. The thing to expect of them was the unexpected, and for this he must be prepared.

He traveled very clumsily. He ran into sticks and things. A twig that he thought a long way off would the next instant hit him on the nose or rake along his ribs. There were inequalities of surface. Sometimes he overstepped and stubbed his nose. Quite as often he understepped and stubbed his feet. Then there were pebbles and stones that turned under him when he trod upon them; and from them he came to know that the things not alive were not all in the same state of stable equilibrium as was his cave; also, that small things not alive were more liable than large things to fall down or turn over. But with every mishap he was learning. The longer he walked, the better he walked. He was adjusting himself. He was learning to calculate his own muscular movements, to know his physical limitations, to measure distances between objects, and between objects and himself.

His was the luck of the beginner. Born to be a hunter of meat (though he did not know it), he blundered upon meat just outside his own cave-door on his first foray into the world. It was by sheer blundering that he chanced upon the shrewdly hidden ptarmigan nest. He fell into it. He had essayed to walk along the trunk of a fallen pine. The rotten bark gave way under his feet, and with a despairing yelp he pitched down the rounded descent, smashed through the leafage and stalks of a small bush, and in the heart of the bush, on the ground, fetched up amongst seven ptarmigan chicks.

They made noises, and at first he was frightened at them. Then he perceived that they were very little, and he became bolder. They moved. He placed his paw on one, and its movements were accelerated. This was a source of enjoyment to him. He smelled it. He picked it up in his mouth. It struggled and tickled his tongue. At the same time he was made aware of a sensation of hunger. His jaws closed together. There was a crunching of fragile bones, and warm blood ran in his mouth. The taste of it was good. This was meat, the same as his mother gave him, only it was alive between his teeth and therefore better. So he ate the ptarmigan. Nor did he stop till he had devoured the whole brood. Then he licked his chops in quite the same way his mother did, and began to crawl out of the bush.

He encountered a feathered whirlwind. He was confused and blinded by the rush of it and the beat of angry wings. He hid his head between his paws and yelped. The blows increased. The mother ptarmigan was in a fury. Then he became angry. He rose up, snarling, striking out with his paws. He sank his tiny teeth into one of the wings and pulled and tugged sturdily. The ptarmigan struggled against him, showering blows upon him with her free wing. It was his first battle. He was elated. He forgot all about the unknown. He no longer was afraid of anything. He was fighting, tearing at a living thing that was striking at him. Also, this live thing was meat. The lust to kill was on him. He had just destroyed little live things. He would now destroy a big live thing. He was too busy and happy to know that he was happy. He was thrilling and exulting in ways new to him and greater to him than any he had known before.

He held on to the wing and growled between his tight-clenched teeth. The ptarmigan dragged him out of the bush. When she turned and tried to drag him back into the bush's shelter, he pulled her away from it and on into the open. And all the time she was making outcry and striking with her wing, while feathers were flying like a snowfall. The pitch to which he was aroused was tremendous. All the fighting blood of his breed was up in him and surging through him. This was living, though he did not know it. He was realizing his own meaning in the world; he was doing that for which he was made— killing meat and battling to kill it. He was justifying his existence, than which life can do no greater; for life achieves its summit when it does to the uttermost that which it was equipped to do.

After a time, the ptarmigan ceased her struggling. He still held her by the wing, and they lay on the ground and looked at each other. He tried to growl threateningly, ferociously. She pecked on his nose, which by now, what of previous adventures, was sore. He winced but held on. She pecked him again and again. From wincing he went to whimpering. He tried to back from her, oblivious of the fact that by his hold on her he dragged her after him. A rain of pecks fell on his ill-used nose. The flood of fight ebbed down in him, and, releasing his prey, he turned tail and scampered off across the open in inglorious retreat.

He lay down to rest on the other side of the open, near the edge of the bushes, his tongue lolling out, his chest heaving and panting, his nose still hurting him and causing him to continue his whimper. But as he lay there, suddenly there came to him a feeling as of something terrible impending. The unknown with all its terrors rushed upon him, and he shrank back instinctively into the shelter of the bush. As he did so, a draught of air fanned him, and a large, winged body swept ominously and silently past. A hawk, driving down out of the blue, had barely missed him.

While he lay in the bush, recovering from this fright and peering fearfully out, the mother-ptarmigan on the other side of the open space fluttered out of the ravaged nest. It was because of her loss that she paid no attention to the winged bolt of the sky. But the cub saw, and it was a warning and a lesson to him—the swift downward swoop of the hawk, the short skim of its body just above the ground, the strike of its talons in the body of the ptarmigan, the ptarmigan's squawk of agony and fright, and the hawk's rush upward into the blue, carrying the ptarmigan away with it.

It was a long time before the cub left his shelter. He had learned much. Live things were meat. They were good to eat. Also, live things when they were large enough, could give hurt.

It was better to eat small live things like ptarmigan chicks, and to let alone live things like ptarmigan hens. Nevertheless he felt a little prick of ambition, a sneaking desire to have another battle with that ptarmigan hen—only the hawk had carried her away. Maybe there were other ptarmigan hens. He would go and see.

He came down a shelving bank to the stream. He had never seen water before. The footing looked good. There were no inequalities of surface. He stepped boldly out on it; and went down, crying with fear, into the embrace of the unknown. It was cold, and he gasped, breathing quickly. The water rushed into his lungs instead of the air that had always accompanied his act of breathing. The suffocation he experienced was like the pang of death. To him it signified death. He had no conscious knowledge of death, but like every animal of the Wild, he possessed the instinct of death. To him it stood as the greatest of hurts. It was the very essence of the unknown; it was the sum of the terrors of the unknown, the one culminating and unthinkable catastrophe that could happen to him, about which he knew nothing and about which he feared everything.

He came to the surface, and the sweet air rushed into his open mouth. He did not go down again. Quite as though it had been a long-established custom of his, he struck out with all his legs and began to swim. The near bank was a yard away; but he had come up with his back to it, and the first thing his eyes rested upon was the opposite bank, toward which he immediately began to swim. The stream was a small one, but in the pool it widened out to a score of feet.

Midway in the passage, the current picked up the cub and swept him downstream. He was caught in the miniature rapid at the bottom of the pool. Here was little chance for swimming. The quiet water had become suddenly angry. Sometimes he was under, sometimes on top. At all times he was in violent motion, now being turned over or around, and again, being smashed against a rock. And with every rock he struck, he yelped. His progress was a series of yelps, from which might have been adduced the number of rocks he encountered.

Below the rapid was a second pool, and here, captured by the eddy, he was gently borne to the bank and as gently deposited on a bed of gravel. He crawled frantically clear of the water and lay down. He had learned some more about the world. Water was not alive. Yet it moved. Also, it looked as solid as the earth, but was without any solidity at all. His conclusion was that things were not always what they appeared to be. The cub's fear of the unknown was an inherited distrust, and it had now been strengthened by experience. Thenceforth, in the nature of things, he would possess an abiding distrust of appearances. He would have to learn the reality of a thing before he could put his faith into it.

One other adventure was destined for him that day. He had recollected that there was such a thing in the world as his mother. And then there came to him a feeling that he wanted her more than all the rest of the things in the world. Not only was his body tired with the adventures it had undergone, but his little brain was equally tired. In all the days he had lived it had not worked so hard as on this one day. Furthermore, he was sleepy. So he started out to look for the cave and his mother, feeling at the same time an overwhelming rush of loneliness and helplessness.

He was sprawling along between some bushes, when he heard a sharp, intimidating cry. There was a flash of yellow before his eyes. He saw a weasel leaping swiftly away from him. It was a small thing, and he had no fear. Then, before him, at his feet, he saw an extremely small live thing, only several inches long—a young weasel, that, like himself, had disobediently gone out adventuring. It tried to retreat before him. He turned it over with his paw. It made a queer, grating noise. The next moment the flash of yellow reappeared before his eyes. He heard again the intimidating cry, and at the same instant received a severe blow on the side of the neck and felt the sharp teeth of the mother-weasel cut into his flesh.

While he yelped and ki-yi'd and scrambled backward, he saw the mother-weasel leap upon her young one and disappear with it into the neighboring thicket. The cut of her teeth in his neck still hurt, but his feelings were hurt more grievously, and he sat down and weakly whimpered. This mother-weasel was so small and so savage! He was yet to learn that for size and weight, the weasel was the most ferocious, vindictive, and terrible of all the killers of the Wild. But a portion of this knowledge was quickly to be his.

He was still whimpering when the mother-weasel reappeared. She did not rush him, now that her young one was safe. She approached more cautiously, and the cub had full opportunity to observe her lean, snakelike body, and her head, erect, eager, and snakelike itself. Her sharp, menacing cry sent the hair bristling along his back, and he snarled warningly at her. She came closer and closer. There was a leap, swifter than his unpracticed sight, and the lean, yellow body disappeared for a moment out of the field of his vision. The next moment she was at his throat, her teeth buried in his hair and flesh.

At first he snarled and tried to fight; but he was very young, and this was only his first day in the world, and his snarl became a whimper, his fight a struggle to escape. The weasel never relaxed her hold. She hung on, striving to press down with her teeth to the great vein where his life-blood bubbled. The weasel was a drinker of blood, and it was ever her preference to drink from the throat of life itself.

The gray cub would have died, and there would have been no story to write about him, had not the she-wolf come bounding through the bushes. The weasel let go the cub and flashed at the she-wolf's throat, missing, but getting a hold on the jaw instead. Then the she-wolf flirted her head like the snap of a whip, breaking the weasel's hold and flinging it high in the air. And, still in the air, the she-wolf's jaws closed on the lean, yellow body, and the weasel knew death between the crunching teeth.

The cub experienced another access of affection on the part of his mother. Her joy at finding him seemed greater even than his joy at being found. She nozzled him and caressed him and licked the cuts made in him by the weasel's teeth. Then, between them, mother and cub, they ate the blood-drinker, and after that went back to the cave and slept.

Ernest Hemingway

THE SHORT HAPPY LIFE OF
FRANCIS MACOMBER

It had started the night before when he had wakened and heard the lion roaring somewhere up along the river. It was a deep sound and at the end there were sort of coughing grunts that made him seem just outside the tent, and when Francis Macomber woke in the night to hear it he was afraid. He could hear his wife breathing quietly, asleep. There was no one to tell he was afraid, nor to be afraid with him, and, lying alone, he did not know the Somali proverb that says a brave man is always frightened three times by a lion; when he first sees his track, when he first hears him roar and when he first confronts him. Then while they were eating breakfast by lantern light out in the dining tent, before the sun was up, the lion roared again and Francis thought he was just at the edge of camp.

"Sounds like an old-timer," Robert Wilson said, looking up form his kippers and coffee. "Listen to him cough."

"Is he very close?"

"A mile or so up the stream."

"Will we see him?"

"We'll have a look."

"Does his roaring carry that far? It sounds as though he were right in camp."

"Carries a hell of a long way," said Robert Wilson. "It's strange the way it carries. Hope he's a shootable cat. The boys said there was a very big one about here."

"If I get a shot, where should I hit him," Macomber asked, "to stop him?"

"In the shoulders," Wilson said. "In the neck if you can make it. Shoot for bone. Break him down."

"I hope I can place it properly," Macomber said.

"You shoot very well," Wilson told him. "Take your time. Make sure of him. The first one in is the one that counts."

"What range will it be?"

"Can't tell. Lion has something to say about that. Won't shoot unless it's close enough so you can make sure."

"At under a hundred yards?" Macomber asked.

Wilson looked at him quickly.

"Hundred's about right. Might have to take him a bit under. Shouldn't chance a shot at much over that. A hundred's a decent range. You can hit him wherever you want at that. Here comes the Memsahib."

"Good morning," she said. "Are we going after that lion?"

"As soon as you deal with your breakfast," Wilson said. "How are you feeling?"

"Marvellous," she said. "I'm very excited."

"I'll just go and see that everything is ready," Wilson went off. As he left the lion roared again.

"Noisy beggar," Wilson said. "We'll put a stop to that."

"What's the matter, Francis?" his wife asked him.

"Nothing," Macomber said.

"Yes, there is," she said. "What are you upset about?"

"Nothing," he said.

"Tell me," she looked at him. "Don't you feel well?"

"It's that damned roaring," he said. "It's been going on all night, you know."

"Why didn't you wake me," she said. "I'd love to have heard it."

"I've got to kill the damned thing," Macomber said, miserably.

"Well, that's what you're out here for, isn't it?"

"Yes. But I'm nervous. Hearing the thing roar gets on my nerves."

"Well, then, as Wilson said, kill him and stop his roaring."

"Yes, darling," said Francis Macomber. "It sounds easy, doesn't it?"

"You're not afraid, are you?"

"Of course not. But I'm nervous from hearing him roar all night."

"You'll kill him marvellously," she said. "I know you will. I'm awfully anxious to see it."

"Finish your breakfast and we'll be starting."

"It's not light yet," she said. "This is a ridiculous hour."

Just then the lion roared in a deep-chested moaning, suddenly guttural, ascending vibration that seemed to shake the air and ended in a sigh and a heavy, deep-chested grunt.

"He sounds almost here," Macomber's wife said.

"My God," said Macomber. "I hate that damned noise."

"It's very impressive."

"Impressive. It's frightful."

Robert Wilson came up then carrying his short, ugly, shockingly big-bored .505 Gibbs and grinning.

"Come on," he said. "Your gun-bearer has your Springfield and the big gun. Everything's in the car. Have you solids?"

"Yes."

"I'm ready," Mrs. Macomber said.

"Must make him stop that racket," Wilson said. "You get in front. The Memsahib can sit back here with me."

They climbed into the motor car and, in the gray first daylight, moved off up the river through the trees. Macomber opened the breech of his rifle and saw he had metal-cased bullets, shut the bolt and put the rifle on safety. He saw his hand was trembling. He felt in his pocket for more cartridges and moved his fingers over the cartridges in the loops of his tunic front. He turned back to where Wilson sat in the rear seat of the doorless, box-bodied motor car beside his wife, them both grinning with excitement, and Wilson leaned forward and whispered,

"See the birds dropping. Means the old boy has left his kill."

On the far bank of the stream Macomber could see, above the trees, vultures circling and plummeting down.

"Chances are he'll come to drink along here," Wilson whispered. "Before he goes to lay up. Keep an eye out."

They were driving slowly along the high bank of the stream which here cut deeply to its boulder-filled bed, and they wound in and out through big trees as they drove. Macomber was watching the opposite bank when he felt Wilson take hold of his arm. The car stopped.

"There he is," he heard the whisper. "Ahead and to the right. Get out and take him. He's a marvellous lion."

Macomber saw the lion now. He was standing almost broadside, his great head up and turned toward them. The early morning breeze that blew toward them was just stirring his dark mane, and the lion looked huge, silhouetted on the rise of bank in the gray morning light, his shoulders heavy, his barrel of a body bulking smoothly.

"How far is he?" asked Macomber, raising his rifle.

"About seventy-five. Get out and take him."

"Why not shoot from where I am?"

"You don't shoot them from cars," he heard Wilson saying in his ear. "Get out. He's not going to stay there all day."

Macomber stepped out of the curved opening at the side of the front seat, onto the step and down onto the ground. The lion still stood looking majestically and coolly toward his object that his eyes only showed in silhouette, bulking like some super-rhino. There was no man smell carried toward him and he watched the object, moving his great head a little from side to side. Then watching the object, not afraid, but hesitating before going down the bank to drink with such a thing opposite him, he saw a man figure detach itself from it and he turned his heavy head and swung away toward the cover of the trees as he heard a cracking crash and felt the slam of a .30–06 220-grain solid bullet that bit his flank and ripped in sudden hot scalding nausea through his stomach. He trotted, heavy, big-footed, swinging wounded full-bellied, through the trees toward the tall grass and cover, and the crash came again to go past him ripping the air apart. Then it crashed again and he felt the blow as it hit his lower ribs and ripped on through, blood sudden hot and frothy in his mouth, and he galloped toward the high grass where he could crouch and not be seen and make them bring the crashing thing close enough so he could make a rush and get the man that held it.

Macomber had not thought how the lion felt as he got out of the car. He only knew his hands were shaking and as he walked away from the car it was almost impossible for him to make his legs move. They were stiff in the thighs, but he could feel the muscles fluttering. He raised the rifle, sighted on the junction of the lion's head and shoulders and pulled the trigger. Nothing happened though he pulled until he thought his finger would break. Then he knew he had the safety on and as he lowered the rifle to move the safety over he moved another frozen pace forward, and the lion seeing his silhouette now clear of the silhouette of the car, turned and started off at a trot, and, as Macomber fired, he heard a whunk that meant that the bullet was home; but the lion kept on going. Macomber shot again and every one saw the bullet throw a spout of dirt beyond the trotting lion. He shot again, remembering to lower his aim, and they all heard the bullet hit, and the lion went into a gallop and was in the tall grass before he had the bolt pushed forward.

Macomber stood there feeling sick at his stomach, his hands

that held the Springfield still cocked, shaking, and his wife and Robert Wilson were standing by him. Beside him too were the two gun-bearers chattering in Wakamba.

"I hit him," Macomber said. "I hit him twice."

"You gut-shot him and you hit him somewhere forward," Wilson said without enthusiasm. The gun-bearers looked very grave. They were silent now.

"You may have killed him," Wilson went on. "We'll have to wait a while before we go in to find out."

"What do you mean?"

"Let him get sick before we follow him up."

"Oh," said Macomber.

"He's a hell of a fine lion," Wilson said cheerfully. "He's gotten into a bad place though."

"Why is it bad?"

"Can't see him until you're on him."

"Oh," said Macomber.

"Come on," said Wilson. "The Memsahib can stay here in the car. We'll go to have a look at the blood spoor."

"Stay here, Margot," Macomber said to his wife. His mouth was very dry and it was hard for him to talk.

"Why?" she asked.

"Wilson says to."

"We're going to have a look," Wilson said. "You stay here. You can see even better from here."

"All right."

Wilson spoke in Swahili to the driver. He nodded and said, "Yes, Bwana."

Then they went down the steep bank and across the stream, climbing over and around the boulders and up the other bank, pulling up by some projecting roots, and along it until they found where the lion had been trotting when Macomber first shot. There was dark blood on the short grass that the gun-bearers pointed out with grass stems, and that ran away behind the river bank trees.

"What do we do?" asked Macomber.

"Not much choice," said Wilson. "We can't bring the car over. Bank's too steep. We'll let him stiffen up a bit and then you and I'll go in and have a look for him."

"Can't we set the grass on fire?" Macomber asked.

"Too green."

"Can't we send beaters?"

Wilson looked at him appraisingly. "Of course we can," he said. "But it's just a touch murderous. You see we know the lion's wounded. You can drive an unwounded lion—he'll move on ahead of a noise—but a wounded lion's going to charge. You can't see him until you're right on him. He'll make himself perfectly flat in cover you wouldn't think would hide a hare. You can't very well send boys in there to that sort of a show. Somebody bound to get mauled."

"What about the gun-bearers?"

"Oh, they'll go with us. It's their *shauri*. You see, they signed on for it. They don't look too happy though, do they?"

"I don't want to go in there," said Macomber. It was out before he knew he'd said it.

"Neither do I," said Wilson very cheerily. "Really no choice though." Then, as an afterthought, he glanced at Macomber and saw suddenly how he was trembling and the pitiful look on his face.

"You don't have to go in, of course," he said. "That's what I'm hired for, you know. That's why I'm so expensive."

"You mean you'd go in by yourself? Why not leave him there?"

Robert Wilson, whose entire occupation had been with the lion and the problem he presented, and who had not been thinking about Macomber except to note that he was rather windy, suddenly felt as though he had opened the wrong door in a hotel and seen something shameful.

"What do you mean?"

"Why not just leave him?"

"You mean pretend to ourselves he hasn't been hit?"

"No. Just drop it."

"It isn't done."

"Why not?"

"For one thing, he's certain to be suffering. For another, some one else might run onto him."

"I see."

"But you don't have to have anything to do with it."

"I'd like to," Macomber said. "I'm just scared, you know."

"I'll go ahead when we go in," Wilson said, "with Kongoni tracking. You keep behind me and a little to one side. Chances are we'll hear him growl. If we see him we'll both shoot. Don't worry about anything. I'll keep you backed up. As a matter of fact, you know, perhaps you'd better not go. It might be much better. Why don't you go over and join the Memsahib while I just get it over with?"

"No, I want to go."

"All right," said Wilson. "But don't go in if you don't want to. This is my *shauri* now, you know."

"I want to go," said Macomber.

They sat under a tree and smoked.

"Want to go back and speak to the Memsahib while we're waiting?" Wilson asked.

"No."

"I'll just step back and tell her to be patient."

"Good," said Macomber. He sat there, sweating under his arms, his mouth dry, his stomach hollow feeling, wanting to find courage to tell Wilson to go on and finish off the lion without him. He could not know that Wilson was furious because he had not noticed the state he was in earlier and sent him back to his wife. While he sat there Wilson came up. "I have your big gun," he said. "Take it. We've given him time, I think. Come on."

Macomber took the big gun and Wilson said:

"Keep behind me and about five yards to the right and do exactly as I tell you." Then he spoke in Swahili to the two gun-bearers who looked the picture of gloom.

"Let's go," he said.

"Could I have a drink of water?" Macomber asked. Wilson spoke to the older gun-bearer, who wore a canteen on his belt, and the man unbuckled it, unscrewed the top and handed it to Macomber, who took it noticing how heavy it seemed and how hairy and shoddy the felt covering was in his hand. He raised it to drink and looked ahead at the high grass with the flat-topped trees behind it. A breeze was blowing toward them and the grass rippled gently in the wind. He looked at the gun-bearer and he could see the gun-bearer was suffering too with fear.

Thirty-five yards into the grass the big lion lay flattened out along the ground. His ears were back and his only movement was a slight twitching up and down of his long, black-tufted tail. He had turned at bay as soon as he had reached this cover and he was sick with the wound through his full belly, and weakening with the wound through his lungs that brought a thin foamy red to his mouth each time he breathed. His flanks were wet and hot and flies were on the little openings the solid bullets had made in his tawny hide, and his big yellow eyes, narrowed with hate, looked straight ahead, only blinking when the pain came as he breathed, and his claws dug in the soft baked earth. All of him, pain, sickness, hatred and all of his remaining strength, was tightening into an absolute concentration for a rush. He could hear the men talking and he waited, gathering all of himself into this preparation for a charge as soon as the men would come into the grass. As he heard their voices his tail stiffened to twitch up and down, and, as they came into the edge of the grass, he made a coughing grunt and charged.

Kongoni, the old gun-bearer, in the lead watching the blood spoor, Wilson watching the grass for any movement, his big gun ready, the second gun-bearer looking ahead and listening, Macomber close to Wilson, his rifle cocked, they had just moved into the grass when Macomber heard the blood-choked coughing grunt, and saw the swishing rush in the grass. The

ext thing he knew he was running; running wildly, in panic
n the open, running toward the stream.

He heard the *ca-ra-wong!* of Wilson's big rifle, and again
n a second crashing *carawong!* and turning saw the lion,
orrible-looking now, with half his head seeming to be gone,
rawling toward Wilson in the edge of the tall grass while the
ed-faced man worked the bolt on the short ugly rifle and
imed carefully as another blasting *carawong!* came from the
nuzzle, and the crawling, heavy, yellow bulk of the lion stiff-
ned and the huge, mutilated head slid forward and Ma-
omber, standing by himself in the clearing where he had run,
olding a loaded rifle, while two black men and a white man
ooked back at him in contempt, knew the lion was dead. He
ame toward Wilson, his tallness all seeming a naked re-
roach, and Wilson looked at him and said:

"Want to take pictures?"

"No," he said.

That was all any one had said until they reached the motor
ar. Then Wilson had said:

"Hell of a fine lion. Boys will skin him out. We might as
ell stay here in the shade."

Elizabeth Marshall Thomas

THE TRIBE OF TIGER

Perhaps the most dramatic evidence of cat sociability i
their vocalizations—a logical means for animals whos
economic needs drive them apart even as their emotional need
draw them together. People who have both dogs and cats ca
verify the statement: when called, the common response o
dogs is to come, and of cats is to answer.

Lions certainly answer. During a period in the 1950s whe
I was in Nyae Nyae, in the Kalahari Desert of southern Africa
the lions kept in touch by roaring. One would roar, and afte
a short while another lion, very far away, would reply. O
certain nights the lions would spread out through the bush i
a line perhaps a mile long or even longer and seemed to kee
their line straight and in order by answering in turn. Th
farthest would roar, then the next and the next, until six o
eight had made themselves known. This way they could te
if all were present and if their line was reasonably straight. I
the rainy season, these lions even answered thunder. I love
that: a dark night, the endless, rain-soaked bush, a flash o

lightning, a cosmic crash of thunder, a little pause, and then, faint and far, a lion's roar!

"WHERE ARE YOU, MY LION?"

". . . (*me?*) . . . I'M HERE!" . . .

Our first encounter with lions was on our first trip, at the edge of the Kalahari, far to the west of /Gautscha, just after we had camped for the night. With us was a young Afrikaner man, a former smallpox-control officer, who had come to show us the way to a place where he once had found and vaccinated some Bushmen. (In those days, almost no non-Bushmen had contact with the Bushmen, or even had any idea where they were.) In the dark, a group of five lions came quietly up to us. Beyond our fire we saw their shining eyes, which were so high above the ground that we thought at first we were seeing donkeys. When I realized that we were seeing lions, I was overcome with excitement and ran around the fire to see them better. Just then, a bullet whizzed by my ear, shots ran out, and the eyes vanished. Before anyone realized what the young Afrikaner was doing or could stop him, he had shot two of the lions.

That was all he did, too. He wouldn't even go to see if he had killed them. When the rest of us found tracks and splashed blood but no dead lions, we realized the extent of the problem created by the young man—two wounded lions nearby in the dark. We asked him what he was going to do about it. Nothing, he said. It was, after all, nighttime. It would be dangerous to follow up the lions. So the task fell to me, my brother, and a man named William Cam, who had come with us as a mechanic.

We set off on foot in the starlight, moving very quietly so that we might hear the lions breathing or the low, mumbling growl that a wounded lion might make. We also tried to catch their scent. At last we heard a soft moan. We followed the sound, turned on the flashlight, and found a lion—a male, full grown but still too young to have a mane or to have left the pride. Badly wounded, he was lying on his side, unable to get up. He was evidently in pain, for he had been biting the grass. We had to shoot him several times before we could kill him and each time a bullet hit him he cried. One of the worst moments of my life, that scene is as fresh in my mind today as it ever was, and as painful. The lion turned his head aside, to look away from us as we stood over him and shot him. I wonder now if by averting his gaze he was hoping to limit our aggression.

We couldn't find the other lion, and after many hours of searching we gave up, to try again in the morning. When the sky grew pale, at the place where the lions had been when the young man fired, my brother and I found the tracks of a lion who had taken a great leap. Not fifty feet from camp, at the end of the next leap, lay the body of a lioness shot through the heart. She, like the lion, seemed young: she still had spots on her white belly. Her fur and the grass around her were cold and set with dew. Or mostly cold and wet with dew. Right beside her we found a warm, dry place where the grass lay flat. Looking around, we saw a dark trail through the grass where something had knocked off the dew. Then on the trail we saw a grass stem starting to rise after being pressed down, then another, and another, and under the slowly lifting grass stems we found the round footprints of an enormous lion, who had left only moments before. So we knew that while the dew fell, this huge lion or lioness had stayed beside the dead lioness, within sight of our camp, listening to all our comings and goings, listening to the shots and cries. During the night the watching lion or lioness had groomed the body of the dead lioness, turning her fur the wrong way.

Our next encounter took place on the first night of our second trip to /Gautscha. We had come in vehicles after much hard traveling. We were too tired to pitch tents so, about fifty feet from the Ju/wa encampment, we threw down our sleeping bags and without even bothering to build a fire went immediately to sleep. During the night, we heard the Ju/wasi saying some strong words to someone, but we didn't pay much attention. We were too tired. In the morning, we found the footprints of lions all around us. Several lions had come to investigate us as we slept and had even bent down to sniff our faces. We found the huge, round prints of lions' forefeet, toes pointed at us, right by our heads.

Afterward, the lions had gone on to the Ju/wa encampment and had stared over the tops of the little grass shelters at the people there. Unlike us, who stayed awake all day and slept all night, the Ju/wasi took naps during the day and got up often at night. Hence they were virtually never all asleep at the same time. Even in the depth of night someone would be awake, getting warm by the fire, having a snack or a sip of water or a chat with someone else. When the people who were awake saw the burning green eyes, they got smoothly to their feet and firmly told the lions to leave. Since the Ju/wasi would hardly take a low, commanding tone with one another, the unusual voices woke everyone else. At first, the lions didn't want to leave, but the people insisted, and at last shook burning branches at them. Eventually, the lions went.

On several occasions, lions seemed to have strong feelings about us, about something we had done or were doing. As I look back, the interesting thing about the episodes is not that they were frightening, which they were, or dangerous, which they could have been, but that the lions seemed to be trying hard to communicate with us, perhaps simply to give expression to their feelings, perhaps to make us do something.

Unlike the lions, who correctly understood, and even obeyed, the spoken and gestured commands of the Ju/wasi—words and gestures that were designed for other human beings and then merely applied to lions—we human beings were not able to understand the lions. Not even the Ju/wasi understood them, and they knew them better than anyone else. Why could the lions of /Gautscha understand the requests of the people but the people not understand the requests of the lions? Are lions better than people at understanding interspecific messages? Are people better than lions at conveying messages? No one really knows. It came to me, however, that our kind may be able to bully other species not because we are good at communication but because we aren't. When we ask things of animals, they often understand us. When they ask things of us, we're often baffled. Hence animals frequently oblige us, but we seldom oblige them. Elephants are different, but then, elephants can motivate people as no other animals can. Once, an elephant who didn't want me near him threw gravel at me so hard it felt like buckshot. I understood at once what he wished to communicate, and thereafter I paid scrupulous attention to his boundary, which was, incidentally, not the bars of his cage or the edge of the sidewalk but a creation of his own mind and seemed to be expressed by an unchanging but invisible line.

Of course, each time an animal tries to communicate with a human being, the animal is pioneering, since there are no established ways. Sometimes the animal tries something that is familiar and that works with his or her own kind—a dog who wanted something might, for instance, bark or stare or whine, all ways in which he might successfully communicate with another dog. But not all animals are satisfied with the familiar. Cats are particularly inventive in communicating with human beings, and most of us can see plenty of examples in the efforts of our own cats. Our cat Orion, perhaps having noticed that at night I would investigate noises on the stairs, once jumped hard from step to step, and repeated the procedure so successfully that I thought the sound was being made by a heavy person, and I got out of bed to investigate. Orion had, I saw, been jumping on the top three stairs only, and when he got to the third step from the top, he would go back up and do his jumps over again. He was just starting over for the fourth or fifth time when I arrived. He then looked at me and *meowed*. He had food, he had water, he had a cat box. In short, he lacked nothing that I ordinarily would provide for him. It occurred to me that he wanted to go out, and needed me to open the cat door for him. But we had long since begun keeping our cats indoors at night, for fear of a coyote, and I couldn't oblige him. I said aloud, "I'm sorry, but I can't let you out." His eyes lingered on mine, as if he were taking in what I had told him, and then he turned his head and went on down the stairs in perfect silence. Did we communicate what I believe we communicated? Had he really wanted to go out? Had he understood my remark, or some of it, and deduced the rest from the tone? Possibly—he was certainly communicating something, and I may or may not have picked it up.

But in my experience, the most dramatic episode involving cat's attempt at communication took place one hot, moonless night in the rainy season at /Gautscha, when a lioness came to our camp. Most of our people and also many of the Ju/wasi were elsewhere. I happened to be alone in a tent in our camp, and my mother and brother happened to be visiting people in the Ju/wa camp, about thirty yards away. I was working on my notes by lantern light. At the Ju/wa camp, about six small fires burned. We had been in residence there for almost a year and in no sense could be considered newcomers.

At about ten o'clock that night a lioness suddenly appeared between the two camps and began to roar. The loudness of lions cannot be described or imagined but must be experienced. My body was so filled with the sound that I couldn't think or breathe, and in the brief silences between roars my ears rang. The earth and the walls of the tent seemed to be shaking. Terror-stricken and confused, I tried to collect my wits. There was nowhere to go that gave more protection than the places we were already in—I in a very flimsy tent but at least not completely exposed, the other people all together beside fires. Climbing a tree was out of the question—there were no trees whose upper branches the lioness couldn't reach by standing on her hind legs. At last, with trembling hands, I carried the lantern outside the tent, partly so that its light would shine on the tent rather than through the tent, to make the fabric seem solid rather than transparent, with me quivering inside like a shadow puppet. I also wanted to illuminate the lioness so the other people could see where she was, because her roars were so deep and so loud that they gave no direction. To judge from her roars, she was all around all of us—anywhere, everywhere.

She seemed to have in mind something in the Ju/wa camp, since she was looking in that direction. She seemed not to notice the lantern. With her ears half up and turned sideways, with her tail taking great, full sweeps, she seemed angry and edgy; a lioness whose patience was at an end. Sometimes she would pace back and forth, and once she leaped out of the lantern light, only to leap back into it again. It is sometimes claimed that lions roar at other creatures to confuse or stampede them, making them easy prey. That night, such an explanation seemed improbable. Long ago, natural selection would have removed from the general population any people unwise enough to leave their fires and weapons and scatter in the dark, especially at the urging of a lion. Even Western people don't necessarily stampede under such conditions. Not knowing what to do or where to go, they simply remain rooted to the spot with terror. That was what happened to me. As for the Ju/wasi, the lioness certainly got their attention but perhaps didn't frighten them as badly as she frightened me. Cool but alert, they awaited developments. Anyway, there wasn't anything anyone could do. The lioness certainly didn't seem in the mood to consider a firmly spoken request from the Ju/wasi, and that night they didn't offer any; they maintained a tactful silence. It seemed to me terribly important to notice how long the lioness stayed there, so I timed her. She roared intermittently for almost thirty-five minutes. Then she left, with swift, impatient strides. And there the episode ended. She never came back, or not in any obvious manner, and no one ever knew what it was she had wanted of us.

Another time, lions combined their investigation of newcomers with unexplained roaring. The event took place on the second night my mother and I, along with some of the Ju/wasi, spent camped at Tsho//ana, a Kavango cattle post by a ravine about fifty miles north of /Gautscha. Up the ravine and into our camp came a great group of lions, and they began to roar in unison. Some began to roar as others ended, so that no gaps appeared in the appalling sound. Again the earth shook and the tent rattled. Noise so loud literally robs the breath and stuns the senses. We were paralyzed. At last, as suddenly as the noise began, it stopped. Then came a long silence, more terrifying than the roaring. The lions must have been listening, surely to learn the effects of their aggressive bellows. I held my breath and tried to keep my jaws apart so the lions wouldn't hear my teeth chattering. The lions apparently heard nothing and began to roar again.

As frightened as I was, I couldn't help pointing my flashlight's quavering beam around in the hope of sighting some of the lions. But they were right behind the tent, where I couldn't see them. Instead, out of the night, out of the deafening, thundering din, came one of the Ju/wa men. He had been on the far side of the ravine when the roaring began and, armed only with his little spear, he had crossed the ravine to be with his wife and children. Walking silently on bare feet, he had actually woven his way among the roaring lions in the dark.

Roger Caras

ANIMALS IN THEIR PLACES

Kodiak Island, all 3,465 square miles of it, huddles in the northern sector of the great Alaskan Bay like an enormous amoeba waiting to envelop the smaller islands of the archipelago that bears this island's name. Cut off from the Arctic Ocean by the Alaskan Peninsula, Kodiak Island is under the comparatively mild spell of temperate southeastern Alaska rather than in the harsher grasp of the land of Eskimos and polar bears.

One hundred and three miles long, fifty-seven miles wide, rain-drenched for much of the year, the Island is situated between 56° 40' and 58° north latitude, 152° and 155° west longitude. High in the east and covered with conifer and hardwood forests of Sitka spruce and cottonwoods, the Island decends over four thousand feet toward the tundrous west with its uniform cover of muskeg grass. Here only scattered clumps of alders break the monotony.

It is a wild land. Although long settled it has never been tamed. The city of Kodiak, huddling in the northeast part of the Island, is the sixth largest settlement in Alaska and dates from 1794, when it was the capital of Russian America. Yet only a few miles away it is possible for even an experienced woodsman to get hopelessly lost in a tangle of land that rises and falls like a stormy sea.

This blue-gray land, serenaded by a chorus of gulls a million strong, has over a thousand miles of coastline that resembles, often enough, Norway's fjord-indented shores. The treacherous Shelikof Strait to the north separates the Island from the great land mass of the Alaskan Peninsula by thirty miles. A graveyard for unwary sailors, these waters and those along the Island's other shores roll inward in high, fast tides that swallow the rocky beaches and seaweed flats in greedy gulps. Kodiak Island's granite, slate and even sandstone have so far withstood the sea's intrusion. It owes its shape and the long shadows of its ragged hills to the carving power of prehistoric sheets of glacial ice.

A history measured in millions of years, with the intermingling influences of sea and quake, glacier and wind, makes it hard to tell how a given feature of the land was formed. It may have once been two islands, for the largest fjord to slash her coast, Uyak or Windy Bay, west of the Island's middle in the north, cuts forty miles inland and all but meets Deadman Bay in the south.

Kodiak Island shows many scars, only the least of which were made by man. The quarries that had been cut into her hills, the roads on their sides and the light cosmetic touches to her natural bays are of little account. More momentous things have shaped this land. From June 6 to June 8 in 1912, Mount Novarupta on the Alaskan Peninsula to the north showered millions of tons of raw volcanic ash on Kodiak Island, in many places to a depth of twelve or more inches. All the changes wrought by all the men who have ever stepped ashore on this island are as nothing compared with the force let loose upon it in those few hours.

When the winds are high, and they often are, and when the sea is angry with the land, rain does not simply fall on Kodiak

Island; it is hurled against this intruder in the sea like shrapnel. Fog banks engulf her like living things. This island is like a ship at sea, and often she sails uneasily through unaccountable weather fronts. There are days, though, when the land sails out of the mists and drifts on calm and sunlit waters. On such days men know why they have come to this place.

Such a land as this, raw one moment and steaming the next, provides a garden in which giants can grow.

———————

The female bear eased slowly into the clearing on the south side of the hill. She was seven years old and had attained her maximum growth. Her head and body together were over seven feet long and when she stood square on her pillar-thick legs she was over four feet at the shoulders. She weighed about seven hundred pounds. Since it was still mid-May her lustrous golden bronze coat was prime. Only a few—perhaps 5 or 6 percent—of the bears on the Island had coats of this color. In another six weeks she would be ragged from the shedding and rubbing that would continue through August. Still fresh from her winter's rest, however, her fur was thick and lush.

Her humped shoulders distinctive as she stood, she rotated her head on her short, muscular neck, her nose pointing straight up. Her small, close-set eyes could tell her little, but her keen ears and sensitive nose would report most of what she had to know. The unrelenting demands of survival had sorted these things out over thousands of centuries of evolution.

Her ears, small, round and erect, set far apart on her broad skull, twitched as a downy woodpecker chinked metallically in a tree nearby. Her lips rolled back and she woofed hoarsely. Her somewhat pointed jaws, loosely articulated for grinding vegetation, moved easily and she stooped to graze on some meadow barley, then shuffled forward to where the favored bluejoint grew. These preferred grazing plants and others as well, beach rye, the sedges, nettle and seacoast angelica, had brought the sow down from the mountains for the first phase of her spring feast.

She stopped often to listen, for she was seeking more than food. The preceding summer she had had cubs of a previous mating still with her and their sucking stimulus had inhibited ovulation. Free now, and alone once again, her seasonal estrus had begun. Descending ova were ready for fertilization and the sow's behavior would be dictated by the compelling instinct to mate again. Nature, intent on the propagation of her wonders, arranged such matters carefully.

Abruptly the sow stopped grazing, raised her head, sniffed, woofed softly, then bawled. Her call ended in a whine that mixed intricately with a loud chopping of her jaws. Although she could not pick out his shape she knew a boar stood back among the trees examining those of her secrets that could be wind-borne. The mating play had begun and would not be concluded until nature had assured herself of another generation of brown bear cubs. These two giants had survived many dangers and difficulties; the price of their survival was more of their kind.

The female stood in the middle of the clearing, woofing hoarsely and occasionally whining. The male moved toward her cautiously. He had been following her for hours. His nose told him she was in heat and ready to break her solitude. Still, instinctively, he knew that if he was wrong and if this was a sow with cubs, he could expect an explosive reaction to his approach. Males are often cannibalistic toward cubs, their own as well as those of other boars, and females can be quick and savage in defense of their offspring.

The big chocolate bear, more typical of brown bear color than the bronze sow, tested the wind continuously as he shuffled toward his prospective mate. If she was the sow who had laid down the tantalizing trail, her standing fast in the clearing was a good sign. If she was a different animal, it was a dangerous situation, because it meant she had decided to fight. Few females will stand up to a boar, but those that do have the advantage of a determination more fierce than a male's hunger for cub flesh.

Satisfied at last that this was the sow he had been following, having sorted her out from the scents of other bears that had passed through the clearing earlier in the day, he quickened his gait.

As they came together they woofed and rubbed noses in a gesture surprisingly gentle for such formidable animals. In a few minutes they were feeding side by side in a most sociable manner. In fact, only on this occasion would either of them seek out or even tolerate the company of another mature bear. Between matings they lived solitary and short-tempered existences.

There was no breeding that day or the next, the time being spent in companionable foraging. Late the following afternoon, however, the male began to exhibit more precise interest in the sow and she was obliged on several occasions to plunk her ample bottom down hard to stop the rude intrusions of his nose. He was becoming more persistent. She was slow to respond but the critical business which they were about had softened their dispositions and there was no brawling. That would come later.

On their second night together the pair did not bed down apart as they had done the night before. There was a growing intimacy and as they lay close in the dark on the side of the hill they nibbled at each other's lips and occasionally slapped each other with ponderous paws. Their dark brown claws, recurved, strong and ever available, had grown long during the winter denning and were not yet worn down. They were not brought into play, though, and the slapping was good-natured with broad, plantigrade feet. Paws that could smash small trees with a single blow were used for caressing, and so the night passed.

There seemed to be an understanding reached during the playful hours of the second night. On the morning of their third day the sow submitted easily as the great boar covered her. The surrounding woods echoed with the wonderful range of their voices. They came apart after a few minutes and began to feed on tender spring plants almost immediately. Later that afternoon, when the boar covered her with his great bulk a second time, they remained locked together for nearly an hour. Erectile nodes blocked the vagina and kept the precious sperm from being lost.

During the days that followed they copulated several times more. When the sow showed signs of wanting to break loose, the male would plant his paws in front of her hips with his head lying along her neck. Her wriggling was to no avail and only when she began to whip her head back and forth and make violent chomping sounds with her jaws, only when he could sense her mounting anger, would he release her. By the end of the first week, she was far less tolerant of the male's insistent appetite.

Early in the second week the female watched with marked indifference as the boar, an experienced warrior of eleven breeding seasons, chased a smaller male away after giving him a vicious beating. The pair had been feeding apart for several hours each day since the end of the first week and the young male had approached the bronze sow as she grazed alone on an easy slope. The sudden appearance of the older boar on a ridge above startled the less experienced male, who was soon routed. The hunter who was to take the smaller boar's life the following year would wonder how he came to be missing an ear.

The big male returned to the female's side to find no recognition of his valiant deeds. Whether to reprimand her, or just because the fray had shortened his temper, the boar cuffed his mate rather too violently and she ran off and sat down among some nearby trees to sulk. It was two days before he saw her again. When they met she allowed him to mount her for the last time. During the ensuing ten days they met often, fed together for hours on end, and even bedded down close to each other on several occasions, but their sexual interest in each other had all but evaporated. At any time now their innate need for solitude would repossess them and they would drift apart permanently.

In the middle of the fourth week they met for a brief hour of feeding, but that part of them that demanded solitude had gained dominance over their sexual pattern, and they dissolved their union without ceremony.

The next morning found the sow moving in a westerly direction. Two fertilized eggs inside her uterus had already started to develop but would undergo a dormant stage before becoming implanted. Although the month was June it would not be until December that the embryos, potentially great beasts that could weigh almost three quarters of a ton, would be three quarters of an inch long. Since nature had ordained that all bear cubs around the world be born during the last week in January or the first week in February, the delay in development was essential to the schedule.

Alone, now, and hostile to all other bears, cubs and adults alike, the sow moved off and began feeding in earnest. The year was 1950 but it could have been any one of the four and a half million that have passed since the Pleistocene, when the species emerged. Its origin is traceable to a time twenty million years ago when *Hemicyon,* part dog, part bear, stalked lesser Miocene fauna. The more direct ancestor of the species was *Uasavus,* a wolf-sized bear of Europe as it was fifteen million years ago. A few million years later, in the Pliocene era, *Ursus arctos,* the European brown bear, was on the scene and from it descended all the brown bears and grizzlies whose ranges circle the globe in the Northern Hemisphere. When man was still only a vague potential in an ape's loins, the basis of the bear's mating ritual was already millions of years old. The precision of its formula stems from that antiquity. Although the bear is an intelligent and adaptable creature, in matters as critical as this neither of these two qualities is required. Nature does not trust such basics to choice. In mating the bear is guided by instinct; its behavior is rigidly controlled.

There was no specific plan to the sow's general movement toward the west and south. She had moved down into the valley from her winter denning site, mated, and was now continuing her wandering without conscious concern for her goal. She was biding her time before the start of the salmon run that would take her to certain streams in the area. Spring was passing into summer with its inevitable battle of white versus green and brown. White would lose and retreat to the highest hills in the east and north. The blue lupine, the white windflower, ragwort, four species of orchids, yellow violets, blue irises, flowers shaped like bells and others like stars, flowers sweet and some with poisonous roots, grew in wild profusion. Color was creeping back into the land and overhead the activities of the birds became frenetic.

Without regard for the havoc she created, the sow wandered from larder to larder. Birds challenged her whenever she passed a nest or brushed against a favored tree. Year-round residents, the magpie, black-capped chickadee, the varied thrush and the crossbill, cocked their heads and worried about her size. Summer visitors, violet-green swallows, the hermit thrush, pine grosbeaks, redpolls, and dozens more that had been goaded into their perilous journey to the Island by a fury and drive they could not understand, discussed her ever move. As she moved by day, slept by night, she was abused and cursed by a shrill chorus of countless voices. Several times she was mobbed by a mass of swallows who flew at her in a steady stream. Bewildered and frustrated by their dive-bombing tactics, she shuffled off in sullen dignity.

East of Deadman Bay the sow reached the coast. She argued with some raucous gulls and took possession of the carcass of a Pribilof fur seal. An old warrior of many seasons, the bull had sickened at sea and wandered too far to the east. Infested with hookworm and doomed to die, he had crawled ashore and remained half alive while a dozen tides came and went, first washing over him and then leaving him wedged between sea-battered rocks. The gulls had started to feed on him before he was dead. His eyes were taken first. He had lost both the will and the strength to resist, yet the power of life within him was too strong to allow an easy surrender. The natural order of things began drawing his chemistry back into the cauldron while he still lived.

The sow drove the gulls away and began to feed after ending the seal's misery with a single blow of her great paw. That night she bedded down in a clump of trees at the head of the cove and reclaimed the carcass the following morning. A hundred gulls moved among the rocks nearby and hovered overhead, maintaining their lament. Her indifference seemed to anger them further. Beyond the tide pools more gulls floated on the momentarily gentle swells, blue, gray and white corks, animated and shrill. A pair of bald eagles perched like sentinels on a nearby tree. Despite their aloof and perhaps noble appearance they hungered for carrion no less than the other birds.

As summer approached, the sea birds along the coast increased in numbers and variety. Summer visitors, the common snipe, rock sandpiper, mew gull, black-legged kittiwake and Arctic tern, added their endless movement and noise to those of the permanent shore residents, the glaucous-winged and herring gulls. The magnificent golden eagle, a summer visitor only, appeared and matched aerobatics with the bald eagle who was king year-round. Loons, grebes, albatrosses, shearwaters, petrels, and cormorants, geese, ducks, whistling swans, sandhill cranes, murrelets, puffins, scoters, oystercatchers, some resident, some purposefully present, some transient, and others accidental, appeared by the thousands and turned the great Island into a vast aviary. Short-tailed weasels and red foxes worked their way along ledges and into brush piles to harry the ground nesters, and destroyed thousands of eggs and fledglings. The Island feasted on its own abundance. A billion times a billion food chains took microscopic form in the soil and the sea. On land the great bear was the largest creature and in the sea it was the whale, but each depended, ultimately, on animals too small to be seen by the naked eye to supply the chemicals upon which the whole complex scheme of life was based. . . .

The world of change into which the cubs emerged was already far advanced. Cubs of previous seasons, the yearlings, sows that had not bred the summer before, and the unpredictable males were about. The influx of bird life and the offshore flow of marine mammals heading for the newly liberated Arctic Ocean pastures were in progress. Rain was a daily and sometimes hourly occurrence and the ground underfoot was mushy. Spring was unmistakable on all sides and summer was on the way. Her advance scouts were everywhere.

Shortly after leaving the cave, ahead of her cubs and extremely alert to the possible appearance of a mature bear, the sow began to eat cathartic grasses and herbs and quickly voided the black, resinous plug that had blocked her intestinal passage. Her feet were tender from the long period of inactivity and she limped slightly. During the first days she stayed close to her den, eating what she could find on the higher slope. Not at all unlike a cow, she would take a mouthful of grass and crop it by a slightly abrupt lift of her head. She was still fat but would lose weight rapidly during the first two weeks. Following that she would again begin to lay on fat against the needs of her coming sleep.

This concentration on food is typical of bears. The demands increase as spring progresses into summer and the sow, never a fastidious eater, took whatever she could find. While she might consume surprisingly little for so large an animal at any one feeding, her meals were so frequent as to be almost continuous. The total volume of food consumed was larger than might be suspected by the casual observer.

Seeking the tender pooshka, or wild parsnip, the sow would grasp a mouthful of vegetation and plant her front paws firmly on the ground. With a convulsive movement she would thrust backward with her body until a clump of sod tore loose. Turning it over with her paw she freed the roots, up to a half inch or more in diameter, and slowly ate them. In her quest for these tender morsels, and for grubs and beetles as well, she turned over whole areas of the hillside until it looked as if it had been plowed by a drunken farmer. Food-getting for a bear is more a matter of drudgery than of reliance on keen senses. Having given the bear a varied appetite, having delivered it from the agony other predators know when game is short, nature has either taken back or denied altogether the razor-edge alertness that wolves, weasels, and cats must have to survive.

At regular intervals the sow returned to her cubs, for their feeding demands were no less insistent than hers. Unlike their mother, however, they could accomplish nothing on their own.

Often, as she worked the fields close to the mouth of the cave, she would leave her cubs at its entrance, but she was never out of range and she constantly tested the wind for signs of danger. When she came to them they whined eagerly and climbed over each other to get at her. She would sometimes lie on her side and watch them feed, making the softest of satisfied sounds. At other times she would lie on her back and move her hind legs rhythmically as they tugged and gorged. And at yet other times she would sit square on her bottom with her back against a tree or mound and place a paw on the back of each cub. With her hind legs thrust out in front like a comical old woman she would point her nose straight up and slowly rotate her head as if to exercise a stiff neck. The cubs thrust hard with their hind feet and shuddered with satisfaction at what she gave them. Always she was tender, always alert. Her life was divided between feeding herself, and through herself her cubs, and worrying about their safety. There seemed to be no other forces, no other concerns.

The cubs grew daily. Their emergence weight of fifteen pounds would have to increase to a hundred pounds or more by mid-autumn. By the late fall of their second year they would weigh as much as four hundred pounds. A difference in weight between them would not occur until about their fourth year. For the moment, there was little to distinguish between the two. They were liver-gray in color but it was impossible to predict the tones they would finally achieve. The genes they inherited from their parents had been too confused over the preceding generations by the influx of brown bear color variation to take a predictable form. Since no survival factor had existed in any one tone before man arrived there was no particular trend. Before nature can make that miraculous adjustment man will almost certainly see to it that the bear is extinct.

As the cubs' size and strength grew and as their coordination improved the sow increased the length and duration of her excursions. Calling to them and constantly bolstering their confidence with the sounds she made, she took them further and further away from the cave. At last she began keeping them away for days and nights at a time, always bedding down before dark in the deepest cover she could find. Their demands on her never faltered and their treks were often interrupted for a feeding session. The further they moved away from their den site the more alert she became. She seldom relaxed for more than a few minutes at a time.

One afternoon as the family was edging down through a clearing between two rings of stunted alders that girded a hill, the sow stopped short and rose to her hind legs. The movement was smooth and effortless. Straining against the inadequacy of her vision she moved her head from side to side. The cubs came tumbling up against her legs and began to frolic. She issued three rapid, harsh commands and in a comic imitation of their mother they attempted to rise up to see what had caught her attention. The longer she held the position the more nervous the cubs became. They sank to all fours and moved in close against her legs. The female cub began to whine and again the sow grunted peremptorily. She was listening to the winds and sampling their chemistry. She sensed another bear in the vicinity—and it was close by.

On the lower portion of the slope, another sow stood among the alders and stared myopically up to where the bronze female towered. Victim of a natural freak, this bear had *four* cubs huddled by her legs. This extremely rare occurrence does happen from time to time and the sows involved are generally all but overwhelmed by the ordeal. With so much more to do, with so much more to worry about, their whole attitude is one of profound bewilderment.

A small current of moving air that had begun at sea and picked its way across seaweed-covered rocks, through patches of brush and trees, was working up the slope. The energy behind it was reinforced by other currents from over the surface of the water and it flowed and rippled across the clearing. It passed the sow in the alders, snatched away her secret and eddied past the female on the slope peering down, alert but uninformed. Instantly, the bronze sow located the intruder in the valley. Her sudden head movement and grunt caused the stranger to move, and to shift her position ever so slightly. The bronze sow was able to detect the movement and determine her shadowy outline. She gave a sharp bark and lumbered two steps forward on her hind legs before dropping to all fours, facing downhill. Her cubs were already on their way up to the ridge. They bawled in terror as they ran.

With front legs stiff, each step jarring her great frame, the sow hurried down the slope.

In the alder growth the other female, too, had gone to all fours and, determining that her cubs were well concealed, started out into the open.

The two sows faced each other over a distance of a couple

of dozen yards and circled slowly until they were on the same level. In a kind of displacement activity, as if to relieve the unbearable tension that had been mounting, the intruder stopped and pulled free a mouthful of grass. Jerking her head up she quartered away and stood with her head turned to the side, looking in the direction of her opponent with the grass drooping comically from the corner of her mouth. In an imitative movement the bronze sow did the same.

Then, without warning, after having given it all the thought of which she was capable, the bronze sow charged. She hurtled across the intervening yards and caught the intruder in the shoulder as she turned and half rose to bring her great forepaws into play. They slapped ineffectually as she was rolled over twice by the weight of the impact. Her reflexes had been a beat too slow and the blood flowed from an open wound where the sow had sunk her teeth.

The momentum of her charge carried the bronze sow well beyond her target and when she pulled up and whirled about to charge again she was struck by the intruder barreling down on top of her. She felt a terrible, stunning shock as a paw as large as a platter with powerful claws spread wide and angry descended with the full force of half a ton behind it. One of the bronze sow's cheeks was opened and her teeth showed through the wound. Again she charged, snapping furiously, but the intruder had already begun to retreat. She caught up with the darker female and managed to sink her teeth into her rump before she vanished into the brush. The crashing of her great body sounded as if a truck were hurtling through the growth.

The sow patrolled the edge of trees, coughing and grunting. She didn't dare enter the thicket with an opponent so aroused and with the benefit of cover. The air currents between the trees could not be trusted and her eyesight would be all but useless.

The bronze sow's two cubs and the intruder's four had witnessed the battle huddled in two groups a hundred yards

apart. They would have played together had they been al-
lowed, for they were still endowed with a social sense that
enabled them to tolerate their littermates. They would lose it
in time, though, and were learning the lesson of distrust that
would stay with them as long as they lived.

Both females bedded down almost immediately after re-
turning to their cubs. They were no more than a hundred and
fifty yards apart in the two groups of alders that bounded the
small clearing. Throughout the night they both remained
awake, sniffing, listening for the sound of any movement. On
several occasions each moved to the edge of the trees and
stood facing each other, although neither could know for sure
the other was there.

On the following morning the sows again spotted each
other. They did not clash, although some short charges were
made by each as gestures of threat. They drifted apart after a
few minutes and did not see each other again for several
hours, when once again they came within sensing distance of
each other. Several defiant movements were made, but again
there was no direct conflict.

On the morning of the third day, shortly after feeding her
cubs their first meal of the morning, the bronze sow moved
down to the edge of the trees. There, not more than a dozen
feet away, the intruder grazed with her four cubs strung out
behind her. The wind was blowing again from the sea and
the scent and sound of the intruder carried clearly and unmis-
takably. The sow sank back on her haunches and sorted out
the messages. With a wild roar, almost a scream, she burst
from her cover. The four cubs scattered but one was too slow.
Snatching it up in her great jaws she ended its life with a
single snapping action, dropped its small body and spun again
to re-enter the woods where her own cubs were wailing.

Whether or not it was immediately clear to the intruder that
she had lost her smallest cub we cannot know. Her remaining
three were running and tumbling down the slope in abject
terror. The charge of the great bronze sow out of the brush

so close at hand came with stunning impact. Only their training enabled them to break away from the paralyzing effect of the attack and get away at all.

The intruder spun around, perhaps seeing the body of her cub lying limp and oozing blood, and crashed into the brush after her opponent. Roaring, wailing, grunting, and chopping her jaws, she smashed down brush and with a gesture of wild defiance clubbed a sapling an inch and a half thick to the ground with one sweep of her forepaw. Rising to her full height, her jaws still chopping in anger, the great sow circled slowly, worrying everything in her way. In her passage she destroyed the nests of three ground-nesting birds. The yellow yolks from a dozen shattered shells seeped out and the parent birds circled overhead, bemoaning their loss. Diminutive mammals of several species fled before the onslaught and a mouse nest toppled, spilling its pink inhabitants to the ground. When the sow had passed a weasel emerged and took the little bodies before the female mouse could find them.

The furious charge of the intruder into the brush was to no avail. While she beat her way through the bushes and between the trees the bronze sow and her cubs had vanished over the ridge above and were close to a mile away when the intruder emerged grunting and coughing on the downslope side to sit wailing beside her dead cub. She left the valley that day and never returned.

As if her cruelly violent deed had reminded her of the danger that surrounded her own two cubs, the sow was unusually alert in the days that followed. She was even short-tempered with her charges and their obedience had to be ever more unquestioning to satisfy her. She cuffed them often and bit one on the flank hard enough to make it whimper for several minutes. Thoroughly cowed, it returned to her to be fed and found her forgiving.

Five

FELLOW CREATURES

Walt Whitman

Song of Myself

I think I could turn and live with animals, they are so
    placid and self-contain'd,
I stand and look at them long and long.
They do not sweat and whine about their condition,
They do not lie awake in the dark and weep for their
    sins,
They do not make me sick discussing their duty to God
Not one is dissatisfied, not one is demented with the
    mania of owning things,
Not one kneels to another, nor to his kind that lived
    thousands of years ago,
Not one is respectable or industrious over the whole
    earth.

Fred Bodsworth

LAST OF THE CURLEWS

The curlew held to a course that was almost due south. When the tumbling Labrador hills dropped from sight behind, the last orienting landmark was lost, but the curlew led the flock unerringly on. Somewhere in the cosmic interplay of forces generated by the earth's rotation and magnetic field was a guide to direction to which hidden facets of his brain were delicately tuned. He held direction effortlessly, without conscious effort. An unthinking instinct, millenniums old, was performing subconsciously a feat beyond the ken of the highest consciousness in the animal world.

The night was but yet half spent when white surf outlined the craggy coastline of Nova Scotia's Cape Breton half a mile below. On some other years the curlew had stopped here, but the season was late and there was no thought of stopping now. It had taken five hours to cross the Gulf of St. Lawrence and the flock pushed now without pause across the tip of Cape Breton to the 2,500-mile misty maw of the Atlantic beyond.

The curlew dropped back for rest to an easier flight spot in the body of the flock and stayed there an hour while one of the plovers led. Then a cold front of air, moving eastward off the Canadian mainland, enveloped them in an area of turbulent air currents and the curlew moved forward to the lead again. The warm lower layers of air were being lifted by the heavier cold air pushing beneath. In the colder temperature of higher altitudes, the warm air's moisture began condensing, first into misty rain then, as its temperature dropped, it became snow.

Erratic air currents buffeted the flock and the formation broke up. The snow, light and sparse at first, became thicker. The flakes grew into large, loose, damp clusters that caked into the birds' wing feathers and made flight difficult. The curlew, reacting instinctively, led the flock upward in a steep spiraling climb. The air turbulence decreased as they climbed, but the snow clouds grew denser. The quieter air permitted them to line up in formation again, but they had to form ranks more by the feel of the wingtip air whorls than by sight, for now the snow was so thick that frequently even the bird next ahead was hidden. They stopped climbing and leveled off again.

There was no way of detecting how fast the cold front was moving eastward, but the curlew knew—partly from half-remembered experiences of previous migrations, but mostly by an instinctive intuition—that their 50-mile-an-hour flight speed would take them back through the front and keep them ahead of it, because the storm's front would be moving at a speed slower than theirs. But they would have to turn and fly with the storm, and that was eastward toward mid-Atlantic.

The curlew veered eastward and the double rank of plovers behind followed his deflecting air trail, though only the front few birds had been able to see the curlew turn. The snow clung to their wings, packed into the air slots between the flight feathers. Wings that a few minutes before had responded deftly to the gentle, rhythmic flexing of the breast muscles were now heavy and stiff, and they beat the air futilely like lifeless paddles, driving air downward in a waste of energy instead of deflecting it rearward for the horizontal airflow essential to flight. Their flight speed dropped until they were hovering almost motionless in a disorganized, bewildered cluster, now almost a mile above the sea. Then the curlew led them eastward again by angling slowly downward and drawing from gravitational pull the flight speed that their soggy wing feathers could no longer produce unaided. Now their flight speed was normal once more, but they were sacrificing altitude rapidly to maintain it. Up from the grey void below, the sea was rising steadily toward them.

The curlew led them on a long gradual, seaward incline, adjusting the downward flight angle to the pressure of the airflow on its sensitized wings so that normal speed was maintained with the minimum of altitude loss that would accomplish it. Occasionally the snow thinned and for brief intervals almost level flight was possible. Then it thickened again and their wings grew heavy and the curlew would have to angle sharply downward.

Behind them, but cut off probably by several flight-hours of impenetrable snow, were the coastlines of Nova Scotia and New England. Ahead, perhaps only minutes, was the storm front with warmer undisturbed air before it. But even if the storm front were overtaken and passed there was only a limitless Atlantic beyond into which they would have to keep flying to stay ahead of the snow clouds now pressing them implacably towards the wavecrests below. All this the curlew knew, not from any process of reasoning but via the same nebulous channels of instinct which told him too that somewhere a mate of his own species was waiting for another breeding time to green the tundra lichens again.

Even the curlew's thick breast muscles and wing tendons, stronger by far than those of the smaller plovers he led, were aching and burning now from the abnormal energy output demanded to overcome the effect of the crusting snow on their wings. Their downward flight course took them into the lower layers of turbulent, bumpy air once more. The flock was thrown out of formation again. They clung together by calling sharply and constantly to each other. Each bird was alone in a gusty white world of its own, unseen and unseeing, but the quavering chatter of flight notes was a nexus that held them together.

For a long time the blind, numbing flight continued and the curlew fought to maintain height until not only his breast muscles but every fibre of his body throbbed with agonizing fatigue. To the lisping murmur of flight notes from the plovers behind there was soon added a sibilant hissing that came from below. The hissing grew stronger. It was the sound of snow striking water.

Then through the white curtain the curlew could see it. Waves with silvery caps curling upward appeared first ahead of the flock, paused momentarily below as they were overtaken, then disappeared behind. The snow had cleared slightly and now the plovers became visible again strung out haphazardly to the curlew's rear. The hindmost, weaker birds were lover, closer to the sea. They had had to sacrifice altitude faster to keep up with the stronger flyers ahead. Glutinous snow clung to their wingtips, the melting rate from body heat barely equalling the rate at which new snow accumulated.

The curlew would hold a level plane of flight for several seconds, then as forward speed decreased he would have to dip downward, gain new speed and level off again. The sea was clearly visible now, the white wave crests etched sharply against the black water. At times a higher crest leaped upward to within a few feet of the struggling birds.

A great wave appeared ahead. The curlew fought the lethargy in his wings and lifted over it painfully to drop into the trough beyond. He struggled on. The next crest was lower and curlew mounted it with several feet to spare. Behind him, the great wave lunged into the plover flock. Three of the lower birds fought for height but could do no more than hover helplessly. There was no cry. The wave arched upward momentarily and the birds disappeared from sight. The wave passed and the three plovers didn't re-appear.

Nature, highly selective in all things, is most selective with death. The weak neither ask nor obtain mercy.

The flock slogged on, a few feet above the sea, struggling laboriously over each crest and snatching a few niggardly seconds of partial rest in the quieter, protected air of each trough. Once a long trough lifted into a seething comber many feet higher than those preceding and the spray of its crest lashed the curlew's wings. The curlew had to battle a maelstrom of air currents for several seconds to keep airborne. When the wave passed two more of the plovers failed to re-appear. But the spray melted much of the snow clinging to the curlew's wingtip feathers. For a minute his unburdened wings could bite into the air with all their old power. Then the snow clogged them again. Only the knowledge that somewhere close ahead the cold front terminated kept the curlew plunging on.

The air grew warmer very gradually, so slowly it was difficult to detect the change. But the snow altered to rain abruptly. At one wave crest there was only the swirling white wall of snow ahead, by the next crest the snow was behind and sheets of rain pelted them. The snow melted from their feathers in a few seconds and the curlew led the remnant of his flock upward in a sharp climb. The pain and fatigue drained quickly from their wings and breasts with the resumption of normal flight. The sea disappeared again in the darkness beneath them. After several minutes they broke through the rain front into a quiet mist-roofed world beyond. . . .

———

Now it was corn-planting time on the Nebraska and Dakota prairies and great steel monsters that roared like the ocean surf were crossing and recrossing the stubble fields leaving black furrows of fresh-turned soil in orderly ranks behind them. Most of the shorebirds shunned the growling machines and the men who were always riding them. Yellowlegs and sandpipers would stop their feeding and watch warily when the plowman was still hundreds of yards off, then if the great machine came closer they would take wing, whistling shrilly, and not alight again until they were a mile away. But the Eskimo curlews had little fear. Far back in the species' evolutionary history they had learned that, for them, a highly developed fear was unnecessary. Their wings were strong and their flight so rapid that they could ignore danger until the last moment, escaping fox or hawk easily in a last-second flight. So their fear sense had disappeared, as all unused faculties must, and while other shorebirds relied on wariness and timidity for survival, the Eskimo curlew relied entirely on its strength of wing.

The curlews followed the roaring machines closely, for the white grubs and cutworms that the plows turned up were a rich and abundant food.

All the time their reproductive glands had been swelling in the annual springtime rhythm of development, the development keeping pace with the northward march of spring, so that their bodies and the tundra would become ready simultaneously for the nesting and egg-laying. As the physical development came close to the zenith of its cycle, there was an intensification of emotional development too. With high body temperatures and rapid metabolism, every process of living is faster and more intense in birds than any other creature. When the breeding time approaches they court and love with a fervor and passion that matches the intensity of all their other life processes.

Now many times a day the male curlew's mounting emotion boiled over into a frantic display of love. It had become a much more violent display than the earlier acts of courtship. First the male would spring suddenly into the air and hover on quivering wings while he sang the clear, rolling, mating song—a song much more liquid and mellow now than at any other time of year. After a few seconds his wings would beat violently and he would rise almost straight upward, his long legs trailing behind, until he was a couple of hundred feet above the prairie. There he would hover again, singing louder so that bursts of the song would reach the female, bobbing and whistling excitedly far below. Then he would close his wings and dive straight toward her, swerving upward again in the last few feet above her head and landing several yards away.

Panting with emotion, singing in loud bursts, his throat and breast inflated with air and the feathers thrust outward, he would hold his wings extended gracefully over his back until the female invited the climactic approach. She would bob quickly with quivering wings and call with the harsh, food-begging notes of a fledging bird. Then he would dash toward her, his wings beating vigorously again so that he was almost walking on air. Their swollen breasts would touch. The male's neck would reach past her own and he would tenderly preen her brown wing feathers with his long bill.

It would last only a few seconds, and the male would dash away again. He would pick up the largest grub he could find and return quickly to the female. Then he would place it gently into her bill. She would swallow it, her throat feathers would suddenly flatten, her wings stop quivering, and the love-making abruptly end. For as yet the courtship feeding was the love climax; their bodies were not yet ready for the final act of the mating.

For a couple of hours after each courtship demonstration the passion and tenseness of the approaching mating time would relax, for the love display was a stopgap that satisfied them emotionally while they awaited the time for the physical consummation.

They moved north steadily, a couple of hundred miles each night. The male's sexual development matured first and he was ready for the finalizing of the mating. His passion became a fierce, unconstrainable frenzy and he spent most of each day in violent display before the female. But with each courtship feeding her tenseness suddenly relaxed and the display would end.

It was mid-May and the newly-plowed sections of rolling, Canadian prairie steamed in the warming sun. They followed closely behind the big machine with the roar like an ocean surf. The grubs were fat and they twisted convulsively in the few seconds that the sun hit them before the curlews snapped them up. Now the snows of the tundra would be melting. In the ovaries of the female the first of her four developing eggs was ready for the life-giving fertilization.

The male flung himself into the air, his love song wild and vibrant. He hovered high above the black soil of the prairie with its fresh striated pattern of furrows. The roar of the big machine stopped and the curlew hardly noted the change, for his senses were focused on the female quivering excitedly against the dark earth far below. The man on the tractor sat stiffly, his head thrown back, staring upward, his eyes shaded against the sun with one hand. The curlew dove earthward and the female called him stridently. He plucked a grub from the ground and dashed at her, his neck outstretched, wings fluttering vigorously. He saw the man leap down from the tractor seat and run toward a fence where his jacket hung. Normally, at this, even the curlews would have taken wing in alarm, but now the female accepted the courtship feeding and her wings still quivered in a paroxysm of mating passion. She crouched submissively for the copulation and in the ecstasy of the mating they were blind to everything around them.

The thunder burst upon them out of a clear and vivid sky. The roar of it seemed to come from all directions at once. The soil around them was tossed upward in a score of tiny black splashes like water being pelted with hail.

The male flung himself into the air. He flew swiftly, clinging close to the ground so that no speed was lost in climbing for height. Then he saw the female wasn't with him. He circled back, *keering* out to her in alarm. Her brown body still crouched on the field where they had been. The male flew down and hovered a few feet above her, calling wildly.

Then the thunder burst a second time and a violent but invisible blow blasted two of the biggest feathers from one of his extended wings. The impact twisted him completely over in mid-air and he thudded into the earth at the female's side. Terrified and bewildered at a foe that could strike without visible form, he took wing again. Then the bewilderment overcame his terror and he circled back to his mate a second time. Now she was standing, *keering* also in wild panic. Her wings beat futilely several times before she could raise herself slowly into the air. She gained height and flight speed laboriously and the male moved in until he was close beside her.

He continued to call clamorously as he flew, but the female became silent. They flew several minutes and the field with terrifying sunlight thunder was left far behind. But the female flew slowly. She kept dropping behind and the male would circle back and urge her on with frantic pleas, then he would outdistance her again.

Her flight became slower and clumsy. One wing was beating awkwardly and it kept throwing her off balance. The soft buffy feathers of the breast under the wing were turning black and wet. She started calling to him again, not the loud calls of alarm but the soft, throaty *quirking* of the love display.

Then she dropped suddenly. Her wings kept fluttering weakly, it was similar to the excited quivering of the mating moment, and her body twisted over and over until it embedded itself in the damp earth below.

The male called wildly for her to follow. The terror of the ground had not yet left him. But the female didn't move. He circled and re-circled above and his plaintive cries must have reached her, but she didn't call back.

A long time later he overcame the fear and landed on the ground close to her. He preened her wing feathers softly with his bill. When the night came the lure of the tundra became a stubborn, compelling call, for the time of the nesting was almost upon them. He flew repeatedly, whistling back to her, then returning, but the female wouldn't fly with him. Finally he slept close beside her.

At dawn he hovered high in the grey sky, his lungs swelling with the cadence of his mating song. Now she didn't respond to the offer of courtship feeding. The tundra call was irresistible. He flew again and called once more. Then he leveled off, the rising sun glinted pinkly on his feathers, and he headed north in silence, alone.

THE snow-water ponds and the cobblestone bar and the dwarfed willows that stood beside the S-twist of the tundra river were unchanged. The curlew was tired from the long flight. But when a golden plover flew close to the territory's boundary he darted madly to the attack. The Arctic summer would be short. The territory must be held in readiness for the female his instinct told him soon would come.

Paul Gallico

THE SNOW GOOSE

One November afternoon, three years after Rhayader had come to the Great Marsh, a child approached the lighthouse studio by means of the sea wall. In her arms she carried a burden.

She was no more than twelve, slender, dirty, nervous and timid as a bird, but beneath the grime as eerily beautiful as a marsh faery. She was pure Saxon, large-boned, fair, with a head to which her body was yet to grow, and deep-set, violet-colored eyes.

She was desperately frightened of the ugly man she had come to see, for legend had already begun to gather about Rhayader, and the native wild-fowlers hated him for interfering with their sport.

But greater than her fear was the need of that which she bore. For locked in her child's heart was the knowledge, picked up somewhere in the swampland, that this ogre who lived in the lighthouse had magic that could heal injured things.

She had never seen Rhayader before and was close to fleeing

in panic at the dark apparition that appeared at the studio door, drawn by her footsteps—the black head and beard, the sinister hump, and the crooked claw.

She stood there staring, poised like a disturbed marsh bird for instant flight.

But his voice was deep and kind when he spoke to her.

"What is it, child?"

She stood her ground, and then edged timidly forward. The thing she carried in her arms was a large white bird, and it was quite still. There were stains of blood on its whiteness and on her kirtle where she had held it to her.

The girl placed it in his arms. "I found it, sir. It's hurted. Is it still alive?"

"Yes. Yes, I think so. Come in, child, come in."

Rhayader went inside, bearing the bird, which he placed upon a table, where it moved feebly. Curiosity overcame fear. The girl followed and found herself in a room warmed by a coal fire, shining with many colored pictures that covered the walls, and full of a strange but pleasant smell.

The bird fluttered. With his good hand Rhayader spread one of its immense white pinions. The end was beautifully tipped with black.

Rhayader looked and marveled, and said: "Child, where did you find it?"

"In t' marsh, sir, where fowlers had been. What—what is it, sir?"

"It's a snow goose from Canada. But how in all heaven came it here?"

The name seemed to mean nothing to the little girl. Her deep violet eyes, shining out of the dirt on her thin face, were fixed with concern on the injured bird.

She said: "Can 'ee heal it, sir?"

"Yes, yes," said Rhayader. "We will try. Come, you shall help me."

There were scissors and bandages and splints on a shelf,

and he was marvelously deft, even with the crooked claw that managed to hold things.

He said: "Ah, she has been shot, poor thing. Her leg is broken, and the wing tip, but not badly. See, we will clip her primaries, so that we can bandage it, but in the spring the feathers will grow and she will be able to fly again. We'll bandage it close to her body, so that she cannot move it until it has set, and then make a splint for the poor leg."

Her fears forgotten, the child watched, fascinated, as he worked, and all the more so because while he fixed a fine splint to the shattered leg he told her the most wonderful story.

The bird was a young one, no more than a year old. She was born in a northern land far, far across the seas, a land belonging to England. Flying to the south to escape the snow and ice and bitter cold, a great storm had seized her and whirled and buffeted her about. It was a truly terrible storm, stronger than her great wings, stronger than anything. For days and nights it held her in its grip and there was nothing she could do but fly before it. When finally it had blown itself out and her sure instincts took her south again, she was over a different land and surrounded by strange birds that she had never seen before. At last, exhausted by her ordeal, she had sunk to rest in a friendly green marsh, only to be met by the blast from the hunter's gun.

"A bitter reception for a visiting princess," concluded Rhayader. "We will call her *'La Princese Perdue,'* the Lost Princess. And in a few days she will be feeling much better. See?" He reached into his pocket and produced a handful of grain. The snow goose opened its round yellow eyes and nibbled at it.

The child laughed with delight, and then suddenly caught her breath with alarm as the full import of where she was pressed in upon her, and without a word she turned and fled out of the door.

"Wait, wait!" cried Rhayader, and went to the entrance, where he stopped so that it framed his dark bulk. The girl was already fleeing down the sea wall, but she paused at his voice and looked back.

"What is your name, child?"

"Frith."

"Eh?" said Rhayader. "Fritha, I suppose. Where do you live?"

"Wi' t' fisherfolk at Wickaeldroth." She gave the name the old Saxon pronunciation.

"Will you come back tomorrow, or the next day, to see how the Princess is getting along?"

She paused, and again Rhayader must have thought of the wild water birds caught motionless in that split second of alarm before they took to flight.

But her thin voice came back to him: "Ay!"

And then she was gone, with her fair hair streaming out behind her.

The snow goose mended rapidly and by midwinter was already limping about the enclosure with the wild pink-footed geese with which it associated, rather than the barnacles, and had learned to come to be fed at Rhayader's call. And the child, Fritha, or Frith, was a frequent visitor. She had overcome her fear of Rhayader. Her imagination was captured by the presence of this strange white princess from a land far over the sea, a land that was all pink, as she knew from the map that Rhayader showed her, and on which they traced the stormy path of the lost bird from its home in Canada to the Great Marsh of Essex.

Then one June morning a group of late pink-feet, fat and well fed from the winter at the lighthouse, answered the stronger call of the breeding-grounds and rose lazily, climbing into the sky in ever widening circles. With them, her white body and black-tipped pinions shining in the spring sun, was the snow goose. It so happened that Frith was at the lighthouse. Her cry brought Rhayader running from the studio.

"Look! Look! The Princess! Be she going away?"

Rhayader stared into the sky at the climbing specks. "Ay," he said, unconsciously dropping into her manner of speech. "The Princess is going home. Listen! She is bidding us farewell."

Out of the clear sky came the mournful barking of the pink-feet, and above it the higher, clearer note of the snow goose. The specks drifted northward, formed into a tiny v, diminished, and vanished.

With the departure of the snow goose ended the visits of Frith to the lighthouse. Rhayader learned all over again the meaning of the word "loneliness." That summer, out of his memory, he painted a picture of a slender, grime-covered child, her fair hair blown by a November storm, who bore in her arms a wounded white bird.

Christina Rossetti

TO WHAT PURPOSE THIS WASTE?

And other eyes than ours
Were made to look on flowers.
Eyes of small birds and insects small:
The deep sun-blushing rose
Round which the prickles close
Opens her bosom to them all.
The tiniest living thing
That soars on feathered wing,
Or crawls among the long grass out of sight
Has just as good a right
To its appointed portion of delight
As any King.

Alden Stevens

THE WAY OF A LION

In the African dusk that fades swiftly to night, a dense cloud of tiny birds wheeled with a fluttering roar of wings across the end of the shallow valley and disappeared over the hill.

The tumult of their passing was startling, but it did not disturb the great black-maned lion where he crouched tense in a clump of yellow grass. The dark mass of hair that covered his neck and shoulders stirred with the evening breeze. He lay there in the grass, massive head on outstretched paws. The dark round pupils of his eyes were large now as the darkness gathered. He stared intently up the little valley that lay like a shallow trough between its rounded hills.

Except for the call of a night bird all was quiet. It was not the quiet of peace, however. Perhaps the pose of the beast himself suggested a calm that precedes some storm of action. He waited for something. A ripple ran up the great tawny back, and the flat cords of muscle in his tremendous forelegs quivered and writhed with a contained excitement that pervaded the silent night.

This lion was larger than the average of his kind, weighing

near to five hundred pounds. Stretched flat as he now lay, he measured ten and a half feet from the tip of his broad muzzle to the black, hairy tuft at the end of his tail. Black hair grew low on his forehead, and over chest and shoulders. The barrel of chest curved sharply up into a lean belly. His color ranged from a deep brown along the spine, to a golden yellow. Six years old perhaps, no scar yet marred the smooth beauty of his skin. Muscle overlaid his bones in rippling bands of power. Within him was a swift intelligence and the capacity for lightning action. Here was a creature of beauty and grace, of menace and strength.

The chill wind that blew into the lion's flaring nostrils brought the scent of a little herd of zebra that fed—wary but unalarmed—up there in the darkness. Another message came on the night wind. The lion scented his mate. The familiar odor of her distant body told him that she was playing her part and that her snarling voice would soon shatter the peace of the night.

Just over the crest of one of the hills that bounded the valley, the lioness moved swiftly through the darkness. Her belly swayed as she trotted. From time to time she stopped and listened. At last she reached a point just opposite to where the zebra were feeding. She could see the black mass of them below, less than two hundred yards from where she crouched. Her amber eyes stared intently into the dark and the temptation was strong to charge in and try for a kill. But she knew that the chances were against her. Before she had covered half the distance, the zebra would be aware of her approach. There would be a snort of warning from the leader and then, with a thunder of hoofs, the whole band would be gone over the opposite ridge. The plan of the hunt would be ruined. She thought of her mate, remembering where he waited in the grass at the narrow entrance to the valley. Her powerful body relaxed and she trotted on along the hillside.

Perhaps a quarter of a mile beyond where the zebra fed, the big lioness turned sharply to the left and went down the hill into the valley. Now the feeding animals were between her and her lord. Head thrust forward, she swept down toward her unsuspecting prey. She was less than three hundred yards from the zebra when they became aware of her. There was a loud snort of alarm and warning from the leader, shrill whinnies of fright from the mares as they gathered their colts. Before the oncoming lioness, straight down the valley, the herd of zebra fled in drumming thunder. The wind with its smell of death was at their heels. Death was before them too, waiting there in the grass at the mouth of the valley.

The great black-maned lion tensed himself for the kill. He heard the oncoming beat of hundreds of hoofs. Now he could see them, the mad dark mass of them, rushing directly at him out of the night. Now the sharp smell of sweat, the dust of flying forms about him. Here a fat mare, anxious for the little yellow colt that labored at her heels. There's a fleeting stallion, the whistle of effort in his nostrils.

With a blaring snarl that shook the night air with its depth and ferocity, a giant form shot from the grass and loomed an instant over the fat mare. Steel-like claws closed over her straining face. Others gripped her just below the ears. There was a dexterous twist of mighty muscles, and the sharp report of her breaking neck was followed by a scream of utter agony. The zebra was dead even as she fell, and her colt stumbled over her, his long slender legs kicking in frantic fear. The little creature had just regained his feet when the lioness was upon him. Her fangs closed over the back of his neck and met in a crushing bite that severed spine and flesh.

The herd of zebra was gone. Somewhere on the open plain they would gather trembling, listening, their eyes straining into the night, their nostrils flaring wide to catch the scent of enemies. In the dark hour before dawn, they would feed again.

The big lion growled and the lioness answered him. Then he sniffed at her, their noses touching gently. She dropped on the grass as though tired, then rolled over lazily like a cat and lay extended. Her mate dropped his shaggy head, then raising it suddenly gave forth a tremendous blast of sound, a bellowing roar that filled all the world about. Then he dropped his head again, only to raise it once more as his roar shook the night. Jackals, yapping on the starlit plains, ceased their clamor and it seemed as though every creature within range of that mighty voice, cowered and listened. For a full minute after the last roar, the night hung empty and still as though suspended in the cold spaces among the stars.

There had been a growing radiance along the rim of low-lying mountains to the eastward, and now the edge of a lemon-yellow moon appeared, its rays lighting the scene where the lions surveyed their kill. Lazily, the female watched her mate as his mighty forearm swung the dead zebra into position for the work ahead of him. Holding the striped body in place, with one paw, the lion raked the tender belly in tearing sweeps, ripping through the skin and flesh until an opening appeared. Then, growling fiercely, he scooped again and again, his big paw thrusting into the still warm body until it was completely disemboweled. No human hunter, armed with a knife and spear, could have done it more expertly.

While her mate was engaged in this savage operation, the lioness had watched him, growling deep encouragement. Now she rose slowly to her feet, padded to the edge of a patch of thorny bush and began to dig, her claws tearing through sod and brown earth. The steady sweep of leg and paw soon produced a considerable hole and into it the two beasts tumbled the intestines of the zebra, scraping earth, leaves and grass over the mass until the depression was filled. Thus buried, the swiftly decomposing insides would not taint the air, and alert noses of scavenging hyenas and jackals would be less likely to scent the kill. Here was food for at least two meals, and the killers had no desire to share their meat with lesser beasts who would be lured to the scene by the seductive odor of corruption.

Paws pushing against the strain of clamping fangs, the lions began to feast. They tore first at the meaty insides of the hind legs. Occasionally their bloody muzzles would touch and the lioness would growl fiercely, slapping her mate in a lightning swift jab. Hind quarters reared high, massive head and chest bent low, he ate in noisy satisfaction. She, stretched flat on spreading belly, gripped the prey between razor-keen claws, thrusting her tusks into the tender meat as she fed.

The two had eaten for a very short time when the lioness raised her head and looked about her. Then she rose heavily to her feet. A shiver rippled the skin along the length of her tawny body. There was something of physical weariness in her action as she turned and, with low-hanging head, disappeared into the black shadows of the thorn scrub. The big male stopped his feeding for an instant and stared after her.

Threading her way slowly through the tangled bush, the lioness soon came into an open plain and crossed a flat expanse of short grass to the foot of a low rocky hill that rose abruptly from the land. It was shaped somewhat like a loaf of bread, broad and rounded at the top, several hundred yards wide across its base—perhaps half a mile long. A dim trail zig-zagged upward along the face of the hill, winding amid low growing bush and rocks. Up this faint path the lioness made her slow way. At a point close by a great boulder she stopped and looked out and downward, resting as she gazed.

The flat stare of her yellow eyes encompassed the scene completely; the way she had come, the rolling vastness of the plains, the dark distant line that was forest, the starry bowl of the African sky arching mightily over the silent wilderness. These things she saw, and comprehended them for what they were. But more insistently her gaze focused on the dark patch of bush at the mouth of the little valley. Down there her black-maned mate was snarling over the body of the zebra. Hunger assailed her and a slow clear drool dripped from her black lips, but a need as old and even more urgent than hunger was now upon her. She turned away, following the path that led sharply upward.

Where a tumbled mass of boulders rose beyond a narrow

ledge, a low opening showed black against the moonlit rocks. Without hesitation the lioness went into this case, her belly swaying and almost dragging the ground as she crouched slightly at the dark entrance.

The cave was deep and dry. Lying in a rocky hollow at the far end, the big sinewy body stretched wearily and a sound very like a deep groan came from her. A glaze of pain filmed the clear eyes. Within her the life she had been carrying for nine months struggled urgently for exit into the world. Her cubs were about to be born and she awaited them.

The moon had set and only the stars looked in at the three squirming cubs and the lioness. The cubs—born with eyes wide open—looked out and saw the stars, then huddled close to the warmth of the great furry body that sheltered them, sucking vigorously at the generous breasts of their mother. They drank until filled, then slept to awake and drink again. The lioness, relaxed and content, cleansed the cubs with her rough tongue, stretched out and slept.

Dian Fossey

Gorillas in the Mist

The first years of research at Karisoke were much like the tremendously rewarding first six months at Kabara because I was able to concentrate primarily on daily observations of the gorillas with few interruptions from the outside world. Countless days were spent tracking and observing—usually through binoculars—the shy and as yet unhabituated gorillas. Evenings were spent sitting on the cot in the tent typing up the day's notes on an improvised table made from a packing crate. Usually I was surrounded by dripping clothes hung from lines along the top of the tent as near to the warmth of the hissing kerosene lamp as I could safely arrange them.

I thought of the lamp as a friendly genie, particularly when stepping outside the tent into a bitterly cold, ink-black night. It was awesome to think of this as the only speck of light, other than perhaps occasional poacher fires, within the entire Virunga mountain range. When contemplating the vast expanse of uninhabited, rugged, mountainous land surrounding me and such a wealth of wilderness for my backyard, I considered myself one of the world's most fortunate people.

It was impossible to feel lonely. The night sounds of the elephants and buffalo, who had come to drink at nearby Camp Creek, combined with the squeaky door-screech choruses of the three hyrax (*Dendrohyrax arboreus*), encompassed me as part of the tranquillity of the nights. Those were magical times.

Some six hundred feet from mine was the tent for the three Rwandese assistants, who collected water and firewood and whom I eventually trained as gorilla trackers. Following the natural deaths of Lucy and Dezi, the chickens from Kabara, the crew presented a replacement couple, Walter and Wilma, who shared my tent for several months. Walter was no ordinary rooster. Every morning, much like a dog, he followed me into the field several hundred feet from camp. Every afternoon he would come running to meet me with greeting clucks. At night he roosted on the carriage of my typewriter, never fluttering a feather while being shuttled back and forth across the keyboard.

After a year and a half, the tent was beginning to bulge at the seams. Some European friends from the Rwandan towns of Ruhengeri and Gisenyi decided to build a small one-room cabin for me, complete with an oil-drum fireplace and windows. The thought of a cabin disturbed me at first, for it represented permanency at a time when I still bore the scars of my exodus from Kabara in Zaire. In spite of my lack of faith, the first Karisoke cabin became a reality in only three weeks of cooperative work on the part of all of us. A near-constant line of porters carried up ruler-straight eucalyptus saplings from the villages below to form the cabin's supporting framework. Tin sheeting (*mbati*) was brought from Ruhengeri for the exterior, and handwoven Rwandese grass mats served as insulation for the interior wall, roof, and floor surfaces. From Camp Creek, the four-foot-deep stream running through the meadow, rocks, gravel, and sand were collected to form a stout setting for the very functional oil-drum fireplace. The original crew members and I spent hours sanding and polishing broad planks for work tables and bookcases. We then made curtains from brilliantly colored local cloth for the finishing touches of the first real home I had had since leaving America. Eight additional cabins, each more elaborate than the ones preceding them, were to be constructed during the years that followed. None, however, came to mean as much to me as the first simple structure.

The cabin conveyed a new sense of security. I was finally convinced that I could welcome the company of a puppy needing a home. I named the two-and-a-half-month-old part-boxer female Cindy because of her habit of lying with her nose immersed in the cinders of the fireplace. In no time at all she became an integral part of camp life. (Indeed, two yeas later she would befriend Coco and Pucker, the gorilla orphans.) A great affection quickly developed between the staff and Cindy. She never lacked for human attention when I was out with the gorillas each day. The puppy spent hours playing with Walter, the rooster who thought he was a dog, a teasing pair of ravens, Charles and Yvonne, and even the elephants and buffalo that came to Camp Creek after dusk. Brilliant moonlit nights brought out the gamin in Cindy whenever she heard elephants trumpeting and bellowing around the waterhole. If let out of the cabin, she always ran directly toward the nearest elephant herd, some fifteen to twenty animals, to run playfully between their legs. I'll never forget the sight of the tiny puppy yapping and nipping at elephants' heels like a wearisome fly, yet somehow avoiding being flattened out into an elephant-sized pancake.

Late one afternoon, when Cindy was about nine months old, I returned to camp to be welcomed only by the clucking Walter. Neither Cindy nor any of the staff were to be found. Several hours passed before the men returned dejectedly with the news that Cindy had been "dog-napped" not too far from camp by either cattle grazers or poachers. We followed her pawprints along a muddy trail until they merged with footprints of some six to ten barefooted men and then disappeared entirely. It did not take skilled trackers to see that the puppy had been picked up and carried off.

Though uncertain as to whether poachers or cattle grazers were responsible for taking Cindy, I decided I could retaliate by rustling some cattle grazing illegally in the meadows near camp and hold them as ransom for Cindy's possible return. With no small difficulty, the men and I herded several-dozen head of long-horned Watutsi cattle back to camp, where we began building a corral around the trunks of five huge *Hagenia* trees. While the men cut saplings to fill in the spaces between the trees, I drew on former occupational-therapist skills to weave a knotty fishnet stockade, using every available piece of string in camp. About midnight the ludicrous structure was completed and judged strong enough to hold the seven cows and one bull, all that remained from our initial captive herd. We pushed eight uncooperative rumps into the flimsy corral, nailed tin sheeting over the entrance, rekindled the campfires surrounding the stockade, and wearily began a night-long vigil against rustlers, the cattle's legal owners.

Under a brilliant starry night, the entire scene resembled a bizarre Hollywood Western. The cattle were bawling from the confines of their fire-lit corral, their indignant bellows joined by the curious snorts of passing buffalo and elephants on their way to Camp Creek. The usual tranquillity of the night was also broken by the shouts of my staff, whom I had asked to yell out into the surrounding forest, in Kinyarwanda, that I would kill a cow a day for every day that Cindy was missing. In between messages, I dozed fitfully, dreaming on and off of lassoing elephants from the backs of buffalo or trying to confine elephants within a string stockade. It was nearly dawn before Mutarutkwa, whose cattle I had taken, came out from the shadows of the forest surrounding camp to call out a message to us concerning Cindy's whereabouts. During the night Mutarutkwa had taken it upon himself to track the real culprits and found that poachers, led by Munyarukiko, had taken Cindy to an *ikibooga* high on the slopes of Mt. Karisimbi.

That morning I "armed" my camp staff and Mutarutkwa with firecrackers and Halloween masks for Operation Rescue Cindy. Marine-style, the four men charged the poachers' *ikibooga,* threw firecrackers into the main campfire, and, during the confusion, retrieved Cindy while the poachers fled from the attack site. Cindy's rescuers later told me that she was anything but a dejected captive. They had found her happily ensconced in the midst of all Munyarukiko's dogs cheerfully chewing away on buffalo bones remaining from the poachers' kills. With Cindy restored to camp, I gratefully returned the cattle to Mutarutkwa, thankful that the turn of the events had not called my bluff.

Nine months later Cindy was again stolen by poachers led by Munyarukiko. This time they took her directly to their Batwa village near the park boundary below Mt. Karisimbi, where she was tied up alongside their hunting dogs. Mutarutkwa's dignified father, Rutshema, rescued Cindy and returned her to me, commenting bitterly on the thieving ways of Batwa poachers. Over the years I came to owe a great deal to this Watusi family. Indeed, Matarutkwa was later to join my staff and lead antipoacher patrols throughout the parklands of the Virungas.

A year after Cindy's arrival, and shortly after Coco and Pucker's departure for the Cologne Zoo, I acquired a new companion at camp. At a gas station in the lakeside town of Gisenyi, a shifty-eyed man carrying a small basket sidled up to my car door. He asked the equivalent of thirty dollars for the contents. For a while I feigned lack of interest; then, casually taking the basket, I found inside a small blue monkey (*Ceropithecus mitis stuhlmanni*) about two years old, fearfully huddled at the bottom more dead than alive. Instantly I grabbed the basket, started the car, and threatened the poacher with imprisonment should he ever capture another animal from the park, where such animals are legally protected. As the man fled, I gazed down into a pair of huge brown eyes looking shyly up at me. Thus began a love affair that was to last for eleven years.

All I needed was a monkey living in an environment unsuited for it. There are golden monkeys (*Ceropithecus mitis kandti*) and blue monkeys living in the lower bamboo zones of the Virungas to as high as nine thousand feet, but not to the ten-thousand-foot altitude of Karisoke.

The captive, named Kima, an African word meaning "monkey," was carried to camp the next day, and thereafter camp life was never the same, a fact to which anyone who has ever visited or worked at Karisoke would readily attest.

Kima soon learned to thrive on fruits and vegetables, brought up by porters from Ruhengeri's open market, as well as bamboo shoots carefully selected from lower park altitudes where others of her species live. Within a month Kima had also developed a decided liking for human food such as baked beans, meat, potato chips, and cheese. Her hors d'oeuvres menu expanded to include glue, pills, film, paint, and kerosene.

Kima's natural simian destructive inclinations were mitigated somewhat by her eventually acceptance of "babies" that I first made from old socks. Later I supplied her with stuffed toys from America. The koala bear, with its big shiny button-nose and dark eyes so much like her own, was her favorite. Deprived of others of her own kind, Kima spent hours each day grooming and carrying her stuffed "babies" around camp. Because I do not believe in confining animals, Kima was given the freedom of both house and forest, though she never strayed far from camp. My cabin became extremely neat, for anything left unguarded was bound to end up on top of a *Hagenia* tree or be shredded to pieces.

Kima, Cindy, Walter, and Wilma formed an unusual welcoming committee upon my return from the gorillas to camp each afternoon. During the chilly nights Kima stayed inside my cabin, usually in a wire cage with a two-way door permitting her access to the outside. It was always a most delightful, cozy feeling to type up field notes near the crackling fireplace at night with the two pets dozing nearby, the sounds of the owls, hyrax, antelope, buffalo, and elephant outside.

Two years following Kima's arrival, I had to spend seven months at Cambridge University. During my absence, Kima lost an eye in an accident. She survived that trauma only to succumb nine years later while I was teaching at Cornell University in 1980. Neither camp nor my life will ever be the same without her loving, albeit somewhat impish, personality.

In August 1980 I returned to Karisoke after an absence of five months and found Cindy, then almost twelve and a half years old, near death. Cindy instantly recognized me but could only hobble weakly and feebly wag her tail in greeting. Together we went to the mound near my cabin where Kima had been buried, and Cindy laid her head down on the wooden plaque marked KIMA. It was then that I made the decision to bring Cindy back to America, where she has become "habituated" to civilization and regained her health. Now accustomed to the noise of planes and cars, Cindy remains puzzled only by cats, unknown to her previously, and the raucous barking of neighborhood dogs. During her life in Africa she had only heard barking occasionally from poachers' dogs near camp and, consequently, never acquired the habit of barking. Even now, socializing with other canines, Cindy does not bark.

OVER the years camp harbored other animals, visitors from the surrounding forest. One clear night in 1977 I looked outside the cabin window and thought my vision badly impaired. There was a giant rat (*Cricetomys gambianus*) feeding on chicken corn. Rufus, as I named him, had a body and tail each about twenty inches long. I wondered where the animal could have come from, for, although such rats were common in villages below, it was a long hike to make just for grains of leftover corn. Several weeks later Rufus was joined by Rebecca, then Rhoda, Batrat, and Robin. Soon every cabin had its own family of rats, each reproducing at an alarming rate until I was compelled to deprive them of the sources of food that had attracted them in the first place.

By the end of 1979 camp had grown into a scraggly town of nine cabins separated by small meadow glades and nearly concealed from one another by natural thickets of herbaceous foliage that grew profusely under the shelter of large *Hagenia* and *Hypericum* trees. Walking between the cabins was a sure guarantee of seeing a growing number of duiker (*Cephalophus nigrifons*), bushbuck (*Tragelaphus scriptus*), and buffalo (*Syncerus caffer*). The antelope and buffalo had begun to seek camp proximity as a refuge against poachers. I had never envisioned the shy ungulates becoming habituated to the presence of humans; they are far more subjected to hunting pressures than are gorillas, yet Karisoke seemed to be their last refuge, an unprovisioned one at that.

I named the first duiker resident Primus, after the sparkly and tasty local beer. When she first came into camp with a flickering white tail, huge brown jeweled eyes, and a moist black quivering nose, Primus was about eight months of age. The buds of her horns were submerged in a clownish black headtuft of hair, later growing into two delicate needle-sharp spikes. In the first months of her stay Primus never associated with any other duiker, leading me to believe that she probably had been orphaned. In time it seemed that Primus also had identity problems in not knowing if she was a duiker, chicken, or dog. She frequently followed the chickens around camp because they provided a feather alarm system by clucking whenever supposed danger threatened.

Primus often spent cold overcast days curled up around camp's central outdoor fireplace, something no other duiker has ever done. On bright sunny days she participated in the usual duiker games of head butting, playing hide-and-go-seek in the foliage thickets, and wild chasing pursuits that often ended up in mountings with other duikers. She also playfully chased the chickens or Cindy and was chased by the mischievous

Kima. My dog had long since been trained to understand that duiker are not to be pursued, so she was totally perplexed when Primus took off after her in a teasing manner. On many occasions Walter, Wilma, and other chickens would be scratching idly on the main path between the cabins when Cindy would come running along with Primus on her heels, and often even Kima thereafter. What a flurry of feathers, fur, and screeching these incidents caused!

In time Primus began chasing the humans at camp, taking special enjoyment in seeming to tease the housemen whenever they were balancing a load of dishes or laundry on their heads. Since Primus had never been pursued by humans, she exhibited caution but little fear of unknown people. Of course, this is what a game park should be.

Primus gave much joy, and occasional surprises, to many guests at camp, especially some Africans. One day I was showing the graveyard of gorilla-poacher victims to a group of important Rwandese that included armed soldiers. Our hum of conversation attracted Primus, who emerged from dense vegetation to stroll casually through the crowd on her way to the meadows. Immediately everyone stopped talking. As the men watched the duiker delicately browse, I allowed myself to hope that someday poaching would be a thing of the past and that animals of the park might be able to put their trust in all humans.

On another occasion an extremely surly poacher, temporarily held at camp, was being escorted along the main path between the cabins and saw Primus dozing under a tree at the trail edge. The poacher's astonishment at seeing a duiker quietly lying only a few feet from him was, in a sense, comical. It was also poignant, since the man showed a deep personal delight in having been trusted by the antelope, an animal he had only recognized as prey before.

Bushbuck were far more reclusive than duiker in that they were seen usually only in the early morning or dusk when grazing around camp. The largest resident family of bushbuck grew to seven individuals headed by a huge male of advanced age. His hair was grizzled black and from a distance, in dim light, he resembled a buffalo because of his enormous size. It was remarkable that he or his aged mate had managed to elude the traps, hunters, and dogs throughout their environment.

I discovered aged male bushbuck frequently lead solitary lives except for occasional dependence upon duiker. This relationship was seen at camp, as well as in many other sections of the forest. Duiker serve as sentries by moving ahead of the bushbuck and giving penetrating, whistle-like alarm calls when spotting potential danger. The signaling system might imply that duikers' senses are keener than those of bushbuck. I think it more likely that this satisfactory arrangement evolved to allow more browsing time for the far larger bushbuck than constant solo vigilance would have permitted.

One of the most memorable bushbuck incidents around camp instantly brought to my mind Jody's words from *The Yearling*: "Pa, I done seen me something today!" As usual, upon awakening I looked out of the cabin windows and observed a sight more credible to a Walt Disney movie than to real life. All the hens, led by Walter, were tiptoeing awkwardly toward a young male bushbuck. The chickens' heads bobbed like yo-yos from their stringy necks. The curious antelope minced toward them with a metronomically twitching tail and quivering nose. Each chicken then made a beak-to-beak contact with the bushbuck as both species satisfied their undisguised interest in the other. Just about this time Cindy innocently came trotting up the path and froze, one foreleg suspended in the air, as she gazed at the weird spectacle before her. Her presence was too much for the young buck, who bounded off with a bark, his white-flag tail held high.

Much like the antelope, buffalo around camp were distinctive because of personality traits or physical variations. One lone male that appeared to be in his prime was noticeable because of his pink mottled muzzle and gregarious inclination toward humans. He thus gained the name Ferdinand, and first introduced himself one evening about dusk. Two of the staff and I were completing some carpentry work in front of the cabin, abusing the twilight calm with the noise of hammering and sawing. Just as I felt a faint trembling sensation beneath my feet I turned to behold the incredible sight of the massive bull trotting toward us. One of the men ran into the house immediately, but the second remained outside with me to watch Ferdinand. Stopping about eighteen feet away, the bull stared with unabashed curiosity and not the slightest bit of antipathy or fright. It was as though he wanted to be entertained. My helper and I resumed our hammering and sawing, and Ferdinand watched contentedly for another five minutes before turning away to feed slowly, without as much as a backward glance. Since that time I have met Ferdinand a number of times around Karisoke, most frequently in the early morning, and he continues to react mildly when seeing humans pass him on the camp trail. Like the duiker and the bushbuck, this buffalo is another gift of trust from the forest.

A second bull, an ancient animal initially accompanied by an elderly female, had as startling an appearance as Ferdinand had a personality. From rump to withers his body was scarred like a road map, with countless healed wounds, possibly the results of encounters with poachers, traps, or other buffalo. The heavy boss on his head must have at one time been twice its size, but had been relentlessly chipped away over the years of his life. The remnants of the horns themselves gave evidence of decades of battles and remained only worn and shattered nubbins.

I named the old bull Mzee, meaning "old one" in Swahili. It was an impressive sight to see Mzee following his aged female, who, until her disappearance, seemed to serve as a watchdog when his eyesight began to fail. During his second year around Karisoke the old bull, upon hearing my voice in the early evening hours, would slowly feed toward me as if wanting company and, eventually, allow me to scratch his withered rump. Early one morning the woodman found the old buffalo's body lying in a small grassy hollow next to Camp Creek under the towering silhouettes of Mts. Karisimbi and Mikeno. I could not imagine a more fitting spot for Mzee's final resting place. The serenity of the surroundings matched the dignity of the bull's character. Although he had lived in the shadow of poachers, he had managed to defy them in death.

Ten years before Mzee's natural death, when there were no regular patrols conducted from Karisoke, several buffalo in their prime met horrid endings at the hands of poachers very near camp. The first killing occurred during the second holiday season I had been in Rwanda and before I realized the devastation holidays brought to the park animals. I made the mistake of leaving camp for several days around Christmas 1968 and returned to find that my staff had locked themselves up in my cabin for safety's sake. Nearby, I found the remains of two poachers' dogs smashed up against the side of Camp Creek. The entrails of a buffalo led to a nearby hill where the carcass had been skinned and carried off by poachers. According to the staff, the poachers' dogs had chased the buffalo out of the forest, onto the meadows, and into the creek in front of my cabin. The bull, fighting for its life, managed to gore two dogs to pieces before losing his battle to spears flung from the poachers led by Munyarukiko. This was the last time I ever left camp unprotected during the holiday season.

The second buffalo slaying occurred several months later when the camp staff reported hearing the bellows of a "cow" in pain not too far below Karisoke. Taking a small pistol with me, I followed the men toward the source of the noise and found an adult buffalo wedged into the forked trunk of an old *Hagenia* tree. I regret that poachers also had heard the agonized wails of the trapped animal and had hacked off both its rear legs with their *pangas*. We found the poor beast desperately trying to stand on its two hind stumps amid a wallow of blood and dung. Still, the bull was able to toss his head boldly and snort at our approach. To have to kill such a valiant example of courage, an animal that could fight so bravely even to the last second of its life, was difficult. I returned to camp with the knowledge that one more magnificent creature of the Virunga Volcanoes was dead.

Farley Mowat

A WHALE FOR THE KILLING

The tranquil acceptance of the Fin Whales at Burgeo was in sharp contrast to an incident I witnessed at about this time at St. Pierre, the capital and only port for the French islands of St. Pierre and Miquelon which lie a few miles off the south coast of Newfoundland. Most of the inhabitants there are fishermen too, but St. Pierre itself is full of shops, tourist establishments, ship repair facilities, and people whose loyalties lie with the modern industrial society.

On a moonless night in August 1961, my schooner lay moored to a rotting dock in St. Pierre harbour. About midnight I went on deck to smoke a pipe and enjoy the silence; but the quiet was soon broken by what sounded like a gust of heavy breathing in the waters almost alongside. Startled, I grabbed a flashlight and played its beam over the dark waters. The calm surface was mysteriously roiled in great, spreading rings. As I puzzled over the meaning of this phenomenon, there came another burst of heavy exhalations. I swung the light to port and was in time to see one, three, then a dozen broad black backs smoothly break the oily surface, blow, then slip away into the depths again.

I was seeing a school of Potheads who had made their way into the sewage-laden waters of the inner harbour. They must have had a pressing reason, for no free-swimming animal in its right mind would have entered that cesspool willingly. The skipper of a local dragger later told me he had met a small group of Killer Whales close to the harbour channel on the day the Potheads entered. Killer Whales have been given a ferocious reputation by men; one not at all deserved, but it is true that they will occasionally make a meal of a Pothead calf, and the Potheads in St. Pierre harbour were accompanied by several calves.

When I went to bed, the whales were still circling leisurely. I slept late, to be awakened by the snarl of outboard engines, by excited shouting, and by the sound of feet pounding on my deck. When I thrust my head out of the hatch, I found what appeared to be about half the male population of St. Pierre, accompanied by a good many women and children, closely clustered along the waterfront.

There was a slight fog lying over the harbour. In and out of it wove two over-powered launches, roaring along at full throttle. In the bow of one stood a young man wielding a homemade lance which he had made by lashing a hunting knife to the end of an oar. In the second boat was another young man, balancing a rifle across his knees. Both boats were in furious pursuit of the Potheads which numbered some fifteen adults and six or seven calves.

The whales were very frightened. The moment one of them surfaced, the boats tore down upon it, while gunners on the shore poured out a fusillade of shots. The big animals had no time to properly ventilate their lungs but were forced to submerge after snatching a single breath. The calves, choking for oxygen, were often slow in diving. Time after time the harpooner got close enough to ram his hunting knife into the back of one of them so that long streamers of crimson began to appear on the filthy surface of the harbour. It was obvious that neither the gunfire—mostly from .22 calibre rifle—nor the lance were capable of killing the whales outright; but it did not appear that killing them was the object. In truth, what I was watching was a sporting event.

I was appalled and infuriated, but there seemed to be nothing I could do to end this exhibition of wanton bloodlust. A fisherman friend of mine, Theophille Detcheverey, came aboard and I poured out my distress to him. He shrugged.

"That one in the big speedboat, he is the son of the biggest merchant here. The other, with the spear, he is from France. He came here two years ago to start a raft voyage across the Atlantic. But he don't get out of the bars until today, I think. They are pigs, eh? But we are not all pigs. You see, there is no fisherman helping them with their dirty work."

This was true enough, if of small comfort to the whales. The fishermen of St. Pierre had left for the cod grounds at dawn. When they returned in their laden dories late in the afternoon, the excitement in the harbour had reached a crescendo. All the fast pleasure craft available had joined in the game. The onlookers crowding around the harbour had become so densely packed it was hard to push one's way through. I had chased scores of them off my decks where they sought a better vantage point; and they had responded to my anger with derision. For ten hours, relays of boats had chased the whales. Clusters of men with rifles stood at the pierhead at the harbour entrance and every time the Potheads tried to escape in that direction they were met with a barrage of bullets which now included heavy-calibre slugs. Unable to run that gauntlet, the whales were forced to give up their attempts to escape in the only direction open to them.

Toward evening the whales, most of them now bleeding profusely, had become so exhausted they began to crowd up into the dangerously shoal water at the head of the harbour where the boats could not follow. Here they lay, gasping and rolling, until they had recovered enough strength to return to deeper water. Many times they swam directly under my boat, and they were beautiful . . . superb masters of the seas, now at the mercy of the bifurcated killer of the land.

At dusk the sportsmen called it a day and went home to dinner. The audience departed. The fog rolled in thickly and silence returned. Again I sat on deck, and again the strange sibilant breathing of the whales kept me company. I could not go to my berth, knowing what must await them with the dawn. Finally I untied my little dinghy and rowed out into the darkness of the fog shroud. I had a vague hope that I might be able to drive the herd out of the harbour before daylight brought a renewal of their ordeal.

It was an uncanny experience, and a nerve-wracking one, to row my little cockleshell silently through that dense and dripping fog, not knowing where the whales might be. The size of them—the largest must have been nearly twenty feet long—and their mysterious and unseen presence intimidated me. I felt extraordinarily vulnerable, detached from my own world, adrift on the lip of a world which was utterly alien. I thought, as a man would think, that if there was the capacity for vengeance in these beasts, surely I would experience it.

Then, with heart-stopping suddenness, the entire pod surfaced all around me. A calf blew directly under one upraised oar and my little boat rocked lightly in its wash. It should have been a terrifying moment, but it was not. Inexplicably, I was no longer afraid. I began talking to the beasts in a quiet way, warning them that they must leave. They stayed at or near the surface, swimming very slowly—perhaps still exhausted—and I had no difficulty staying with them. Time after time they surfaced all around me and although any one of them, even the smallest calf, could have easily overturned the dinghy, they avoided touching it. I began to experience an indescribable sense of empathy with them . . . and a mounting frustration. How could I help them to escape from what the morrow held?

We slowly circled the harbour—this strange flotilla of man

and whales—but they would not go near the harbour mouth, either because they knew the Killer Whales were still in the vicinity or because of the vicious barrage of bullets with which men had greeted their every attempt to escape during the daylight hours.

Eventually I decided to try desperate measures. At the closest point to the harbour entrance to which they would go, I suddenly began howling at them and wildly flailing my oars against the water. Instantly they sounded, diving deep and long. I heard them blow once more at the far side of the harbour but they never came close to me again. I had done the wrong thing—the human thing—and my action had brought an end to their acceptance of me.

The whales were still in the harbour when dawn broke. During the long evening in the bars, the ingenious sportsmen of St. Pierre had set the stage for a massacre.

Early in the morning, just as the tide was beginning to ebb, half a dozen boats came out and formed a line abreast at the harbour mouth. Slowly, they began to sweep the harbour, driving the herd closer and closer to the shoals. When the whales sounded and doubled back, they were again met with rifle fire from the breakwater as on the day before. One of the largest beasts seemed to be leading these attempts to escape with the rest following close in its wake. It looked like a stalemate until three small whales became momentarily separated from the pod as it came under the fusillade from the breakwater. They gave way to panic. Fleeing at full speed on the surface, and close-harried by a fast speedboat, they torpedoed across the harbour and into the shoals where the tide was dropping fast. Within minutes they were hopelessly aground.

Howling like the veriest banshees, men and boys armed with axes and carving knives leapt into the knee-deep shallows. Blood began to swirl thickly about them. The apparent leader of the pod, responding to what impulse I shall never know, charged toward the three stranded and mutilated whales.

There was a wild melée of running, falling, yelling people; then the big whale stranded too. The rest of the herd, following close behind, were soon ashore as well. Only one calf remained afloat. It swam aimlessly back and forth just beyond the fatal shoals, and for a few minutes was ignored as the boats crowded in upon the herd and men leapt overboard, jostling one another in their lust to have a hand in the slaughter. Blood from one impaled whale spouted high over their heads—a red and drenching rain. Men flung up their ensanguined faces, wiped the blood away, and laughed and shouted in the delirium of dealing death.

Finally someone noticed the calf. Arms, red and savage, pointed urgently. A man leapt into his speedboat. The engine roared. He circled once at top speed then bore straight at the calf which was in such shoal water it could not sound. The boat almost ran up on its back. The calf swerved frantically, beat its flukes wildly, and was aground.

The slashing and the hacking on that bloody foreshore continued long after all the whales had bled to death. A crowd of four or five hundred people drank in the spectacle with eager appetite. It was a great fiesta in St. Pierre. Throughout the remainder of the day there was a crowd standing and staring at the monstrous corpses. I particularly remember a small boy, who could not have been more than eight years of age, straddling a dead calf and repeatedly striking into its flesh with a pocket knife, while his father stood by and encouraged him.

Nor were the "townies" of St. Pierre the only ones to enjoy the spectacle. Many American and Canadian tourists had witnessed the show and now were busy taking pictures of one another posing beside the dead behemoths. Something to show the folks back home.

It was a grand exhibition . . . but the aftermath was not so grand. Those many tons of putrefying flesh could not be left lying where they were. So, on the following day, several big trucks appeared at the shore where lay the carcasses of twenty-three Pothead Whales. One by one the whales were hauled up by a mobile derrick and either loaded aboard the trucks or, if they were too big, chained behind. Then the trucks carried and dragged the bodies across the island to a cliff where, one by one, they were rolled over the steep slopes . . . and returned to the freedom of the seas.

Diane Ackerman

WHALES

The adolescent whale drifts away from the mother and calf and begins swimming slowly toward us—curious, no doubt, about a black rubber raft with many moving animals inside. Then it blows and, tossing its tail, dives directly under the boat. A long dark shadow, spotted with white at one end, where the head's callosities glow, floats underneath us for what seems like minutes. It surfaces with a blow, rolls onto one side, and curves back toward us. Its tail has a slightly ragged line of notches, probably orca bites.

"Watch the tail," Roger warns. "If you ever see the tail coming down on you, leap fast into the water. Don't even think about it. Just jump. You don't want to get crushed between the boat and the tail." But the whale dives back underneath the boat, rolling onto one side, apparently so it can look at us, then surfaces on the other side and blows a fine mist, which pours over us and smells sweet, like wet fur. The whale circles back again, and this time it swims right alongside the boat. Its huge, dark head, floating at the surface, comes so close I can look into the blowholes, which are open-

280

ing and closing like two hands held palms together and pressing wide apart at fingers and thumbs. A few hairs sprout around the blowholes. The young whale is only about thirty-five feet long. It has thick callosities, with whale lice clinging all over them, and the black skin is streaked with fine lines of the sort one sees on a window after rain. Males tend to have more callosities, and also scrapes along their backs from fighting; we think this is a male. It brings its mouth toward the boat and nudges it. Stretching out a hand over the gunwale, I touch its head delicately with one finger. Its whole body flinches. I wonder how it can be so sensitive. Its skin is startlingly soft, like oiled chamois.

The sound of light artillery in the distance draws our attention to two breaching whales, hurling themselves into the air, half-twisting, like a top running out of momentum, and splashing onto their sides in thick geysers of spume. By now, the adolescent has returned to the other side of the boat and is languidly rubbing one whole flank along the inflated gunwale, as a cat might twine between someone's legs. After several passes, it swims away. The afternoon is almost over, and the data that Tom and Roger want have been collected. The sinking sun has lost a lot of its heat, and we are all starting to feel chilly, so we head back to camp. We watch a whale near shore rolling over and over. There are many shells and pebbles in the shallows, and it may be scratching, the way a dog enjoys rolling in the dirt. It waves a flipper in the air, follows with the semaphore of its flukes. At last, we land on the beach, and drag the Zodiac into the boathouse.

At sunset, the horizon is orange and the sea grows blue-gray. Stretches of wet sand, exposed by the withdrawing tide, shine like an array of hand mirrors. Venus appears overhead, as loud as a whistle blow, with the pinprick light of Mercury at its side. As night falls, the shallows shimmer like ice, and the winds begin to sound like freight trains. The wind has a large vocabulary in Patagonia. It shushes through the thornbushes, it rattles the corrugated-metal walls, it flutes through the arroyos, it makes the cliffs sound as if they are being scoured with a wire whisk. A night heron cries *owow*. A whale sneezes loudly, and the sound suggests an iron patio chair being dragged across a concrete floor. In the distance, three whales blow bushes of mist. Over the apricot horizon, the sky billows upward from pale green, through thick teal, to a translucent wafer of azure blue.

Dinner—by gas lamp—begins late by American standards. By the time everybody finishes a dessert of *dulce de leche* poured over bananas, it is nearly midnight. We all pile plates in the sink; there is no running water, and tomorrow we'll wash them in the ocean. With a flashlight, I hunt my way back to my tent, behind a sheep fence and among a clutch of thornbushes on the ledge of the beach; zip my tent shut; and crawl into my sleeping bag.

Fifteen minutes later, I hear footsteps outside. "Asleep yet?" Kate says. "I think there's an orca calling. Come on down to the beach."

At the shoreline, Tom stands holding a tape recorder that is attached to a hydrophone line running out into the bay. Over the years, Roger has produced a library of right-whale recordings. Right whales make many different sounds: funny, serious, strange; underwater, in the air. Probably they mean a variety of things; it's a mystery that remains to be solved. Under a full moon, sea and sky blur in a creamy fog both eerie and radiant. Small bioluminescent creatures flash green from the shallows. Close to shore, a large right whale blows loudly. Another whale sneezes. The hydrophone picks up a stretched meow. No orcas are calling, but many right whales sigh and bleat through the pallid fog under the brilliant moon. Shivering, we decide to call it a night, and return to our tents and huts for a chilly sleep. . . .

WE say dawn breaks, as if something were shattering, but what we mean is that waves of light crest over the earth. On Wednesday morning, rinsed by those light waves, I walk along the beach, beside overhanging cliffs, and realize what an ancient place the camp is. The cliffs are almost solid fossil—uplifted prehistoric seabeds. Fossil oysters large enough to have held more than a pound of meat jut out from the top, and fossil sand dollars perhaps seventy million years old lie at its base. Also on the beach is an amazing array of dead penguins and other birds. In the tide wrack lie feathers, flippers, mummified animals, and countless shells. To reach the water, I cross dunelike ridges of stones. One thing the ocean does surprisingly well is sort according to size. There are fields of large stones, then ridges of medium-sized ones, then areas of even smaller stones. Looking out at the water, I see a mother and baby whale lolling in the shallows slightly to my left. When did they arrive? Rolling on her side, the mother whale swings a flipper up and nurses the baby. When a pack of seals appears and begins playfully pestering them, the baby snuggles up to its mother and cups its flipper around her. The whales appear to have stopped in the water, but, however fast I walk toward them, they always seen to be just a yard ahead of me. Finally, I leave them and head for the Peludo Palace.

After coffee, cheese, and cereal crackers, Roger, Judy, and I get into a car with Rubén, the pilot, and set out for an airstrip half an hour away, where he keeps a Cessna 182. Each year, Rubén flies Roger and other camp people out over the bays to photograph whales. We climb aboard and head for the southern bay, which is packed with whales. Rubén spots whales in the water, flies straight to them, and does steep turns around them at three hundred feet while Roger crouches on a seat and shoots pictures of each animal. On an outline of the peninsula I pencil in "♀ + ♀ +" (two females with one calf each) at our approximate position and, a little farther along, another "♀ +." As Roger finishes each roll of film, I hand him a fresh one, and mark the number of the roll, and the date, on the used one. After an hour of steep turns, we head back to the airstrip. Rubén rolls out a yellow drum of gas and attaches to it a green hand pump that looks like a coffee grinder, and Judy pumps gas into a hose that Rubén feeds into a can topped with chamois (to filter out contaminating water) and then pumps the gas from the can into the wing. It is a lengthy process. Then Rubén and Judy climb aboard, and in a moment we are airborne again, flying over the great flat deserts. Sheep trails converge and overlap at far-flung water tanks. In a few minutes, Rubén lands on a dirt road, pauses just long enough for me to get out, turns the plane around, and takes off, to spend the rest of the day photographing whales. I begin walking home down roads that resemble gutted riverbeds. A herd of ten guanacos takes flight on spotting me. Two maras ("rabbits with miniskirts," Roger calls them) scamper away as I pass, and lizards swagger under bushes. In an hour, I stand on the rise overlooking camp. Two boat trails leading from the boathouse to the water tell me that the chicos are already out at work. When I get to the house, I'm amazed by the stillness. Everyone is gone. Climbing up to my hut, I take off my jacket and walk out to the cliff hut, a little less than a mile away. An icy morning has turned into a torrid noon, and the temperature will no doubt drop to near freezing by nightfall. From the cliff hut I see below me in the water the same mother and baby I saw earlier. I recognize the mother because she has a large, distinctive wound on one flank, and the callosity on her snout, which would normally be teardrop-shaped, is hollowed out at each side, forming a sort of parenthesis. When I described her during breakfast, I was told that some earlier observer thought the callosity resembled fangs, and thus she was named Fang. Her new calf nestles beside her. They have spent all morning close to camp. The sunlight makes a glittering path over the water. Each time the whales surface, drops of water sparkle around them.

Fang and her calf are close below me, but the whole bay is awaltz with mother whales and baby whales. Right whales are pregnant for only about a year, which seems like a very short time; after all, the elephant gestation period is twenty-two months, and a whale is far larger than an elephant. When an elephant calf is born, it has to scramble up onto its legs, but a whale calf can go straight from the amniotic fluid of its mother's womb into the womb of the ocean; it doesn't have to support itself. Whales, being warm-blooded mammals, who breathe as we do, could, in principle, live on land, but if a whale were on land its organs would be crushed under its own weight. It needs the water to support its massive size— that's one of the reasons stranded whales fare so poorly. Because a whale baby doesn't have to stand up, its bones are flexible: you could take the rib bone of a baby right whale and bend it back and forth as if it were made of hard rubber.

A newborn whale calf does not leave its mother's side but often swims along eye to eye with her. Sometimes the mother whale swims so that her tail touches the calf with every downstroke. Sometimes the calf gets obstreperous and bangs into its mother, or even breaches onto its mother's back. Finally, she will lose her patience and punish it, by rolling over quickly onto her back as the calf is ready to ram her for, say, the fifteenth time, catching the small of its tail under one of her flippers, and rolling back to hold the baby underwater, so that it begins spluttering, wheezing, sneezing, coughing. After a little while, she lets it go. The calf then resumes its eye-to-eye position and swims along docilely. Hungry calves will butt their mothers, climb all over them, and slide off them, trying to get the mother to roll over and nurse. Occasionally, a mother will calm a hyperactive calf by sliding underneath it and turning over to pick it up out of the water and balance it on her chest, holding it between her flippers. Every now and then, a mother, with a flipper the size of a wall of my hut, will reach over and pat the calf sweetly.

For hours, I sit quietly and watch the doings in the nursery bay. Fang rolls onto her weighty side, and her baby nurses. Then the baby gets rambunctious and strays a little too far. Mother lows to it in a combination of foghorn and moo, calling it back within eyeshot. From time to time, Fang submerges slowly, her tail hanging limp and loose and trailing one tip of a fluke in the water. She makes burpy sounds with occasional moans, and I think she may be napping.

When a whale sleeps, it slowly tumbles in an any-old-crazy, end-over-end, sidewise fashion, and may even bonk its head on the bottom. Or it may just be quiet, looking like a corpse. When it rises again, to breathe during its sleep, it comes up as slow as a dream, breaks the surface, breath a few times, and, without diving, falls again slowly toward the bottom. Off Patagonia, right whales sometimes sleep in the mornings on calm days, and some of them seem to be head-heavy, with light tails; they fall forward, and their tails rise out of the water. Humpbacks are rarely visible when they're sleeping, because they are less buoyant and usually sink rapidly, but all the behavior of right whales is easy to study, because they're at-the-surface whales. They're so fat that they float when they're relaxed, and they spend a lot of time with their backs in the air. When they're asleep at the surface, their breathing rate drops tremendously, and, since they don't close their nostrils completely between breaths when they're asleep, sometimes they snore. When they wake, they stretch their backs, open their mouths, and yawn. Sometimes they lift their tails up and twist them, and then they go about their business. Often, on calm days, they sleep at the surface for so long that their backs get sunburned, and then the skin peels the same way human skin does, but on a big, whale-size scale. The loose skin from their backs falls into the water and becomes food for birds. When they breach, they shed a lot of loose skin as they hit the water, and seagulls, realizing this, fly out fast to a breaching whale.

A bizarre habit has developed among the kelp gulls in this bay. Instead of waiting for the whales to shed sunburned skin, they land on the whales back and carve the skin and blubber right off. A gull sweeps down and gouges a piece of skin and blubber from Fang's back, and Fang, in obvious pain, shakes her head and tail simultaneously, flexes almost in half, then dives. The gull flies to a pair of whales nearby, raids them, and flies off. Other gulls—brown-hooded gulls—will harmlessly yank off long strips of skin and actually set up short-lived feeding territories on the backs of their own particular whales. When Roger first started studying right whales at Valdés peninsula, he noticed that only brown-hooded gulls were peeling the skin off the backs of sleeping sunburned whales; soon, however, the kelp gulls not only learned this technique but also began carving holes in backs. The result is that the backs of whales like Fang are pitted with craters made by kelp gulls. When a gull lands on a whale's back, the whale panics. This year, there are fewer whales in the bay, and Roger thinks that the kelp gulls may be chasing them away, to bays where kelp gulls don't yet know the trick of landing on whales' backs.

Juan appears at the edge of camp, on foot, apparently hiking in from a neighboring bay. By the time I get down to the house, he is just arriving there.

"Tired?" I ask, with an inflection that says I really hope he isn't. "Want to go find some whales?"

He grins. "Just let me get a Coke, then *vamos*."

I put on a leotard and tights, and begin crawling into a half-inch-thick wetsuit, which includes Farmer John overalls, a beaver-tail jacket, boots, gloves, and a hood. There is so much neoprene in the suit that I'll need to wear weights around my waist to keep from bobbing on the surface.

Sitting on the porch whale skull, John watches me suit up. He looks anxious. "Be careful," he says. "This morning, I was out in a boat with Tom collecting breath samples, and the calf of that mother over there"—he points to Fang and her baby, just around the curve of the beach—"rocked the boat with its flipper and gave us a scare."

To tell the truth, I'd feel much safer with Roger on board if I'm going swimming, but I've been waiting all week for the water to calm down, and all afternoon for Roger to get back from flying. It's past four now, and I very much doubt whether he'll be back before sunset. So it's now or never.

Juan returns from the Peludo Palace and tugs on a thin wetsuit and boots, and we go down to the beach. Manolo is there, and joins us in the Zodiac. Heading north along the bay, we come upon two mothers and calves, but the mothers, protective of their calves, move them away. Juan would like to find a young adult to work with. He has been collecting loose skin for Judy and then slipping into the water to photograph the heads of the whales it came from in order to identify them. This afternoon, I hope to join him, staying just behind but looking out for loose skin while hoping to get a glimpse of a whale in its element. We search for an hour, but find none in the mood to be approached. Finally, we head back toward camp and, coming around a bend, discover Fang and her calf still playing. We cut the motor about two hundred yards from them. Juan and I slip over the side of the boat and swim toward them, approaching as quietly as possible, so that they won't construe any of our movements as aggressive. In a few minutes, we are only yards from the mother's head. Looking down, I see the baby beside her, underwater, its callosities bright in the murky green water. Slowly, Juan and I swim all the way around them, getting closer and closer. The long wound on Fang's flank looks red and angry. When her large, dark tail lifts out of the water, its beauty stuns me for a moment, and then I yank Juan's hand to draw his attention and we pull back. Fang is forty-five to fifty feet long and weighs about as many tons, so all she would need to do is hit us with a flipper to crush us, or swat us with her tail to kill us instantly. But she is moving her tail gently, slowly. Right whales, with their baleen plates, are grazers: we don't look like lunch. She swings her head around so that her mouth is within two feet of me, then turns her head on edge to reveal a large white patch and, under that, a dark eye shaped like a human eye. I look directly into her eye, and she looks directly back at me, and we hang in the water, studying each other.

"I wish you well," I think, concentrating hard, in case it is possible for her to sense my mood. I don't imagine she can decipher the words, but many animals can sense fear in human beings. Perhaps they can also sense other emotions.

Her dark, plumlike eye fixes me: for a while, we stare deeply at each other. The curve of her mouth gives her a Mona Lisa smile, but that's just a felicity of her anatomy. The only emotion I sense is her curiosity. That shines through her watchfulness—it's apparent in her repeated turning toward us, her extreme passivity, her caution with flippers and tail. She seems to be doing just what we are—swimming close to a strange, fascinating life-form, taking care not to frighten or hurt it. Perhaps, when she heard us slip over the side of the Zodiac she thought it had given birth and we were its young. In that case, she may be thinking how little we resemble our parent. Or perhaps she understands only too well that we are intelligent beasts who live in the alien, dangerous world of the land, where whales get stranded, lose their bearings and equilibrium, and die. A whale's glimpse of us is almost as rare as our glimpse of a whale. Whales have never seen us mating; they have rarely, if ever, seen us feeding; they have never seen us give birth, suckle our young, or die of old age. They have never observed our normal social habits. They would not know how to tell our sex, since we hide our reproductive organs. They would find it hard to distinguish between a clothed, short-haired, clean-shaven man and a clothed, short-haired woman.

When Fang saw us in the Zodiac, we were wearing large, dark plastic eyes. Now we have small eyes shaped like hers—but two on one plane of the head, like a seal, not an eye on either side, like a whale or a fish. In the water, our eyes are encased in a glass jar, our mouths are stretched around a rubber tube, and our feet are flippers. Instead of diving, like marine mammals, we float on the surface. To Fang, I must look spastic and octopuslike, with my thin limbs dangling around me. Human beings possess such immense powers that there are few animals that make us feel truly humble. A whale does, swimming beside you, as large as a reclining building, its eye carefully observing you as it chooses not to devastate you. Although it lives in a gliding, quiet, investigate-it-first realm, it is not benign, like a Zen monk. Aggression plays a big role in its life, especially during courtship. Whales have weapons that are equal in their effects to our pointing a gun at somebody and wiggling a finger and blowing him away. When they strike each other with their flukes in battle, they hit flat, but to display power they sometimes slash the water with the edge. That fluke edge could break a person in two instantly. A whale could slam a person with its tail and break even bone. But such an attack has never taken place in the thousands of times that people have been known to swim with whales. On rare occasions, unprovoked whales have struck boats with their flukes, perhaps by accident, on one occasion killing a man. And there are three reported instances of a whale breaching onto a boat, again resulting in a death. They don't attack swimmers. In many of our science-fiction stories, aliens appear on earth and a terrible fight ensues, in which everyone uses weapons that burn, sting, or blow up. To us, what is alien is treacherous and evil. Whales clearly don't visualize aliens in that way. So, although it is frightening to float beside an animal as large and powerful as a whale, I know that if I show her where I am and what I am and that I mean her no harm she will return the courtesy.

Suddenly, Juan pulls me back a few feet, and, turning, I see the calf swimming around to our side, though staying close to its mother. Although it is as large as an elephant, it still looks like a baby. Only a few months old, it is as frisky as a pup and rampantly curious. It swims right up close, turns one eye at us, takes a good look, then wheels its head around and looks at us with the other eye. When it turns, it swings its mouth right up to my chest, and I reach out to touch it, but Juan pulls my hand back. I look at him and nod. A touch could startle the baby, which may not know its own strength. In a reflex, its tail or a flipper could swat us, or it might not know that if human beings are held underwater—by a playful flipper, say—they can drown. Its large flippers hang in the water by its sides, and its small callosities look like a crop of fieldstones. When it rolls, it reveals a patch of white on its belly and an anal slit. Swimming forward, it fans its tail, and the water suddenly feels chillier: it has stirred up cold from the bottom. The mother swims forward to keep up with it, and we follow, hanging quietly in the water, trying to breathe slowly and kick our flippers as little as possible. Curving back around, Fang turns on one side in order to see us, and waits while we swim up close again. Below me her flipper hovers, as large as a freight elevator. Tilting it very gently in place, she appears to be sculling; her tail, too, is barely moving. There are no sudden gestures, no acts of aggression. Each time she or the baby blows, a fine mist sprays into the air, accompanied by a whumping sound, as of a pedal organ.

We human beings do not have the whale's insulation of blubber to warm us in these frigid waters, and Juan and I, growing cold after an hour of travelling slowly along the bay with Fang and her baby, begin swimming back toward the beach. To save energy, we roll onto our backs and kick with our fins. When we are a few hundred yards away from Fang, she puts her head up in a "spy hop." Then she dives, rolls, lifts a flipper high into the air, like a black rubber sail, and waves it back and forth. The calf does the same. Juan and I laugh. They are not waving at us, only rolling and playing now that we're out of the way, but it is so human a gesture that we automatically wave our arms overhead in reply. Then we turn onto our faces again. Spears of sunlight cut through the thick green water and disappear into the depths, bottom reveals itself as tawny brown about thirty feet below us, and soon the sand grows visible, along with occasional shells, and then the riot of shells near shore, and, finally, the pebbles of the shallows. Taking off our fins, we step from one realm into another: from the whale road, as Homer called the ocean, back onto the land of human beings.

Barry Lopez

CARING FOR THE WOODS

My family has been in the Americas for almost five centuries. Marín López, a shipwright on my father's side, was in the Caribbean with Cortés in 1511. My mother's English and German ancestors began farming on the Pennsylvania side of the Delaware River valley in the 1650s. A scion of that group later moved to Virginia (where the Holston River still bears the family name); his progeny moved into the Carolinas and eastern Alabama where my mother was born on a plantation in 1914. One relative in that clan moved on to New Mexico at the close of the 19th century and then dropped from sight. He is recalled as a man obsessed with killing Indians.

My father's family, originally tobacco farmers in Cuba, eventually came to St. Louis and New York as tobacco merchants, though they maintained close ties with Asturias, their homeland in northern Spain. Neither the Romans nor the Moors, my father is still proud to say, ever conquered Asturias. He traces his lineage there back to Rodrigo Díaz de Vivar—El Cid. In her last years my mother followed her own path back as far, to a baron of Somerset who ratified the Magna Carta at Runnymede.

All these centuries later, the wandering, the buying up, the clearing, the planting, and the harvesting of land in my single branch of the family has come down to a parcel in Oregon: 35 acres of mixed old-growth forest, rising quickly into the foothills of the Cascade Mountains from the north bank of the McKenzie River. These woods harbor Roosevelt elk and mountain lion, suites of riparian and mixed-forest birds, and an assortment of insects, wildflowers, and mushrooms that trails off into a thousand species.

I understand the desire to own the land, the dream of material wealth that brought each of my lines of descent to the Americas. I respect the determination, the tenacity, and the uses to which the land-profit was put—formal education, for example. But I've come to believe, at the age of 49, that sacrificing the biological integrity of land to abet human progress is a practice my generation must end. If we do not, I believe the Americas will finally wash into the sea like Haiti, leaving behind a social nightmare.

My wife, Sandra, and I have lived on the right bank of the river for 24 years. We want to keep this single wooded slope of land in the West undeveloped and uncut. We want to pass it on like a well-read book, not the leavings of someone's meal.

The enormous trees and the river, because of their scale, dominate what we see here, but the interstices of this landscape are jammed with life: hummingbirds, spiders, butterflies, cutthroat trout, wild ginger, skinks, the cascading blossoms of wild rhododendron. In the 1940s some of the larger trees—Douglas fir, western hemlock, and western red cedar, four to six feet in diameter—were selectively logged. The selective logging and a fire that burned a long stretch of the north bank of the McKenzie in 1855 created a forest with a few tall,

Caring for the Woods 293

rotting stumps; dense patches of younger Douglas fir; and several dozen massive, isolated, towering trees, 300 to 400 years old, all standing among many fewer Pacific yew, chinquapin, bigleaf maple, red alder, Pacific dogwood, California hazel, and the odd Pacific madrone.

In 1989 a neighbor who owned this slope put 32 acres of it up for sale. Timber companies that intended to clear-cut the property were the most active bidders, and Sandra and I were forced to match money and wits with them. But in 1990 we were able to add these acres to three we'd bought in 1976. We then completed a legal arrangement to prevent the land from being either logged or developed after we passed away. Good intention toward an individual stretch of land has now become well-meaning of another kind in my family.

We did not set out to preserve these woods. From the start we felt it a privilege, also a kind of wonder, to live here. Twenty-inch spring chinook spawn on a redd in front of the house in September every year. Wild bleeding heart, yellow violets, white flowers such as trillium and wood sorrel, and the red flowers of coralroot are brilliant in the deep, green woods in April and May. I find bear scat, beaver-clipped willows, and black-tailed deer prints regularly on my walks. On the same night we've listened to northern spotted owls, western screech owls, and northern saw-whet owls call. Spotted skunks and a short-tail weasel have tried to take up residence in the house. On summer nights, when we leave the windows open, bats fly through.

From a certain perspective, this wooded hill with its unnamed creek and marvelous creatures—I nearly stepped on a rubber boat one morning on the way to the toolshed—is still relatively unmanipulated; but I try not to let myself be fooled by the thought. The number of songbirds returning each spring I would guess to be half what it was a decade ago. The number of chinook on the redd, though it fluctuates, has also fallen off in recent years. And I've taken hundreds of dead animals off the road along the river—raccoon, brush rabbit, even Steller's jay and mink. People new to the area are apt to log the few Douglas firs left on their property, to roll out fresh lawns and plant ornamental trees in their place. Their house cats leave shrews, white-footed mice, and young birds strewn in the woods like so much litter.

Driftnets that snag salmon in the far-off Pacific, industrial logging in Central America that eliminates migratory-bird habitat, speeding trucks and automobiles, attractive prices for timber—all of it directly affects these acres. There is no way to fence it out.

THE historical detail that might make vivid what, precisely, occurred in the McKenzie River valley after its location in 1812 by Donald MacKenzie—a trapper and kinsman of the Canadian explorer Alexander MacKenzie—is hard to come by, but the story is similar to those told of a hundred other valleys in the West. Beaver trappers were the first whites to sleep in these woods. (Molala and Kalapuya Indians, from the east and west side of the Cascades respectively, apparently camped along the MacKenzie in summer, when salmon were running and openings in the heavily forested mountains were crowded with ripening blue and red huckleberries, soft thimbleberries, strawberries, orange salmonberries, blue and red elderberries, and trailing blackberries.) When the free trappers and the company trappers were gone, gold and silver miners filtered in. Toward the end of the 19th century some homestead settlement followed small-scale logging operations along the river, though steep mountains and dense forests made farming and grazing in the area impractical. Clear-cutting in modern times, with its complicated attendant problems—siltation smothering salmon redds, "predator control" programs directed against black bears—has turned the road between our house and Eugene, 40 miles downriver, into as butchered a landscape as any I know in the Cascades.

In the 1980s, when the price of Douglas fir reached $300 for

1,000 board feet, some small-property owners succumbed—two or three trees might bring them $2,500. The resulting harvest has grown to look like mange on the hills. Hand in hand with that has come real estate promotion, the hundreds of FOR SALE signs along the road a sort of Muzak.

I am not a cynical man, but watching the quick spread of suburban logging and seeing the same house put up for sale every few years—with a little more landscaping, a higher fence, and another $30,000 to $40,000 added to the price—pushes me closer to it than anything else I know. A long-term commitment to the place, knowledge of its biological limits, or concern for the valley's fate—these do not appear to be a part of the transactions. The hacking away at natural growth, the incessant prettifying with rosebushes and trimmed hedges, and the imposition of incongruous antebellum architecture look like a scatter of bad marriages—reigning husbands and presentable wives.

If I had answers to these problems, or if I felt exempt in this mess, I would be angry about it more often than I am. As it is, Sandra and I pace ourselves. We work on initiatives to control real estate development and rein in logging along the river. We provide a place for the release of rehabilitated raptors, including spotted owls. We work amicably with the state highway department and the Bonneville Power Administration (BPA), which maintain corridors across the land we occupy. We have had to threaten a lawsuit to curb the recklessness of the highway department with chainsaws and heavy equipment, and we have had to insist through an attorney that the BPA not capriciously fell "danger trees" along its power-line right-of-way.

But these agencies, whose land-management philosophies differ so strikingly from our own, have slowly accommodated us. Instead of flooding the roadside with herbicides and flailing at it with oversize brush cutters, the highway department now permits us (and others along the river) to trim back by hand what brush actually threatens motor traffic. And the regional director of the BPA wrote into a recent contract that I could accompany his fallers, to be certain no felled tree was sent crashing needlessly into other trees.

Sandra and I ourselves, of course, have not left the place untouched. In January 1991 two windstorms felled about 30 trees. We logged them out with horses and put the money toward the land payment. I have felled standing dead trees that threatened the house. We compost our kitchen waste, laundry lint, and woodstove ashes in the woods. We've planted gardens and built outbuildings. But it is our habit to disturb these acres very little and to look after them in a way only humans can: by discouraging or preventing the destruction other humans bring. I've asked my neighbors to stop dumping refuse on our place. (They had done it for years because it was only "the woods," a sort of warehouse for timber, deer, and fish, and a dumping ground for whatever one wanted to abandon—cars, bedsprings, fuel drums, small packaging.) I've asked another neighbor's children not to shoot at birds or chop down trees. I've asked unwitting fishermen not to walk through the salmon redd. And, reluctantly, I've gated and posted the land to keep out wanton hunters and people in four-wheel-drives looking for something to break down or climb over.

We know we cannot fence off the endangered chinook redd without attracting curious passersby. Neither I nor anyone can outlaw the product advertising (or foolish popular history) that contributes to images of men taming a violent West. Neither I nor anyone, I fear, can soon change human sentiment to put lands that are unharvested, unhunted, unroaded, or untenanted on the same footing with lands that are domesticated or industrialized. So the birds and animals, the fish and spiders, the wild orchids and other flowers will not have these shields.

Piece by piece, however, as a citizen and as a writer, I want to contest the obsessions that I believe imperil American landscapes—the view that they are principally sources of material wealth or scenic backdrops for a more important human drama. I want to consider the anomalies that lie at the heart of our incessant desire to do good. And I want to see how to sidestep despair, by placing my faith in something larger than my own ideas.

Sandra and I know we do not own these 35 acres. The Oregon ash trees by the river, in whose limbs I have seen flocks of 100 Audubon's warblers, belong also to the families in Guatemala in whose forests these birds winter. The bereavement I feel at the diminishment of life around me is also a bereavement felt by men and women and children I don't know, living in cities I've never visited. And the exhilaration I experience seeing fresh cougar tracks in mud by a creek is an emotion known to any person in love who hears one-who-is-loved speak.

There is more mystery to be contemplated, there are more lessons to be absorbed, on these 35 acres than all the people in my lineage going back to Runnymede and medieval Asturias could manage, should the study be pursued another 1,000 years. My generation's task, I believe, is to change the direction of Western civilization in order to make such a regard practicable.

———

When I rise in the morning I often walk down to the riverbank. If it's summer I'm likely to see mergansers, tree swallows, and osprey. I see first light brightly reflected on alder twigs stripped by beaver. I feel the night movement of cool air downriver and see deerhead orchid and blue gilia blooming in the dark-green salal and horsetail rushes.

I am acutely aware, winter or summer, that these waters have come from farther east in the mountains, that in a few days they will cross the bar at the mouth of the Columbia and become part of the Pacific. The ancient history alone of this river, this animate and elusive business of rain and snow and gravity, gives me hope.

Walking back to the house in this serene frame of mind, I know that to love life, to swear an allegiance to what is alive, is the essence of what I am after. I'm moved to forgive whoever does not find in these acres what I do. I glance into the moving picket of trees and shadow, alert for what I've never noticed before, in a woods I'm trying to take care of—as in its very complicated way it is taking care of me.

Albert Schweitzer

THE ETHICS OF REVERENCE
FOR LIFE

A flock of wild geese had settled to rest upon a pond. One of the flock had been captured by a gardener, who had clipped its wings before releasing it. When the geese started to resume their flight, this one tried frantically, but vainly, to lift itself into the air. The others, observing his struggles, flew about in obvious efforts to encourage him; but it was no use. Thereupon the entire flock settled back on the pond and waited, even though the urge to go on was strong within them. For several days they waited until the damaged feathers had grown sufficiently to permit the goose to fly. Meanwhile the unethical gardener, having been converted by the ethical geese, gladly watched them as they finally rose together, and all resumed their long flight.

ACKNOWLEDGMENTS

J. R. ACKERLEY: Excerpt from *My Dog Tulip*, by J. R. Ackerley, is reprinted by permission of Harold Ober Associates Incorporated. Copyright © 1965 by J. R. Ackerley. Copyright renewed 1998 by Francis King.

DIANE ACKERMAN: Excerpt from "Whales" by Diane Ackerman. Copyright © 1990 by Diane Ackerman. Originally published in *The New Yorker*. This selection appeared in slightly different form in *The Moon by Whalelight*, Random House, 1990. Permission to reprint this version is granted by the author.

CLEVELAND ARMORY: Excerpt from *The Cat Who Came for Christmas*, by Cleveland Amory. Copyright © 1987 by Cleveland Amory. By permission of Little, Brown and Company.

ROGER CARAS: Excerpt from *Animals in Their Places*, by Roger Caras. Copyright © 1987 by Roger Caras. Reprinted with permission of Sierra Club Books.

HECTOR CHEVIGNY: Passage from *My Eyes Have a Cold Nose* used by permission of the estate of Hector Chevigny.

DIAN FOSSEY: Excerpts from *Gorillas in the Mist*. Copyright © 1983 by Dian Fossey. Reprinted by permission of Houghton Mifflin Company. All rights reserved. Reprinted by the permission of Russell & Volkening, Inc., as agents for the author. Copyright © 1983 by Dian Fossey.

PAUL GALLICO: Excerpt from *Honorable Cat* by Paul Gallico. Copyright © 1972 by Paul Gallico and Mathemat Anstalt. Reprinted with the permission of Crown Publishers, Inc.

———: Excerpt from *The Snow Goose* by Paul Gallico. Copyright © 1940 by the Curtis Publishing Company and renewed 1968 by Paul Gallico. Reprinted by permission of Alfred A. Knopf Inc.

ROBERT GRAVES: "In the Wilderness" by Robert Graves from *Collected Poems*, 1966. Used by permission of Carcanet Press Limited.

ERNEST HEMINGWAY: Excerpt from "The Short Happy Life of Francis Macomber." Excerpted with permission of Scribner, a division of Simon & Schuster, Inc., from *The Short Stories of Ernest Hemingway*. Copyright © 1936 by Ernest Hemingway. Copyright renewed © 1964 by Mary Hemingway. Copyright © Hemingway Foreign Rights Trust.

BARRY LOPEZ: "Caring for the Woods," by Barry Lopez. *Audubon* magazine, March–April 1995. Reprinted by permission of Sterling Lord Literistic, Inc.

WILLIE MORRIS: Excerpt from *My Dog Skip* by Willie Morris. Copyright © 1995 by Willie Morris. Reprinted by permission of Random House, Inc.

FARLEY MOWAT: Excerpt from *Never Cry Wolf* by Farley Mowat. Copyright © 1963 by Farley Mowat Ltd.; copyright © renewed 1991 by Farley Mowat Ltd. By permission of Little, Brown and Company. Used by permission, McClelland & Stewart, Inc. *The Canadian Publishers*.

————: Excerpt from *A Whale for the Killing* by Farley Mowat. Copyright © 1972 by Farley Mowat Ltd. By permission of Little, Brown and Company. Used by permission of McClelland & Stewart, Inc. *The Canadian Publishers*.

STERLING NORTH: Excerpt from *Rascal* by Sterling North. Copyright © 1963 by Sterling North; renewed copyright © 1991 by David S. North and Arielle North Olson, text. Used by permission of Dutton Children's Books, a division of Penguin Putnam Inc. Reproduced by permission of Hodder and Stoughton Limited.

HOPE RYDEN: Excerpt from *Lily Pond: Four Years with a Family of Beavers*. Copyright © 1989 by permission of Hope Ryden.

MAY SARTON: Excerpt from *The Fur Person* by May Sarton. Copyright © 1957, 1978 by May Sarton. Reprinted by permission of W. W. Norton & Company, Inc., and by A. M. Heath & Co. Ltd on behalf of the estate of the late May Sarton.

FLOYD SKLOOT: "Daybreak," by Floyd Skloot. Copyright © April 1995, *The Atlantic Monthly*. Used by permission of the author.

GARY ALLEN SLEDGE: "My Father's Way" is used by permission of the author.

JOHN STEINBECK: Excerpt from *Travels with Charley*. Copyright © 1961, 1962 by The Curtis Publishing Co.; ©

1962 by John Steinbeck; renewed © 1990 by Elaine Steinbeck, Thom Steinbeck, and John Steinbeck IV. Used by permission of Viking Penguin, a division of Penguin Putnam Inc.

ELIZABETH MARSHALL THOMAS: Excerpt reprinted with the permission of Simon & Schuster from *The Tribe of Tiger* by Elizabeth Marshall Thomas. Copyright © 1993, 1994 by Elizabeth Marshall Tomas Irrevocable Trust. Also with permission of Weidenfield and Nicolson.

JAMES THURBER: "A Snapshot of Rex." From *The Middle-Aged Man on the Flying Trapeze*. Copyright © 1935 by James Thurber. Copyright © renewed 1963 by Helen Thurber and Rosemary A. Thurber. Reprinted by arrangement with Rosemary A. Thurber and the Barbara Hogenson Agency.

JOHN WRIGHT: "Grammar and Two-Tom." Written by John Wright. Copyright © 1990 Southern Living, Inc.